Left Behind

Left Behind

Latin America and the False Promise of Populism

Sebastian Edwards

THE UNIVERSITY OF CHICAGO PRESS | CHICAGO AND LONDON

Sebastian Edwards is the Henry Ford II Professor of International
Business Economics at the Anderson Graduate School of
Management at the University of California, Los Angeles.

The University of Chicago Press, Chicago 60637
The University of Chicago Press, Ltd., London
© 2010 by The University of Chicago
All rights reserved. Published 2010
Printed in the United States of America

19 18 17 16 15 14 13 12 11 10   1 2 3 4 5

ISBN-13: 978-0-226-18478-4 (cloth)
ISBN-10: 0-226-18478-1 (cloth)

Library of Congress Cataloging-in-Publication Data

Edwards, Sebastian, 1953–
    Left behind : Latin America and the false promise of populism /
Sebastian Edwards.
        p. cm.
    Includes bibliographical references and index.
    ISBN-13: 978-0-226-18478-4 (cloth : alk. paper)
    ISBN-10: 0-226-18478-1 (cloth : alk. paper)
    1. Latin America—Economic policy.   2. Populism—Latin
America—History—20th century.   3. Latin America—Economic
conditions.   4. Latin America—Social conditions.   5. Latin
America—Politics and government.   I. Title.
    HC125.E3923 2010
    330.98—dc22

                                              2009051548

⊗ The paper used in this publication meets the minimum
requirements of the American National Standard for Information
Sciences—Permanence of Paper for Printed Library Materials,
ANSI Z39.48-1992.

This book is for Théodore F. E. Manuel

Contents

Preface

For more than five hundred years the economic history of Latin America has been one of sorrow and frustration. In 1700 the colonies of North and South America had roughly the same standard of living. By 1820, however, income per capita in Latin America was about two-thirds that of the United States and Canada. And in 2009 Latin America's income per person was roughly one-fifth that of North America. This gradual economic decline has affected the lives of millions of people and explains why so many among Latin America's youth strive to emigrate from their countries of birth. Every year, around 400,000 Latin American citizens move illegally into the United States, and hundreds of thousands now live without immigration documents in the European Union.

This book is about Latin America's attempt over recent decades to break a vicious circle of economic mediocrity, crises, inflation, poverty, and authoritarian regimes. It is the history of the Latin American reforms of the 1990s and 2000s—sometimes called the reforms of the Washington Consensus—and of the region's struggle to modernize its economy and institutions. It is also a history of the Latin American countries' efforts to improve social conditions and to reduce poverty and inequality. The book deals with the disappointment with globalization felt in many Latin American countries during the first decade of the twenty-first century and with the ascendance of populist politicians such as Hugo Chávez, Evo Morales, Rafael Correa, and Néstor Kirchner. It is also a book about Brazilian president Luiz Inácio da Silva—universally known as Lula—and his rejection of populism. Finally, this book is about Chile's success with modernizing reforms, capitalism, and economic openness. In dealing with these contemporary issues I take a long view and begin the story with an analysis of the institutions that Latin America inherited from Spain; I then compare this colonial heritage with that of the former English colonies of North America. In order to provide the appropriate historical background, I also analyze in detail Latin America's experience with protectionism and industrialization in the half-century from 1940 through 1990. In addition, I deal with the succession of currency crises that have affected the region since the early days of independence from Spain in the 1820s.

In 2006 I delivered the Figuerola Lecture at the Universidad Carlos III in Madrid. On that occasion I read a paper titled "Crisis and Growth in the World Economy: Historical Prospects," in which I argued that the future of Latin America looked rather bleak. I pointed out that the modernizing reforms of the 1990s had stalled halfway and that in most countries they had barely scratched the surface of economic and institutional inefficiencies and backwardness. Most of Latin America, I said, continued to be saddled by red tape, protectionism, lack of competition, and weak institutions.

I argued that an unsuccessful Latin America was bad news for the United Sates and the European Union. A Latin America characterized by low growth, instability, and poverty represents a clear geopolitical risk for the Western world. If some Latin American countries fail, we will see even greater pressure to migrate illegally, and not even the tallest fence or the toughest immigration officers at Barajas Airport in Madrid will be able to quell the flow of people pushing to get in. Failed economies lead to failed states, violence, assassinations, impunity, and drug trafficking. In Mexico we got a glimpse in recent years of what could happen if the institutions of the state are overrun by drug mafias and other outlaws. Failed states harbor terrorists, don't uphold international law, and don't cooperate with international diplomatic initiatives. There is little doubt that it is in the interest of the advanced nations for Latin America to succeed and finally take off economically. But of course no one is more interested in Latin American success than the half a billion people living in the region. So as we look forward, we have to ask ourselves, why has Latin America lagged behind for so long? Why have successive attempts at jump-starting the economy faltered time after time? Why has Latin America's income gap with the advanced countries grown instead of narrowing?

After the Madrid lecture a number of students and colleagues asked me whether I was writing a book on the subject. My answer was that I wasn't, that I already had a very busy research agenda, and that I was planning to write a book on global imbalances. But the idea stayed in my mind, and I occasionally found myself thinking of what a book on Latin America's economic history would look like. In 2007 I came back to the subject of the overall state of the Latin American economies when I delivered the Corden Lecture at the University of Melbourne. I was again asked whether I was planning to turn the material into a book. This time my answer was less definitive: I said that maybe I would. It was in Melbourne that I put together an outline and, during long and delightful conversations with my friend W. Max Corden, realized that I had done research on almost every topic and country that a book like this would cover. The fact that such a book was a natural continuation of my 1995 book *Crisis and Reform in Latin America: From Despair to Hope* (Oxford University Press) made the idea of writing it even more appealing. I am not completely sure when I actually began writing it, but it could possibly have been when I was thirty-five thousand feet high in the sky over the Pacific Ocean as I traveled from Australia to Santiago, Chile.

In the process of writing this book I incurred many debts. I am grateful to Alberto Naudon, Christine Richmond, and Jessica Roldán for their impeccable assistance in Los Angeles. I have benefited from long discussions with my colleagues Edward Leamer, Al Harberger, Romain Wacziarg, and Deepak Lal. I am also grateful to the participants of the Finance Lunch Table at UCLA's Anderson School of Management, where I tried out many of my views on economic development and on Latin America, markets, and populism. Conversations at various times with Andrés Velasco, Roberto Rigobón, Roberto Steiner, Mauricio Cardenas, Ricardo Hausmann, Rodrigo Vergara, Harald Bayer, Juan Andrés Fontaine, Daniel Artana, Carlos A. Rodriguez, Igal Magendzo, Roberto Alvarez, Moisés Naím, Jorge Castañeda, Máximo Langer, Patricio Navia, and José de Gregorio have been very useful and have helped me sharpen some of the points I make in this book. Over the years, I have learned many things from Guillermo Calvo, and I am grateful to him for his patience and generosity. Also, as any perceptive reader will notice, I have a deep intellectual debt to the late Rudi Dornbusch, an intellectual giant, a brilliant coauthor, and a friend I miss almost every day. I also thank a number of students and friends who read parts of this book and gave me comments, support, and encouragement.

In the process of revising the book I have once again marveled at the power and wisdom of the peer review system than governs academic publishing. Every comment I received from the reviewers was useful and helped me improve the final version of the book. I am grateful to each and every one of them. I thank Willie Schavelzon, my agent in Barcelona, for his support and David Pervin, my editor at the University of Chicago Press, for his enthusiasm and many useful comments. But as always, my greatest debt is to Alejandra Cox

Edwards. I tried every one of my arguments and ideas on her, and although she did not always agree with me, she always had an interesting comment and, more important, a word of encouragement.

Los Angeles, California
December 2009

Chapter 1
Latin America
The Eternal Land of the Future

On January 1, 2003, Luiz Inácio da Silva, universally known by his nickname, Lula, was sworn in as Brazil's constitutional president. The occasion was solemn and fraught with symbolism. Lula was the first trade union leader and self-declared socialist elected to the presidency of a Latin American country. For many years his political party, the Workers' Party, or Partido dos Trabalhadores (PT), had advocated nationalization of large firms and banks, deep agrarian reform, and a move toward socialism.[1] Lula's election represented a dramatic change in Brazil's history and a test for the country's young democracy. For more than two decades, from 1964 through 1985, Brazil had been ruled by a military dictatorship that had persecuted, imprisoned, and even tortured its leftist opponents. Lula spent time in jail in the 1970s, and his predecessor, Fernando Henrique Cardoso, an affable academic and the son and grandson of military officers, had been forced into exile in the 1960s.

Lula's inauguration, held in Brazil's modernist capital, Brasilia, was attended by numerous heads of state, dignitaries, and high-ranking officials from around the world. President George W. Bush, however, was not among those in attendance; nor was Vice President Dick Cheney, Secretary of State Colin Powell, or any other prominent member of the U.S. cabinet. The United States' delegation was headed by Robert Zoellick, the U.S. trade representative, who, in spite of being an able official, lacked the political and diplomatic stature that the occasion called for.[2] With his traditional lightheartedness and keen sense of humor, Lula dismissed the slight and said that there would be many occasions for him to meet with his colleague from the North. Other Latin American heads of state and officials, however, were not so casual; they were offended. In their view the absence of an appropriate U.S. representative was a serious diplomatic affront and a clear reminder that, with few exceptions—including Cuba and, possibly, Mexico—Latin America was not

1

a political or diplomatic priority for the United States. To them it confirmed that Latin America was a "forgotten continent."[3]

As it turned out, Lula was right. Four years after his election, the rift between his government and the Bush administration had been mended. Secretary of State Condoleezza Rice attended the inauguration for his second term in office, and he developed a close rapport with President Bush. In 2007 Lula became the first Latin American leader to be invited to Camp David. This improvement in economic and diplomatic relations was largely due to Lula's decision to eschew the left-wing policies that had long been espoused by his Workers' Party. Instead, he followed a market-friendly economic program that reduced inflation, revived credit markets, and attracted considerable volumes of foreign investments. In 2008 Lula's commitment to fiscal prudence, economic stability, trade openness, and market orientation paid off when Standard & Poor's granted Brazil's national debt the "much-sought-after" investment grade classification, which helped the country attract additional foreign investment and allowed it to borrow internationally at significantly lower costs.

But in spite of the happy ending of this Brazilian episode, all is not quiet on the Latin American front. Since the early twenty-first century the Latin American public has moved increasingly to the left and has elected—sometimes by wide margins—presidents who are openly critical of the United States and its economic and foreign policies and who have pushed populist agendas in their respective countries.

Hugo Chávez of Venezuela has been the most vocal among Latin America's populist and anti-American leaders. But he is not the only one: Néstor Kirchner and Cristina Fernández de Kirchner of Argentina, Evo Morales of Bolivia, Rafael Correa of Ecuador, Fernando Lugo of Paraguay, and Daniel Ortega of Nicaragua have been outspoken in their criticisms of the United States and the market system. All of them have relied on populist rhetoric to attack globalization and to argue that the region needs to greatly increase the role of government in economic affairs. Over the last few years in most of these countries private companies have been nationalized, trade barriers have been hiked, and government controls on prices, investment, and business activities have been tightened. In many of these nations—including Bolivia, Ecuador, and Venezuela—new constitutions aimed at paving the path toward a socialist society have been enacted, and legal maneuvers have been initiated or approved to keep leftist presidents in office.[4]

President Chávez has condemned capitalism, foreign investors, and the international business sector; he packed the Venezuelan supreme court with his supporters, closed a TV channel owned by his political opponents, severed diplomatic relations with neighboring Colombia (only to reinstate them a few days later), meddled in other countries' affairs, and became a close ally of ailing Fidel Castro. In a speech at the United Nations in September 2006, Chávez called U.S. president George W. Bush "the devil" and accused him of "acting as if he owned the world." Chavez's criticisms, however, have not been directed exclusively at the United States; in a meeting of the Ibero-American heads of state held in Santiago, Chile, in November 2007, he engaged in a serious argument with King Juan Carlos of Spain and accused Spain's former president José María Aznar of being a "fascist" and "a serpent." Chávez later threatened Spanish multinationals with expulsion from Venezuela. In May 2008 he criticized German chancellor Angela Merkel and said that her Christian Democratic Party shared "the political ideals of Adolf Hitler."[5]

In February 2009, Hugo Chávez won a crucial referendum that will allow him to run for president as many times as he wishes. If things go his way and he is reelected once more, in 2013, he will be president of Venezuela until at least 2019, extending his tenure to no less than twenty-one years, longer than that of most of the region's recent strongmen, including Chile's Augusto Pinochet. Things could go even better for the former army officer, of course, and he could stay in power indefinitely. A few days after winning the referendum Chávez sent military squads to take over rice-producing companies throughout the country. Chávez then proceeded to condemn the government of newly elected president Barack Obama for allegedly maintaining George W. Bush's foreign policies and complained that the U.S. State Department continued to characterize Venezuela's record on human rights as less than pristine.[6]

Of course, not every leftist leader has been as vocally opposed to open markets and globalization as Chávez, nor have all of them pushed populist policies. In contrast to the Bolivarian president and his supporters there is what former Mexican secretary of foreign affairs Jorge Castañeda has called the "New Latin American Left." In addition to Lula, past and current representatives of this moderate left include Fernando Henrique Cardoso of Brazil, Ricardo Lagos and Michelle Bachelet of Chile, Alan García of Peru, and Tabaré Vázquez of Uruguay. These moderates do not demonize globalization but understand the importance of the market—(despite their criticism of some of its excesses, including those that triggered the global crash of 2008) and acknowledge that innovation and efficiency are at the core of economic success. To be sure, they believe that more government intervention and regulation are essential to reducing inequality. However, they are not hard-core socialists; their goal is to adopt the policies of Western Europe's social democracies.[7]

The Economic Future of Latin America and the United States

The economic future of Latin America, a region with a population of more than half a billion people and vast reserves of natural resources, is important for the rest of the world. In particular, a mediocre economic performance in Latin America is bad news for the United States. If incomes, jobs, and wages grow sluggishly in Latin America—or worse yet, if they stagnate—the flow of illegal immigrants into the United States is likely to increase drastically. During the last decade, almost half a million illegal immigrants entered the United States every year. The vast majority of them—more than 80 percent—come from Latin American nations. Illegal immigrants are no longer only Mexicans and Central Americans. They are now arriving from every corner of Latin America: Argentina, Bolivia, Brazil, Colombia, Ecuador, Paraguay, Peru, and Venezuela. Not surprisingly, the harder economic conditions are at home, the larger is the flow of people who cross the border illegally. Illegal immigration also affects the European Union. In the twenty-first century large numbers of Latin Americans—many of them young, unskilled, and poor—have emigrated illegally to Europe, particularly to Spain, Portugal, Italy, and France. Beginning in 2005, European authorities redoubled airport controls in an effort to stem the flow of undocumented Latin American migrants. Since then, scores of Latin Americans of all ages and walks of life have been denied entry, detained, and sent back to their countries of origin.

An unsuccessful Latin America will be mired in poverty and inequality, and the population will blame capitalism and globalization for the region's misfortunes. Policies aimed at increasing protectionism and government controls will be implemented, and multinational corporations based in the United States, along with Spanish banks and European utility companies, will face stiffer regulations, changes in the regulatory landscape, and higher risks of nationalization. Failure is also likely to result in a lower degree of economic cooperation in areas such as intellectual property rights. And, of course, there is always the possibility that some petroleum-producing countries—Venezuela and Ecuador come readily to mind—may disturb the flow of oil and provoke serious economic dislocation in the United States.

In addition, there is the issue of diplomatic cooperation. Although many Latin American countries have been historical allies of the United States, the region has not always supported U.S. initiatives in the United Nations and other international forums. This was the case, for instance, in April 2003, when Secretary of State Colin Powell failed to obtain the support of Chile and Mexico in the UN Security Council on a key resolution on Iraq. Collaboration at such moments would become even more difficult if anti-U.S. sentiments were to become generalized throughout the region.

Moreover, a significant slowdown in the Latin American economies is likely to result in an increase in illicit activities such as drug trafficking, smuggling, counterfeiting, and money laundering.[8] During 2008 and 2009 drug-related violence spiked significantly in Mexico, and according to various reports from law enforcement agencies, the Sinaloa cartel has now infiltrated several U.S. cities. In a scenario of economic distress it is possible that the region would be less vigilant in dealing with terrorism and terrorist threats. The border between Mexico and the United States is very porous and could become a preferred entry point for terrorists , and the "triple border" between Argentina, Brazil, and Paraguay is notorious for concentrating all sorts of unsavory characters, including some with well-known terrorist connections.

Of course, the future of Latin America does not have to be economic gloom and failure. It is possible that some countries will exhibit robust economic growth and improved social conditions in the next two decades and that the region will cease being the eternal "land of the future." For this to happen, however, Latin America will have to encourage innovation, improve efficiency, and modernize its institutions. It will also have to put in place major reforms to improve the quality of education and equip new generations with the skills required in an increasingly sophisticated and competitive world. Whether the region—including its largest country, Brazil—is politically ready to give a new push to modernization is an open question.

From the Washington Consensus to the Resurgence of Populism: A Brief Overview

Latin America's move to the left has been the result of a deep disillusionment with a number of market-oriented reforms implemented during the 1990s. These policies, which came to be known as the "Washington Consensus," called for elimination of fiscal deficits, reduction of inflation, dismantling of restrictions on international trade, privatization of public enterprises, and deregulation of markets that for decades had been subject to a surreal array of controls, red tape, and restrictions that stifled investment and bred corruption.[9]

The reforms of the Washington Consensus represented a dramatic change in policies throughout the region. Since the 1940s every country in Latin America had shunned the free market and had relied on massive tariff walls to protect its domestic industries. Most had also run large fiscal deficits, experienced runaway inflation, and faced recurrent currency crises. By the late 1980s Latin America had come to a standstill: average income per capita growth was *negative* for a decade—the so-called lost decade—unemployment was very high, and a number of countries had triple-digit inflation; in addition, the region had one of the most unequal income distributions in the world and an astounding incidence of poverty. It was at this time that, in country after country, politicians decided to embark on a major change in direction: suddenly the countries of Latin America welcomed foreign investment, lowered import tariffs, began to deregulate businesses, reduced fiscal deficits, and privatized state-owned companies.

During the early 1990s the Washington Consensus reforms bore fruit: inflation declined substantially, growth accelerated, and, adjusted for inflation, wages increased throughout the region.[10] Optimistic observers, including officials of the International Monetary Fund (IMF) and the World Bank, believed that Latin America would stop being "the land of the future" and would finally take off. It was expected that growth, improved social conditions, and prosperity would replace decades of meager economic performance, pervasive and growing inequality, and recurrent economic and political instability. Throughout most of the region the first half of the 1990s was a period of hope and high expectations.[11]

Progress, however, was short lived. Neither efficiency nor investment in equipment, machinery, and infrastructure increased sufficiently to sustain economic growth over the long run. Institutions were not reformed, property rights were not protected sufficiently, and there was scant improvement in the rule of law. Poverty did not decline significantly, and income distribution remained as skewed as in the past. Moreover, widespread policies that pegged the value of local currencies to the U.S. dollar at artificially high levels reduced exporters' competitiveness by lowering the number of pesos or other local currencies they received per dollar for foreign sales. In addition, many countries were unable to lower expenditures or raise taxes—and thus to control their public finances—and continued to run large government deficits. Eventually, deep currency crises exploded in countries as diverse as Argentina, Brazil, the Dominican Republic, Ecuador, Mexico, and Uruguay. Beginning in 1998 many Latin American nations entered severe recession and experienced heightened unemployment and increased levels of poverty. Between 1998 and 2002 Latin America's income per capita grew on average merely 0.2 percent; during the same period income per capita in emerging Asian nations—including China and India—grew *ten times faster*, at almost 2 percent per annum, and that of the so-called Asian Tigers (Hong Kong, Indonesia, Malaysia, Singapore, South Korea, Taiwan, and Thailand) grew an average of 1 percent per year.

The crises of the 1990s and early 2000s resulted in disappointments and frustration. The Washington Consensus and international institutions—in particular the IMF—were blamed for the currency collapses, increase in unemployment, decline in wages, and rising incidence of poverty. Populist politicians used nationalistic and egalitarian rhetoric to justify increases in protectionism; harassment of foreign investors and businesses; nationalization of foreign companies; taxation of exports at almost expropriatory rates; hikes in regulations, red tape, and bureaucracy; and increases in the power of the executive branch of Latin American governments.

Populism, of course, is not new to Latin America. Some historical examples of strong populists include Juan Domingo Perón of Argentina, Getulio Vargas of Brazil, Luis Echeverría and José López Portillo of Mexico, and Alan García in his first presidency in Peru. Chile under Salvador Allende and Nicaragua under Daniel Ortega and the Sandinistas are examples of socialist governments that undertook populist policies.[12] Historically, populist leaders have had charismatic and strong personalities. Many of them have had weak connections to traditional political parties. Historical populists also had a streak of authoritarianism and often rejected the rules and institutions of liberal democracies.

In 1991, MIT economics professor Rudi Dornbusch and I defined *economic populism* as "an approach to economics that emphasizes growth and income distribution and deemphasizes the risks of inflation, external constraints, and the reaction of economic agents to aggressive nonmarket policies."[13] We went on to argue that while populist experiments often begin with great euphoria and popular support, sustained prosperity cannot be financed with unlimited government debt or by simply printing money. As a result, populist episodes end up invariably leading to rapid inflation—or, in some cases, hyperinflation—higher unemployment, and lower wages. Time after time these policies ultimately fail, hurting those groups—the poor and the middle class—that they were supposed to favor. It is all the more distressing that this pattern is in the process of repeating itself, and paradoxically the global crash that began in 2008 seems likely to increase the appeal of populists precisely at the time when their policies are least likely to work—and most likely to backfire.

Before I proceed further, it is important to emphasize that Latin America is a large, diverse, and complex region. This means that any study that focuses on "Latin America" or on the "typical" Latin American nation is likely to oversimplify matters. However, by addressing the region as a whole I am able to concentrate on some of the structural and institutional features that are common to most countries. In order to provide as much context as possible, throughout the book I discuss a number of country-specific experiences and cases. In particular, I provide detailed discussions of the experiences of Argentina, Brazil, Chile, Colombia, El Salvador, Mexico, and Venezuela.

The Main Argument: A Summary

Contrary to the generalized view among analysts, journalists, and academics, during the 1990s and 2000s most Latin American countries made only limited progress in modernizing their economies. In most nations economic reforms have been incomplete, and thus it is not surprising that they have not transformed Latin America into an economic powerhouse.

A detailed analysis of the evidence shows that in spite of all the media attention, the so-called Washington Consensus reforms only scratched the surface of Latin America's inefficient policy environment. In fact, most Latin American national economies continue to be among the most regulated, distorted, and protectionist in the world. In many of them it is very costly to start a business, red tape is asphyxiating, and taxes are very high. With very few exceptions, institutions continue to be extremely weak: property rights are not protected adequately, the judiciary is inefficient, contracts are difficult to enforce, corruption is pervasive, and the rule of law is wanting. Moreover, throughout the region governments continue to be very large, powerful, and highly inefficient and fail to provide basic services such as quality education and infrastructure and support for research and development. Governments continue to be overreaching and incompetent; they often protect monopolies and are often the source of corruption.

Latin America's mediocre performance during the late 1990s and early 2000s was the result of *not* having implemented market reforms that were deep enough and *not* having adopted policies and institutions that would strongly encourage innovation, productivity enhancements, and lasting economic growth. Latin America, with very few exceptions, clearly suffers from fractured and incomplete economic reform. The region's setbacks during this period were not the result of a deep market-oriented reform program but of policies that, in country after country, pegged the value of local currencies to the U.S. dollar at *artificially high* levels. This meant that foreigners had to pay an excessively large number of dollars in exchange for pesos or other regional currencies (reals, córdobas, colones, and so on). As a result, many Latin American exports were priced out of the global marketplace, and sales shrank. Many countries experienced stagnation of exports, increasingly large trade deficits, and, eventually, deep currency crises that generated soaring unemployment, declining wages, and large income contractions. For example, in Mexico unemployment more than doubled after the collapse of the peso in December 1994, and in Argentina the incidence of poverty shot up to 40 percent of households after the 2001–2 currency crisis.

That so many countries pegged their currencies to the U.S. dollar at artificially high values is particularly ironic, given that this policy was neither a necessary condition for market orientation nor a central component of modernizing reforms. In fact, following Milton Friedman, it is possible to argue that pegging the value of the local currency to the U.S. dollar rather than allowing it to vary according to market forces contradicted the basic tenets of market orientation. These mistakes in the area of exchange-rate policy resulted from a combination of hubris and political expediency. During the 1990s many Latin American technocrats believed in certain economic propositions with religious zeal and labeled those who disagreed with them old-fashioned or ignorant. One of the ideas embraced with quasi-religious fervor was that pegging currency values to the U.S. dollar provided a credible way of eliminating inflation. Evidence that contradicted this view was dismissed as irrelevant or was simply ignored. As I show in the chapters that follow, not only was this belief mistaken but it also encouraged speculation and ultimately contributed to the succession of currency crises that afflicted the region during the 1990s and early years of the twenty-first century. Political impatience also played a role, as many policy makers were convinced that pegging the value of the local currency to that of the United States would generate rapid price adjustment and that double-digit inflation would be eliminated in short order—in two years at most—generating great political gains.

Because the reforms of the 1990s and first decade of this century were superficial and incomplete, most Latin American countries continue to this day to be inefficient and to have low productivity and a high incidence of poverty. Low productivity means that most of these countries have difficulty competing in the global marketplace. This is true in most sectors, with the exception of commodities—copper, petroleum, iron ore, soybeans, beef, and coffee among others—where the region has strong natural advantages. The problem is that even if the demand for raw materials is very strong—as it was from 2003 to 2008—high commodity prices cannot generate lasting and generalized prosperity. A sustainable acceleration in economic growth and a comprehensive increase in wages and income require producing and exporting goods that have a certain degree of sophistication, or what economists call "high value added." This, in turn, necessitates a skilled labor force and incentives—policies and institutions—that foster innovation and efficiency. However, as I show in this book, both in their policies bearing on competition and in their national institutions Latin American nations have done poorly for long periods of time—including the years of the Washington Consensus. Moreover, they are likely to do as badly in the future as they have done in the last two decades. The reality is that most Latin American countries show no political will to embark on the reforms required to generate a jump in productivity.

It is highly likely that in the next ten to fifteen years we will see a three-speed Latin America. There will be a first group of countries that will embrace populism. In these nations the quality of education will continue to be low and institutions weak; these countries will experience almost no improvements in productivity or efficiency. Policies that discourage entrepreneurship and innovation will be put in place in the name of the poor and the indigenous people. Economic growth is likely to be very low, unemployment will increase, black markets will emerge, inflation will accelerate, and social conditions—

particularly the incidence of poverty—will worsen. Insecurity is also likely to rise, and the institutions of the state will lose ground in their struggle with organized crime and drug mafias.

A second group will consist of those countries that will neither fall for the populist temptation nor implement the policies required to generate large efficiency gains. Politicians in these countries will understand that government controls and intrusion, inflation, and protectionism are not the way to reduce poverty and achieve higher standards of living. However, they will not have the boldness or the political ability to implement the policies required to generate a massive jump in efficiency and growth. In these countries economic performance will conform to the Latin American historical norm; that is, it will be mediocre at best. The reduction of poverty will be slow, inequality will continue to be significant, and people's aspirations will be frustrated.

Finally, there will be a third, small group of countries that will embrace the path to innovative economic development. These will be the countries that will experience substantial income growth, improved social conditions, and reduced poverty and inequality. These countries will strengthen their institutions and will increasingly separate themselves from the rest of the Latin American region. They will see a convergence of their income and standards of living with those of the advanced nations of North America, Europe, and Asia.

Of course a key question is which countries are likely to fall in each of these three categories. Which countries will belong to this latter group, and which will belong to the other two? Which nations will thrive, and which will stagnate? Which ones will experience growth and prosperity, and which ones will retrogress? I address these and related questions in great detail in the chapters that follow.

A Conceptual Framework: The Prosperity of Nations and the Mechanics of Successful Growth Transitions

Economists have worked, especially during the last several decades, to understand differences in income levels and prosperity between countries. Their research has asked question such as, why is the standard of living so much higher in Australia than in Argentina? or, why did Ireland grow much faster during the last two decades than Costa Rica? or, why have the nations of Southeast Asia been more productive than Latin American countries?

After considerable research, a number of generally accepted principles regarding long-term income levels from country to country have been established. First, *institutional strength and transparency* play key roles in explaining differences in long-run performance. Institutions that promote the rule of law, protect property rights, encourage rapid conflict resolution, and keep corruption at bay help promote growth and prosperity.[14] Second, national economic policies matter: *policies that promote competition, efficiency, and exports* tend to result in higher rates of economic growth than policies that protect local industries behind tariff walls. And third, *keeping inflation under control and avoiding major currency crises* have important effects on long-term economic performance and growth.[15]

Economists define productivity as the "effectiveness with which factors of production [that is, machines and workers] are converted into output."[16] From a practical point of view this means that if Australia has a higher level of productivity than Argentina, the Australian economy will be able to produce more than Argentina, even if both countries have the same number of machines and workers of comparable skills. That is, if Australia has a higher level of productivity, it uses the resources at hand more efficiently than Argentina does. Economic historians have established that differences in prosperity and income levels between countries are mostly the result of the way in which productivity has evolved; countries with high productivity growth—that is, countries that are quicker to improve efficiency—do better over time than countries that have low productivity growth. It has been estimated that in some countries productivity growth—or improvement in efficiency—accounts for as much as half of overall economic growth over long periods of time (several decades).[17]

Efficiency improves—and thus productivity grows—if there is political, social, and economic stability, if the institutional setting supports learning and innovation, and if economic policies encourage competition. In the Latin American story that emerges in the pages that follow, all of these factors will play very important roles, and, as will be seen, the region does quite poorly in all of them. Worse yet, as noted previously, the reforms of the Washington Consensus were not deep enough and were unable to generate jumps in productivity growth. Two factors in addition to productivity improvements are also important determinants of long-term economic performance: (1) the expansion of productive capacity through investment in machines, equipment, and infrastructure and (2) the employment of more workers with better skills. These factors will also be at the center of this book's investigation of the causes behind Latin America's long-term economic performance.

It is important that property rights are protected for all citizens and not only for the elite. In that regard, a greater degree of democracy will tend to encourage efficiency and productivity growth.[18] In the same vein, a society with an independent and efficient judiciary system will be able to solve conflicts among parties in an efficient way, without negatively affecting the innovation process.[19]

Austrian economist Joseph Schumpeter was one of the first to argue, almost a century ago, that innovation and productivity improvements were the basic forces behind economic progress. He also pointed out that the process of economic growth is not always gentle or beautiful. Sometimes progress and technological advances result in the collapse of old ways of life and the disappearance of older technologies. This is what Schumpeter called "creative destruction."[20]

Extensive research on the performance of scores of countries over long periods of time has supported Schumpeter's contention and has provided important clues about what is required for economic systems based on innovation and productivity improvements to succeed.[21] First, it should be easy to form or dissolve a business. Registering a new business should be a simple task; paperwork and red tape should be minimized, and it should be easy to hire workers and to dismiss them if necessary. There should be access to credit, but bankruptcy procedures should also be simple, efficient, and expeditious. Second, successful innovators should be able to reap the fruits of their efforts. This requires rule of law, protection of property rights, and enforcement of contracts. The judiciary needs to be independent, honest, and efficient and should resolve conflicts fairly and promptly. Moderate tax rates and a regulatory framework that encourages competition are also necessary to encourage innovation. Third, competition should prevail, and monopolies—public or private—should be avoided through dynamic, intelligent, and nonintrusive regulation. International competition and openness serve to reduce the power of monopolies. In order to foster competition, lobbying for special treatment and tax exemptions should be discouraged, as should criminal activities such as extortion and bribery. Fourth, a serious effort should be made to avoid allowing interest groups—including trade associations, large corporations, regional interests, and labor unions—to control regulators or to influence the ways in which regulations are implemented and enforced. And fifth, economic policies should provide the incentives for firms and individuals to continually innovate. It is not enough to adopt productivity-enhancement innovations only occasionally. A flow of new ideas and techniques should be facilitated at all times. In the emerging countries, imitation and the adoption of new techniques first developed in more advanced nations are also important sources of productivity growth. This means that foreign investment should be welcome, trade should be very open, and the educational system should be of high quality at every level.

From a policy perspective, however, it is not enough to understand that good policies and strong institutions are needed for long-term economic success; it is equally important to have a clear notion of the historical patterns of successful *growth transitions*, or episodes in which a particular country moves from very poor performance to rapid economic growth that is sustained over many years—a decade or more. There are a number of historical cases of countries that have undergone successful growth transitions; some of these are recent, while others are more distant in time. Examples include South Korea, the Republic of Ireland, Spain, Italy, China, and Japan. In Latin America, Chile provides an example of successful growth transition over the past twenty-five years.

As it turns out, economists know less about what determines successful growth transitions than about long-term income differentials between countries. It is one thing to say that successful countries have historically had strong institutions, monetary and fiscal stability, and good economic policies that encourage innovation; it is a very different thing to prescribe in detail exactly which specific policies and reforms should be implemented and in what sequence they should be put in place for a particular country to take off and become successful.

The difficulty in understanding growth transitions stems from two factors: First, the broad notion of "good policies and strong institutions" does not correspond to any precise and detailed checklist of policy measures and economic legislation. And second, in reality it is very difficult to devise comprehensive reform policy packages. Complex questions such as which policies to implement first, whether to proceed gradually or in a rapid fashion, and how to handle political opposition to reform have to be addressed. In addition, cultural traits and national traditions often determine what is politically feasible in terms of economic reform. Put in the language of mathematics, the effects of policies are not additive, in the sense that a little more of a certain policy— say, reducing the number of days needed to register property—will generate a little more growth. Quite the contrary: policies and institutions interact in a complex and intricate way; they relate to each other in a subtle *multiplicative* or nonlinear fashion. This means that it is possible that a country is doing most things right but has failed to enact some key aspect of reform and thus has failed to take off economically. The failure to put one key policy in place can be equivalent to multiplying by zero: no matter how much effort a country has put into the other components of reform, the end result will still be zero.

These difficulties for analysis and planning are compounded when one realizes that both "good policies" and "strong institutions" are multidimensional concepts, with many components and potential trade-offs. Different countries could very well have different combinations of these components and still have similar overall policies or institutions. For instance, it is perfectly possible for two countries with different degrees of openness to international competition to have a similar overall policy stance. This would be the case, say, if the nation with the higher import duties avoids an artificially strong currency or has better regulatory policies for public utilities or less red tape and bureaucracy than the country with the higher degree of openness. It is important to emphasize, however, that this does not imply that protectionist and isolationist policies are conducive to good performance.[22]

In short, there are various ways of promoting competition and developing strong institutions. One size definitely does not fit all. This of course does not mean that anything goes. What it does mean, however, is that diversity of experiences should be accepted and that obviously "bad" policies—policies that choke competition, creativity, and innovation and that protect monopolies and promote corruption—should be avoided. Countries should implement market-oriented policies on their own terms, taking into account their own culture, traditions, and realities. Policies that result in inflation and large fiscal or trade imbalances should be avoided, as should policies that artificially strengthen the national currency, which invariably lead to severe and very costly currency crises.

An analysis of a multitude of historical episodes—including those of Japan, Germany, Italy, Spain, and the Asian Tigers among others—indicates that there are three (sometimes overlapping) phases in successful growth transitions. Most Latin American countries have not gotten past the first phase of growth transition and have therefore been frustrated in their aspirations for economic reform. Indeed, it is possible to argue that at the time of this writing Chile is the only country in the region that has successfully gone through all three phases.

During the first phase of a growth transition, a country that has historically done poorly implements important changes in its economic policy: basic modernization reforms are put in place, and measures toward achieving or maintaining price stability are implemented. Very often these economic reforms are triggered by major political events, such as a major financial crisis or a change in the political system—the end of a dictatorship or of a civil conflict, for example. As a result of such broad political or economic changes, the population can devote more time to innovation and adopting new technologies. During this first phase of economic transition, output expansion and income growth are mostly *productivity driven.* To put it simply, economic growth during this first phase is not the result of using more machines and additional workers but of doing things more efficiently. This is precisely what economists mean by productivity growth.[23]

After the reforms of the 1990s, most Latin American countries entered into this productivity-driven phase, in which more efficient use of existing resources led to rapidly expanding output even in the absence of higher investment in machinery, infrastructure, and equipment. Most countries, however, did not move past this first phase; after a few years the initial productivity spurt died off, and the overall rate of economic growth subsided to its historical mediocre trend. Countries that became mired in this first phase include Argentina, Colombia, the Dominican Republic, El Salvador, Mexico, Peru, and Uruguay among others.[24]

During the second phase of growth transition, improvements in efficiency and productivity growth are still strong, and the overall economy continues to grow quickly. In contrast to phase one, during this phase investment in machinery, structures, roads, and ports becomes an important additional source of growth. That is, in addition to greater efficiency, during this phase there are more machines and workers with better skills to support production. During this second phase a virtuous cycle is developed: high growth generates enhanced profit expectations; this results in increased investment in equipment, machinery, and infrastructure, which, in turn, results in even greater growth. The most important characteristic of the second phase of successful growth transition is that the reform process is broadened to include *institutional reforms*. Property rights become more secure (this helps attract foreign investors), the rule of law improves, modern regulatory frameworks aimed at promoting competition are put in place, the judiciary becomes more independent and efficient, and the degree of corruption declines. This second stage of growth transition is also characterized by an upgrading of the educational system and an improvement in labor force skills.[25]

There is no strict blueprint to be followed during these two initial phases of a reform transition. That is, there is no predetermined checklist that, if mechanically implemented, will assure success and prosperity. What is necessary, however, is that during these two early phases progress be made on both the competition policy and institutional fronts and that major mistakes—particularly mistakes that lead to currency crises—be avoided.

During the third phase of successful growth transition, productivity growth—which during the first two phases has been very rapid and a fundamental source of economic growth—begins to decelerate, declining to levels that are more in line with long-term international trends. At this time, however, the institutional reforms initiated during phase two become consolidated, generating a sustained increase in foreign and domestic investment in equipment, machinery, and infrastructure. During this third phase, *accumulation of capital*—both physical capital and human capital—becomes the most important source of growth, helping sustain a (relatively) high rate of economic expansion. Sometimes this third phase is followed by new structural or technological changes that unleash new jumps in productivity growth, and the process discussed above goes through a new, more ordered cycle.[26]

As I show in this book, the vast majority of Latin American nations have not gotten past the first phase of growth transition. Further progress has been frustrated by a combination of factors, including opposition to reforms by groups negatively affected by them—public-sector unions, industrialists who benefited from high trade barriers, companies that enjoyed monopolistic power, employees of state-owned enterprises, members of the judiciary, and teachers' unions—and the public's reaction to the corruption that in many cases has surrounded the privatization of public-sector enterprises. But the most important factor in voters' reactions against reforms has been the wave of severe currency crises that affected the region between 1994 and 2004 and that resulted in income contraction, heightened unemployment, lower wages, and increased poverty.

After these massive and crippling crises the people of Latin America were not able—or willing—to make fine distinctions between modernization and the effects of exchange-rate policies. To them, opening up the economy, privatizing public institutions, and fixing the value of the domestic currency all seemed components of a grand neoliberal scheme. All of these policies were bundled together under the big umbrella of the Washington Consensus. The fact that the fixing of the currency was neither a necessary nor a sufficient component of the modernization reforms—or, worse, that currency fixing contradicted the whole idea of relying on markets—did not matter: all the people knew was that they had been promised stability, growth, and prosperity but that instead major currency crises and devaluations had erupted. Many people became unemployed, and dreams of a better standard of living were shattered. Not surprisingly, this devastating reality resulted in increased popular support for populist leaders and rhetoric in the first decade of this century.

Part I

A Long Decline

From Independence to the
Washington Consensus

Chapter 2
Latin America's Decline
A Long Historical View

Henry Kissinger once dismissed Latin America's importance in world affairs by referring to Chile, which at the time was flirting seriously with the Soviet camp, as a minor irritant; he then memorably added that Chile was "a dagger pointed to the heart of Antarctica."[1] This quip reflects quite accurately Latin America's historical position in global geopolitics: neither too powerful to be a political or diplomatic force nor too rich to represent an economic challenge. Over the years, not even Brazil and Mexico, the two largest countries in the region, have been considered major international players. To be sure, many multinational companies and banks have done business in the region, but in modern times the Latin American countries have not captured the imagination of investors, international analysts, or politicians in the way other nations, including the Asian Tigers, China, and India, have. Indeed, for decades Latin America has been known for its economic and political travails and a long history of authoritarian politicians and tyrants, successive coups d'état, galloping inflation, financial crises, entrenched poverty, and unequal distribution of income. It is not an exaggeration to say that Latin America's modern economic history has been one of modest growth, crises, inequality, and poverty.[2]

A Gradual and Persistent Decline

One of the deepest questions in Latin American history is, why has a region so rich in natural resources done so poorly over the years? Another way of putting it is, why have countries with vast endowments of land and minerals and extensive seacoasts uniformly underperformed what we call today the "advanced world"? According to data assembled by Angus Maddison, in 1492, when Europeans first arrived in the Americas, the indigenous communities that lived in modern-day Bolivia and Peru had a higher standard of living than those in North America. Maddison also estimates that in 1700 the average income per capita in Latin America was roughly the same as in North America. Since then, however, the nations of Latin America have consistently lagged behind the advanced countries, including the United States and Canada. In the year 2000 average income per capita in Latin America was roughly 20 percent of that of the United States.[3]

For a long time the generally accepted view among historians was that Latin America's relative economic stagnation had its origins in the period from 1820, when many colonies obtained independence from Spain, to 1870. Economic decline during these five decades was mostly the result of political instability, successive civil wars, and power struggles. In 1878, H. W. Bates, an early observer of South America, wrote: "With but few exceptions the history of these lands, from the time of their severance from the mother country, has been an unbroken succession of internecine wars and lawlessness, attended by every conceivable horror and atrocity."[4] According to Maddison's data, in 1820 income per capita in Latin America was almost 60 percent of that of the United States; by 1870 it had declined to only 31 percent.[5]

Adam Przeworski has estimated that in the year 2000 the combined costs of political turmoil and delayed independence explained between one-third and three-fourths of the income gap between Latin American countries and the United States. For example, if Brazil had become independent the same year as the United States (1782) and had had the same degree of political stability, in the year 2000 its income gap relative to the United States would have been only $10,000 per capita, rather than the actual figure of $22,000 per capita. Przeworski suggests two reasons that delaying independence may have retarded growth in the former Spanish colonies: first, by restricting trade with other powers—England, France, and the Netherlands—the Spanish stifled innovation; second, early independence allowed the United States to take full advantage of the advances that were unleashed in England with the Industrial Revolution. Of course, as will be seen below, other explanations have been offered, including some involving culture and religion and others involving Spain's zeal for centralized decision making.

Around 1870, after almost half a century of civil conflict, the institutions of the new Latin American national states were consolidated, and political instability declined significantly. With peace came investment, productivity improvements, an expansion of international trade, and an acceleration of economic growth. According to Maddison's data, between 1870 and 1890 Latin America's six largest countries grew almost 2 percent per year in income per capita. During the first decade and a half of the twentieth century Latin America continued to grow rapidly: income per person expanded at an average annual rate between 2.6 and 3.1 percent in the region, which was indeed significantly faster than the growth of income in the United States during the same period.[6] From the Great War until the eruption of the Great Depression in 1929, most of Latin America still performed relatively well (the exceptions were Cuba and the nations of Central America) and grew on average as quickly as the advanced nations.[7]

Until recently most economic historians argued that growth in Latin America continued to be quite fast, in comparative terms, during the period 1940–80, an era characterized by protectionism and government-led development policies aimed at rapidly industrializing the region. According to this view the income gap with the United States remained relatively stable (or even declined a little) throughout these years. Economic historians Pablo Astorga, Ame R. Berges, and Valpy Fitzgerald have said that "the four decades in the middle of the century [1940–80] stand out for the outstanding progress made by nearly every country in the region. . . . It is difficult to avoid the conclusion that greater reliance in the domestic market was a major source of growth during the so-called 'import substitution' phase of state led industrialization." And according to English economist Rosemary Thorp, "Latin American economic performance during the three decades that followed the Second World War was outstanding."[8]

In an important 2007 study, economic historian Leandro Prados de la Escosura criticizes Maddison's data and challenges the mainstream interpretation of the timing of Latin America's economic decline. He maintains that the roots of Latin American "backwardness" lie not in the distant past but in more recent policies.[9] He uses newly constructed historical data to analyze the long-term evolution of Latin America's income per capita and compares his data with the same for a group of what today we call advanced countries. According to this analysis, in 1820 average income per capita in five leading Latin American countries was approximately 40 percent of that of the advanced nations. By 1870, Latin America's income per capita had declined to 27 percent of the advanced countries', and it stayed at about that level until 1938. However, after 1938 the gap in average income between the advance countries and those in Latin America widened: by 1960 Latin American income per capita had declined to 22 percent of that of the advanced countries; by 1970 it was even lower, at 21 percent, and by 1990 it was only 17 percent of the advanced countries' income per capita. After analyzing these new data exhaustively, Prados de la Escosura concludes that "blaming Latin America's long-term backwardness on the post-colonial epoch seems far fetched. Contrary to a widely held view, Latin America's retardation appears to be *a late-twentieth century phenomenon* that should be explored if we want to understand why Latin America remains a backward region in a global world."[10]

These results strongly suggest that the causes for the region's poor long-term performance go beyond delayed independence and heightened political instability from 1820 to 1870; indeed, they suggest that policies undertaken in the aftermath of the Great Depression—including the protectionist-based push toward industrialization—played an important role in Latin America's underdevelopment. The fact that Latin America's decline has been persistent over three centuries also indicates that long-term institutional features of the region—including weak protection of property rights, excessive bureaucracy, centralized decision making, a low regard for the rule of law, an inefficient and ineffective judiciary system, and high levels of corruption among others—played a role in the region's relative decline. An explanation of Latin America's poor performance that relies on a combination of poor policies and weak institutions is compelling and persuasive and provides important clues for understanding the launching of the Washington Consensus reforms of the 1990s, as well as the direction that policies are likely to take in the years to come.

The Poverty of Institutions and Long-Term Mediocrity

There is broad agreement among scholars that institutional weakness has contributed significantly to Latin America's mediocre long-term performance. Francis Fukuyama has said that "one of the most critical sources of the development gap lies in weak Latin American institutions."[11] And according to political scientist James A. Robinson, "the best explanation for Latin America's economic trajectory is its institutions."[12] A crucial question, then, is, why have institutions in Latin America been, historically, so weak? Why have they failed to provide law and order and protect property rights? Why has the rule of law been so tenuous in Latin America? Why has corruption been so much more pervasive in the Latin American nations than in the Asian Tigers and southern European countries? And why have the vast majority of the Latin American countries been unable to reform and strengthen their institutions during the last twenty to thirty years?

A number of answers have been offered to these questions. Some have argued that institutional quality responds to religion and culture, while others have concentrated on the role of ideology; some have emphasized the importance of history, and yet others have argued that, in the final analysis, the answers lie in politics and struggles over power and the distribution of income and wealth.

In an essay published in 1840, Lord Thomas Babington Macaulay was an early proponent of the idea that culture and religion were key determinants of the vast differences in economic conditions between the two Americas:

> The colonies planted by England in America have immeasurably outgrown in power those planted by Spain. Yet we have no reason to believe that, at the beginning of the sixteenth century, the Castilian was in any respect inferior to the Englishman. Our firm belief is that, the North American owes its great civilization and prosperity chiefly to the moral effect of the Protestant Reformation, and that the decay of the southern countries of Europe is to be mainly ascribed to the great Catholic revival.[13]

This religion-based argument became increasingly accepted in the twentieth century as a result of the popularity of Max Weber's analysis of protestant ethics and the development of capitalism.[14] Those that believe in culture's centrality have often quoted David Hume, who in his essay "Of National Characters" wrote that "the same set of manners will follow a nation, and adhere to them over the whole globe. . . . The Spanish, English, French and Dutch colonies, are all distinguishable even between the tropics."[15] Writing in 1878, H. W. Bates, then the assistant secretary of the Royal Geographical Society, argued that Mexico's instability and backwardness were the result of the attempt to impose an alien political culture, in the form of a constitution tailored after that of the United States. According to Bates the people of Mexico were culturally unprepared for this political experiment:

> [T]he introduction of a constitution modeled on such a prototype, involved a complete rupture with the past. The men that had been kept in the apronstrings of political pupilage to Spain, who had been drilled after a strict and

uniform fashion, and governed with irresponsible despotic power by the mother country, were suddenly called upon to play the part of free citizens, to conform to the principles of self-government, voluntarily to submit to the necessary restrains thereby entailed. . . . It needs no great knowledge of human nature to see that such an experiment must invariably lead to the most disastrous results.[16]

In discussing the long-term institutional differences between South and North America, it is important to recognize that the Spanish and English colonization efforts were separated by almost a hundred years. Hernán Cortés's expeditionary force sailed from Cuba toward Mexico in early 1519, while Christopher Newport led his three ships out of London and sailed toward what we know today as New England in late 1609. The fact that such a long time separated the two colonial enterprises is important in at least two respects: first, during those nine decades there were remarkable political and religious changes in Europe, including expansion of the Reformation; second, as historian John H. Elliott has pointed out, because the English initiated their colonization of North America after the Spanish did, they were able to learn from tribulations and mistakes of the Spanish.[17]

Some of the most serious mistakes made by the Iberian colonizers included the imposition of strict trade restrictions (the colonies were forbidden to trade with other European powers), reliance on an inefficient bureaucracy, and the imposition of a highly centralized political system. When the Bourbons tried to reform and decentralize the colonial system in the eighteenth century, it was too late, as bureaucracy and red tape were already ingrained and had become a fundamental part of life and culture in the colonies. The Catholic Church also contributed to creating a culture of centralization and dirigisme. "Nonbelievers" were forced to convert, and Native Americans were not allowed to join the priesthood.[18] The English noted the problems and setbacks faced by the Spanish and made an effort to avoid a burdensome bureaucracy and religious intolerance, at the same time developing a community-based, decentralized political system. As Elliott has noted, this "proved to be a successful formula for unlocking the door to economic growth."[19]

Some authors—including historians Ronald Syme and James Lang—have argued that the contrasts between North and South American institutions stemmed from the differing objectives of the Spanish and English colonial projects. While Spain's was an "empire of conquest," England's was an "empire of commerce." Under this interpretation, institutions in the respective colonies evolved in a way that was useful for fulfilling these different goals: centralization, protectionism, and bureaucracy served Spain's conquest objective well, while a lean, decentralized, and tolerant system based on the rule of law helped England encourage its commercial enterprise.[20] This view has been disputed by James A. Robinson, who has argued that the colonies of North America developed differently than those in South America not because the English had a different motive than the Spanish colonizers but because neither geography nor demography—including population density—allowed the English to replicate the Spanish colonial model. According to Robinson, "a colonial model involving the exploitation of indigenous labor and tribute systems was simply unfeasible in these places [the North American colonies] because of the lack of a large indigenous population."[21]

There is little doubt that culture was important in the development of Latin America's institutions. The question is, how important? Sociologist Claudio Véliz resorts to a metaphor borrowed from philosopher Isaiah Berlin to explain the divergent paths followed by North and South America since the seventeenth century.[22] As Berlin's famously wrote, "The fox knows many things, but the hedgehog knows one big thing."[23] According to Véliz the Spanish were like Berlin's hedgehog, in that they were obsessed with only "one big thing"; the English, on the other hand, were like the fox: open-minded, versatile, flexible, and, especially, good at many things. Véliz is so committed to this metaphor that in an early book he wrote that "Latin America is a hedgehog that since the middle nineteenth century has been desperately trying to be a fox."[24]

For Véliz, the Spanish hedgehog's one big obsession was shaped by the Counter-Reformation and consisted of defending and furthering the Catholic faith. In order to accomplish this goal the Crown developed a system of highly centralized and bureaucratic "councils" that dictated, in great detail, what was to be done under almost every possible circumstance. Both the Inquisition and the Jesuits, two highly centralized and hierarchical institutions, contributed to the enterprise pushed with great fervor by Philip II—whom Véliz calls "the arch-bureaucratic Prudent King"—and his descendants on the throne Philip III and Philip IV. According to Véliz, the historical event that best reflects the foxlike culture of the English is the Industrial Revolution. This remarkable historical period, Véliz tells us, originated in England precisely because the English were tolerant and flexible, loved change, and, most important, were good at many things. These qualities of the English were passed on to their colonists in North America.

In spite of their appeal, explanations based on culture suffer from limitations that call into question David Landes's assertion that "culture makes almost all the difference."[25] In particular, Claudio Véliz's theory, with all its elegance and erudition, faces two challenges. First, there is a significant chronological gap between the Counter-Reformation and the Industrial Revolution, the historical events that, according to him, best exemplify the hedgehog and fox character of the two colonial powers. Although it is not easy to date major historical trends precisely, several decades, at the very least, separate the beginnings of the Industrial Revolution from the end of the Thirty Years' War. Second, any explanation based mostly on culture needs to address what may be called "the Caribbean riddle." The countries of the Caribbean were colonized by the same "foxes" that colonized North America and inherited the same institutions as the North American colonies. And yet their economic performance resembles that of the South American nations much more closely than that of the United States or Canada. Of course, this does not mean that cultural explanations are not important. All it means is that other factors have also played an important role in shaping the Americas' institutions; indeed, in some cases, factors other than culture may have played the most important role in shaping different countries' economic paths.

One such factor is political institutions. Geographer H. W. Bates argued in 1878 that the citizens of the newly independent Spanish colonies were unprepared for self-rule. For more than two centuries they had lived under a highly centralized government, where almost every decision was made in the mother country by a strict and inflexible bureaucracy. In the Spanish colonies the *cabildo* was the basic local government institution. Cabildos, however, were hardly democratic and did not provide experience in self-government, as members were either appointed or purchased their posts. In 1556 it was decided in Santo Domingo that outgoing cabildo members would name their replacements, and in 1595 some positions in Mexico City's cabildo were sold to the highest bidder. With time this practice became quite common, and there is evidence of positions having been sold in Puebla, Veracruz, and Merida, as well as in Córdoba and Buenos Aires in the Viceroyalty of the Río de la Plata. By the late eighteenth and early nineteenth centuries the cabildos were discredited throughout South America.[26] In short, from the start the political institutions in the Spanish colonies were nonrepresentative; they quickly became corrupt, and they soon lost legitimacy. The situation was very different in the North American colonies. As Alexis de Tocqueville wrote:

> In America . . . the township was organized before the county, the county before the State, the State before the Union. In New England townships were completely and definitively constituted as early as 1650. The independence of the township was the nucleus around which the local interests, passions, rights and duties collected and clung. It gave scope to the activity of a real political life most thoroughly democratic and republican. . . . The towns named their own magistrates of every kind, rated themselves and levied their own taxes.[27]

Another factor is income inequality and struggles over income distribution. Recently, Daron Acemoglu, Simon Johnson, and James A. Robinson have argued that social conflict is at the root of historical differences in institutions between countries. Generally speaking, those with power are interested in developing institutions that protect and perpetuate their supremacy and their share of national income. According to Acemoglu and his coauthors, social conflict often leads to institutions that are less than optimal. This may happen even if those with political and economic power recognize that the existing institutional arrangements leave much to be desired; most societies will have imperfect institutions that reflect the structure of power and income distribution.[28]

The way in which the banking system developed in Mexico and the United States provides an illustration of the social-conflict theory of institutions. During the first decade of the twentieth century the United States had approximately twenty thousand banks that competed actively—and sometimes ferociously—among themselves to provide credit to the nascent industrial sector. In contrast, in 1910 there were only forty-two banks in Mexico, each with monopolistic power, earning huge profits, and offering a limited supply of credit. According to historian Stephen Haber, these differences were the result of the way in which political power was distributed: In the United States suffrage had been broaden significantly by the 1850s, and the people demanded that existing restrictions to the creation of new banks be lifted. In contrast, in Mexico there was manifest political instability and limited democratic rule, a situation that eventually led to Porfirio Díaz's dictatorship in 1884. Power in Mexico rested with a few industrial and financial groups that protected their own power and restricted the entry of new banks into a lucrative industry. In the late nineteenth and early twentieth centuries, the expansion of the banking sector in the United Sates was followed by the creation of stock exchanges, legislation that encouraged limited liability and joint-stock companies, and laws and regulations that promoted competition and protected the rights of minority investors. In contrast, in most of Latin America stock exchanges were extremely slow to develop, and the rights of minority stockholders were barely protected.[29]

One of the key tenets of economic theory is that the way in which wealth—including land, skills, and capital—is initially distributed among individuals is an important factor in economic outcomes, including the type of institutions that develop and eventually prevail. Economic historians Stanley L. Engerman and Kenneth L. Sokoloff have relied on this principle in developing a compelling theory of institutions to explain the differences between North and South America. They argue that societies that had a more unequal distribution of wealth during colonial times developed an institutional setting that favored the elites and helped them preserve their power.[30] Engerman and Sokoloff distinguish between three types of colonies in the Americas: those whose climate and soil were suitable for producing sugar and other crops that required very large-scale operations and the use of slaves; those with rich mineral resources that required significant capital and a large labor force, made up mostly of indigenous people, for their extraction; and those whose climate and land quality was best suited for crops that did not require extensive labor. It was precisely in this last type of colony where "owing to the abundant land and low capital requirements, the great majority of adult men were able to operate as independent proprietors."[31] Such colonies, which were established mostly in the northern United States and Canada, developed more egalitarian institutions, including an educational system that catered to the population at large. According to Engerman and Sokoloff, "in societies that began with extreme inequality, the elites were both inclined and able to establish a basic legal framework that ensured them a disproportionate share of political power and to use laws and other government policies that gave them greater access to economic opportunities than the rest of the population."[32]

The distribution of land in the late nineteenth and early twentieth centuries supports Engerman and Sokoloff's theory. In 1910 only 2.4 percent of heads of households in rural Mexico owned land; approximately 19 percent of Argentinean rural households owned land in 1895. In contrast, in 1900 almost 75 percent of rural heads of household in the United States owned land. Of course, not everyone in the northern colonies had access to land, and not everyone who did could afford or finance equally large holdings. However, evidence from a number of sources, including political scientist Tatu Vanhanen, who collected data on the percentage of family-owned farms since the 1850s, shows that access to land was significantly more generalized in northern colonies than in southern colonies.[33]

One of the strengths of Engerman and Sokoloff's approach is that it successfully deals with what I have called the Caribbean riddle. Although the European settlers in the Caribbean isles shared the culture of North America's colonizers, they were endowed with very different natural resources. The climate and quality of soil in the Caribbean were suitable for the cultivation of sugar, which requires large landholdings and a very significant labor force. In that regard, the Caribbean had more similarities with the South American nations than with the colonies north of the Chesapeake.

Daron Acemoglu, Simon Johnson, and James A. Robinson have argued that institutions are persistent through time. That is, deep features of institutions developed long ago—in the colonial times, say—tend to survive. This is the case even if, on the surface, it appears that countries have gone through important milestones, such as independence, the expansion of voting rights, the expansion of the labor movement, the creation of independent courts, and so on. This institutional persistence is the result of political forces that, while evolving with the times, strive to maintain the existing balance of power and distribution of wealth. A vivid historical example can be seen in the fact that after losing the U.S. Civil War in 1865, the southern states in the Union managed to maintain an economic system that, in spite of not relying on slavery, was not greatly different from that of the antebellum period. Similarly, after the Bolivian Revolution of 1952, which resulted in the nationalization of the large tin mines and deep agrarian reform, Bolivia returned to a system with weak institutions and arbitrary policies that maintained the country's unequal income distribution and level of poverty. Similar outcomes followed the Mexican Revolution of 1910 and the nationalization of oil in Mexico in 1938 by President Lázaro Cárdenas.

The existence of institutional inertia raises the question of whether societies can truly break the grip of history. That is, is it possible to radically change the institutional base in a way that creates a new beginning? Are there historical events that allow countries to change its institutions drastically? To the extent that institutions reflect the distribution of power and income, a way of achieving major and sustainable change is precisely through political developments that significantly alter the balance of power. But as the examples of the U.S. Civil War and the Mexican and Bolivian revolutions suggest, not all major political events result in deep institutional transformations. Sometimes they do, sometimes they don't. Some historical examples of major political events leading to very significant institutional transformations include the transformation of Japan after Commodore Perry's expedition and again after World War II, of South Korea after the Korean War, and of China after the rejection of the Cultural Revolution. As I show in chapter 5, since the Pinochet coup d'état and the diaspora of the left in the 1970s and 1980s, Chile has been able to make major institutional changes that have allowed it to become Latin America's undisputable superstar. As I argue in the rest of this book, for Latin America the challenge is to break away from its institutional inertia and adopt new institutions that encourage efficiency improvements, investment in machinery and equipment, and a quality educational system that will allow the region to move toward prosperity and improved social conditions.

Currency Crises, Instability, and Inflation

Modest growth and weak institutions are not the only historical characteristics of Latin America. From early on—indeed, since soon after obtaining independence from Spain—many countries have experienced rapid inflation and recurrent crises in which the local currency lost most of its value relative to gold or a stable currency such as the British pound sterling or the United States dollar. Over the years, large devaluations, debt moratoria, and runaway inflation seemed to be the norm rather than the exception in Latin America. With time the Latin American countries came to be considered such unreliable debtors that in Oscar Wilde's play *An Ideal Husband*, one of the characters says, referring to suspicious investment, "This Argentine scheme is a commonplace swindle."[34]

In the 1820s more than a dozen foreign loans to Latin American nations were defaulted on, including loans to Mexico and Peru. In 1826 Colombia defaulted on 50 percent of its international debt, Ecuador defaulted on 22 percent of its debt, and Venezuela on almost one-third. The smaller countries of Central America—Costa Rica, Guatemala, Honduras, Nicaragua, and El Salvador—defaulted on their foreign debts in February 1828. Sporadic defaults continued during the nineteenth century. For example, in 1873 more than fifteen loans entered into moratorium, including loans to Bolivia, Paraguay, and Uruguay.[35]

After each default, long and protracted negotiations ensued. In most cases settlements that implied significant losses to investors were reached after years of haggling and give and take. In 1875, for example, the government of Bolivia defaulted on its 1872 loan for £1.7 million; eight years later, in 1880, bondholders received a payment for less than one-half of the original debt—£793,000. As defaults mounted, negotiators used new and creative mechanisms in the restructuring process. In 1837, for example, Mexico's congress offered to exchange land in a number of states, including Texas and California, for defaulted bonds. The exchange price was four pounds sterling per acre. There were few takers, however, as British investors thought that holding on to the defaulted securities was a better risk than taking over distant and unknown parcels of land. In 1885 holders of defaulted Paraguayan bonds with a face value of £1.5 million received new bonds for £800,000 plus 2 million hectares in land. And in 1890, British holders of defaulted Peruvian bonds for £33 million received stock in the Peruvian Corporation, a company that owned railways, land, and mining concessions.[36]

Argentina provides the clearest historical example of the extent of instability in Latin America. In the 1820s, barely a decade after declaring independence, Argentina faced its first currency crisis: the peso began to lose value rapidly with respect to gold. In 1827 the peso was devalued by 33 percent; it was devalued again by 68 percent in 1829. In 1838 there was a new currency crisis, and the peso was devalued by 34 percent; a new crisis occurred in 1839 when the peso lost 66 percent of its value. It was again devalued by 95 percent in 1845 and suffered a 40 percent devaluation in 1851. Between 1868 and 1876, in an effort to put an end to macroeconomic instability Argentina implemented a currency board system, which allowed the monetary authorities to issue paper currency only if it was fully backed by gold.[37] In 1876, however, largely as a result of fiscal profligacy, the currency board was abandoned; between

1875 and 1878 the peso was devalued by almost 30 percent with respect to the U.S. dollar. In 1885 there was a new crisis when the peso was devalued with respect to the dollar by 43 percent. Four years later it was devalued again by 64 percent, and in 1890 it was devalued by 32.6 percent during the "Barings Crisis."[38]

In 1891, the Argentine congress approved the Conversion Office Law, and Argentina once more implemented a currency board. Once again, however, the experiment collapsed due to a lack of fiscal restraint. The currency board was suspended in 1914 when World War I erupted; it was reinstated in 1927 and abandoned in 1929. The peso was devalued by 26 percent in 1920 and by 29 percent in 1931. New currency crises occurred in 1938, 1948, and 1949. Macroeconomic instability continued through the 1950s and 1960s; there were currency crises in 1951, 1954, 1955, 1958, 1962, 1964, and 1967. In 1971 the peso was devalued by 117 percent. Between 1974 and 1979 Argentina entered a period of even greater instability. Inflation rose to 444 percent in 1976. This recurrence of crises and currency devaluations had a negative impact on growth: income per capita *contracted* at an annual rate of 1.7 percent between 1975 and 1985. By 1985 inflation was 672 percent, and between 1981 and 1991 the rate of devaluation of the peso averaged a staggering 1,346 percent per year.[39]

Throughout its history Argentina restructured its national, provincial, and municipal external debt several times, imposing severe losses on international investors. An early massive episode of external debt restructuring took place in the 1890s during the Barings Crisis. National government bonds were renegotiated in 1891 and again in 1893. In 1896, international railroad guarantees were restructured, and from 1896 to 1899 foreign bondholders incurred losses of £6 million, when a series of provincial bonds were restructured. In 1897, the municipality of Buenos Aires restructured its bonds, and in 1899 the municipality of Córdoba followed suit. In 1900 it was the municipality of Rosario's turn, and in 1905 Santa Fe's bonds were restructured. In 1906, foreign investors lost approximately one-third of their original investment when the *cédulas hipotecarias* of the province of Buenos Aires were restructured.[40]

Currency instability and inflation were not unique to Argentina. Chile, its neighbor to the west, had one of the highest average rates of inflation in the world during the hundred years from 1878 to 1978. Inflationary pressures were first unleashed in 1878–79, when the peso was devalued by 25 percent and convertibility to gold was abandoned.[41] The peso was further devalued by 20 percent between 1879 and 1888, and by 1898 it had lost another 33 percent of its value. Between 1898 and 1907 the peso was devalued an additional 40 percent. According to Princeton economist Frank W. Fetter, writing in the early 1930s, Chile's inflationary experience during the first decade of the twentieth century was unique, as the government issued increasing amounts of paper money without any need to do so. According to Fetter this deliberate inflationary policy was the result of pressure from Chile's ruling class to obtain abundant and cheap credit. What made Chile's case anomalous was that the massive printing of paper money was supported by conservative politicians and not by liberals or radicals as in the rest of the world.[42] During the Great War, international prices of Chile's exports increased considerably, and the peso experienced a gradual strengthening. This situation, however, was short lived, and in 1921 the peso was depreciated by more than 50 percent. By 1925 the currency had lost 60 percent of its value in 1918. During the next sixty years Chile experienced a chronically high rate of inflation, and attempts to stabilize the economy failed time and again.[43]

Inequality and Poverty

In 1961 anthropologist Oscar Lewis published *The Children of Sánchez*, a book that shocked the world with its vivid portrait of poverty in Latin America. In the introduction Lewis wrote: "This book is about a poor family in Mexico City, Jesús Sánchez, the father, and his four children: Manuel, age thirty-two; Roberto, twenty-nine; Consuelo, twenty-seven; and Marta, twenty-five. My purpose is to give the reader an inside view of family life and what it means to grow up in a one room in a slum tenement in the heart of a great Latin American city which is undergoing a process of rapid social and economic change."[44] In more than five hundred pages Lewis presented the sorrows and frustration, the destitution and the lack of hope of the Sánchezes in the family members' own words. The book documented the recurrent violence of the poor on the poor and the utter failure of the institutions of the state to provide minimum public services. The story moved readers to the core and deeply embarrassed the leadership of successive Mexican governments led by the Partido Revolucionario Institucional (PRI). It was, however, an accurate depiction of the region's social conditions.

The degree of inequality in Latin America is indeed legendary and has been at the heart of many of the region's political and social problems since colonial times. Historical evidence on the distribution of land shows that in the mid-nineteenth century 60 percent of North American farmers owned land, while in Latin America only 5 percent of farmers owned land. In 1850 land ownership by farmers was lowest in Chile (1 percent) and highest in Costa Rica (25 percent). In the early twentieth century land ownership by farmers had increased slightly in Latin America but still lagged significantly behind the United States and Canada. In 1900 family farm ownership in Latin America was as follows: in Argentina it was at 7 percent; in Bolivia, 2 percent; in Brazil 4, percent; in Chile, 2 percent; in Colombia, 5 percent; in Costa Rica, 15 percent, down from 25 percent fifty years earlier; in Mexico, 1 percent; and in Peru, 2 percent.[45]

Economists use a number of tools to measure the extent of income disparity. The most popular is the Gini coefficient, a statistical index that ranges from 0 to 1, with higher values denoting a greater degree of inequality. Under the hypothetical case of absolute inequality, the index takes a value of 1; if, on the other hand, income is distributed in an exactly even way, the Gini coefficient is 0.[46] In the advanced Western democracies the Gini coefficient has tended to vary between 0.30 in more egalitarian societies such as the Scandinavian nations and 0.40 in the United States. Gini coefficients have been much higher in the Latin American countries.[47]

In 1938 Colombia was the first Latin American country to undertake a systematic study of income distribution. Its Gini coefficient was 0.45, one of the highest values recorded in the world to that time. In the years to come it became evident that Colombia's unequal income distribution was not an aberration but the norm for the region. In the 1950s and 1960s a series of studies showed extremely high Gini coefficients for most countries: 0.57 in Brazil, 0.46 in Chile, and 0.59 in Mexico. Only Argentina appeared to have an income distribution that was not remarkably skewed; its Gini coefficient was 0.37 in the 1950s and 0.41 throughout the 1960s, a level that was not very different from that attained by the advanced Western democracies.[48]

By the early 1970s, a decade after the launching of the Alliance for Progress, a vast social program sponsored by the United States whose aim was to improve social conditions in Latin America, income had not become more evenly distributed. On the contrary, in many nations inequality had increased. The Gini coefficient was 0.63 in Brazil (up from 0.57 a decade earlier),—0.47 in Chile, 0.52 in Colombia, 0.44 in Costa Rica, and 0.49 in Venezuela. Only in

Argentina and Uruguay did income continue to be more equally distributed, with Ginis of 0.42 and 0.33 respectively.

Ten years later things had not improved, and in the early 1990s, at the end of the so-called lost decade and after years of military dictatorships, inequality had reached staggering levels in most Latin American countries. In Argentina the Gini coefficient increased from 0.37 to 0.52 over a forty-year period (1950 through 1990); in Brazil it went from 0.57 to 0.65; in Chile, from 0.44 to 0.54; and in Uruguay, from 0.33 to 0.41. Mexico was the only country that experienced a decline in inequality between the 1950s and 1990s. In spite of this achievement, in the early 1990s Mexico's Gini coefficient was still 0.52, one of the highest in all of Latin America.

Many economists have argued that it is misleading to focus attention on inequality. What matters, they point out, is *poverty*. It is perfectly possible for income to be evenly distributed and for the vast majority of the population to live in abject poverty, as is the case in Democratic People's Republic of Korea (North Korea). Likewise, it is possible for income to be unevenly distributed in a country where everyone enjoys a very comfortable standard of living. The debate over the importance of income distribution and poverty has sometimes developed ideological undertones, obscuring the fact that both of these concepts are relevant and play a role in the evaluation of a country's economic and social performance. What is important for our analysis is that when poverty measures—as opposed to inequality indexes—are used, the story of Latin America's social conditions appears to be equally discouraging. In 1970 almost one in two Brazilians lived below the poverty line. This was also the case in Colombia and Peru. The incidence of poverty was an incredible 65 percent of the population in Honduras, 39 percent in Panama, 34 percent in Mexico, 25 percent in Venezuela, 24 percent in Costa Rica, and 17 percent in Chile. Argentina was the only country in the region with a single-digit level of poverty incidence, at 8 percent of the population.[49]

A decade later, in the early 1980s, things had barely improved. Those living in poverty exceeded 40 percent of the population in Brazil, Colombia, Honduras, and Peru. The incidence of poverty differed widely between geographical areas within particular countries. Areas populated primarily by the indigenous peoples of Peru, Colombia, and Ecuador were particularly poor, as were the states of Oaxaca, Guerrero, and Chiapas in Mexico and Brazil's northeastern region.[50]

Other social indicators—including literacy, life expectancy, health provision, and the coverage of education—improved somewhat during the 1950s and 1970s. They did so slowly, however, and Latin America's social gap with other nations continued to be extremely large, noticeable, and substantial.[51]

So Far from God, and So Close to the United States

Since the early nineteenth century, South American thinkers have discussed—sometimes obsessively—the differences between their region and the former colonies of North America. One of the most influential early contributors to this debate was Argentine intellectual, politician and educator Domingo Faustino Sarmiento. In his 1845 book *Facundo: Civilization and Barbarism* Sarmiento argued that the young nations of Latin America had to decide whether to remain backward, remote, and undemocratic, as they had been during the colonial period and the early years of independence, or to do what the United States had done, embracing the ideas and institutions of the Enlightenment and the French Revolution. According to Sarmiento, immediately after independence "barbarism" prevailed throughout most of Latin America, in the form of despotic rule wielded through brute force by local and provincial strongmen, warlords, and caudillos.[52] The subtitle of the first English translation of *Facundo*, published in 1868, captured the thrust of the argument vividly: *Life in the Argentine Republic in the Age of the Tyrants*. In contrast to Latin America, Sarmiento argued, the United States had opted from the early years of its independence for "civilization" and had striven to build the political institutions required to promote this goal.

In a second book, published in 1849, *Travels in Europe, Africa and the United States*, Sarmiento furthered these ideas and argued that it was in the United States, not Europe, that the civilized ideals of liberty, equality, and fraternity had truly taken hold.[53] He saw political decentralization as one of the United States' greatest strengths, allowing its citizens to have control over the educational system, banking, and other public services. But Sarmiento was not content with offering broad descriptions of the United States during its early years or with comparing its institutions with those of Latin America; he wanted his country, Argentina, to emulate the United Sates, to rid itself of despotism and fully embrace civilization. Sarmiento's admiration for the United Sates is captured with clarity in the following assertion from *Travels*:

"This inconceivable extravaganza [of the United States] is grand and noble, occasionally sublime, and always follows its genius."[54]

Over the years many Latin American intellectuals have disagreed with Sarmiento's views and with his admiration for the United States and its way of life. José Enrique Rodó, an intellectual and writer from Uruguay, published in 1900 what is perhaps the most compelling—but certainly not the only—criticism of the United States' values and culture ever written by a Latin American.[55] In this short essay titled "Ariel," Rodó argued that by embracing utilitarianism the United States had turned its back on spiritual pursuits, beauty, and nature.[56] He contrasted the crudeness of the United Sates, where everything—even the arts and the sciences—had to have a practical application, with the values of ancient Greece. He went on to argue that a mechanical application of democratic principles—which he associated with Benjamin Franklin—resulted in crass materialism and encouragement of a mediocre, lowbrow culture.

Rodó's was not a blind criticism of the United States; he was too clever and cultured for that. He recognized many positive traits, including a "sleepless and insatiable instinct of curiosity, an impatient eagerness for the light." He also praised the United States' goal of educating the masses. And yet for Rodó this was not enough: inventiveness and prosperity were vulgar and ultimately failed to generate an enlightened people and harmonious society. He wrote: "Their culture, while far from being spiritual or refined, has an admirable efficiency so far as it is directed to practical ends and their immediate realizations. And while they have not added to the acquisition of science a single general law, one new principle, they have done wonders in its application."[57]

Rodó deplored the attempts by North Americans to spread their views to the rest of humanity. In his view, most United Sates citizens believed that their way of life was "predestined to all humanity." This, said Rodó, South Americans had to resist; they had to stand up to Caliban and the glorification of material prosperity; South America's youth had to pursue the highest aspirations of the spirit, nature, culture, and Western civilization. South Americans could do so because they, like their European forefathers, carried on the traditions and teachings of Athens.

In a remarkable act of dialectical rhetoric, and to the delight of Latin American elites, Rodó put Sarmiento on his head. It was not North America that represented "civilization" and the South "barbarism"; Sarmiento got it all wrong: it was exactly the opposite. The United States, with its relentless pursuit of material progress was, in the final analysis, the country of crudeness, frivolity, and—why not say it?—barbarism. Maybe the nations of the South were backward and lacked the curiosity, dynamism, and energy of the North, but their people still cultivated the spirit; they practiced the nearly lost art of conversation, admired nature, and pursued beauty for its own sake. This was precisely their strength, and it should not be lost. This was what, according to Rodó, made them the representatives of "civilization" in the vast land mass called the Americas. He told his young audience not to fall for the glitter of the North; he told them to resist its siren songs. He wrote: "I see no good in denaturalizing the character of a people—its personal genius—to impose on it identity with a foreign model to which they will sacrifice the originality of their genius. . . . In societies, as in art and literature, blind imitation gives us but an inferior copy of the model."

Although Rodó's book was almost completely ignored in the United Sates—it was only translated and published in 1922, after Rodó's death—it quickly had an effect on Latin American intellectual circles. Some have argued that the times influenced Rodó's views and those of his followers. The United States had just defeated Spain in the Spanish-American War, and Cuba, the Philippines, and Puerto Rico had fallen under its influence. All of a sudden the United States appeared to be a menacing imperial force, flexing its muscles in the neighborhood, ready to impose its will and gain economic advantage, maybe even ready to gobble up new territories.

Regardless of whether the Spanish-American War affected his rhetoric, Rodó's book was extremely influential, and his views became part of Latin America's ethos. Generations of Latin Americans were brought up with the idea that North Americans were crass and uncultured, lacking in manners and sophistication, poorly read, overly materialistic, and naïve. This was contrasted with Europeans, who were seen as sophisticated and refined and the true heirs of classical culture.[58] As a result, South American elites gravitated for a long time toward Europe. Until quite recently South America's rich were educated in Europe and traveled often there. It was in Europe—Paris, Rome, Madrid, Cannes, Monte Carlo—that they played and vacationed. And often, if they were on the wrong side of political developments, it was to Europe that they went into exile. More important, perhaps, Rodó provided a highly convenient "Yes, but" argument to South America elites. They could now say, "Yes, our countries are less productive and materially advanced than the United Sates, but we have avoided their tackiness and vulgarity; instead of being concerned with productivity and material achievements, we care about the developments of the spirit." This argument, of course, was deeply flawed, and with time became untenable. By the mid-twentieth century it was increasingly apparent that most countries of South America lacked the most basic institutions required to further culture and the cultivation of the spirit. The educational system was mediocre at best, universities lagged behind, and museums were half-empty buildings without curators or collections or visitors. A succession of coups d'état and dictatorships was hardly what the cultivation of the spirit needed, and the income gap between the North and the South became too large to be ignored or to be justified by an ethereal argument based on the beauty of Athenian ideals.

The ambivalent—and sometimes openly hostile—views of Latin Americans toward the United States were in part the result of diplomatic blunders by different United States governments. Examples abound, including Woodrow Wilson's support of the conspiracy that resulted in the assassination of Mexican president Francisco Madero in 1913. Over time, different United States administrations supported a succession of despots, including Anastasio Somoza in Nicaragua, Marcos Pérez Jiménez in Venezuela, Leónidas Trujillo in the Dominican Republic, and a long list of generals in Argentina and Brazil. It was president Franklin Delano Roosevelt who, referring to Somoza in 1939, supposedly said: "He may be a son of a bitch, but he is our son of a bitch." At a different level, for a long time Latin Americans have resented—as they continue to do today—the United States' appropriation of the terms *America* and *American*. We are all Americans, they repeat again and again south of the Rio Grande—those from the South, and the Center, and the isles, as well as those from the North. Certainly, that is what Rodó had in mind when he dedicated "Ariel" to "America's Youth" in 1900. Latin Americans also rejected—maybe because they didn't quite understand it—the Monroe Doctrine. Did "America for the Americans" mean that the entire hemisphere—North and South America—was to be dominated by the United States? That would be rampant imperialism, the monster Caliban at his worst. And although it was formulated by President James Monroe in 1823, decades before the publication of either *Facundo* or "Ariel," the doctrine—along with the specific policies that have stemmed from it—continues to be seen as a clear confirmation that

Sarmiento got it all wrong: it is the North Americans, not their neighbors to the south, who are the barbarians.

"To Roosevelt," a poem by Nicaragua's Rubén Darío, captures vividly the way many South American intellectuals felt about their neighbor to the north at the beginning of the twentieth century.[59] This work was published in 1905, only five years after Rodó's "Ariel" and two years after President Theodore Roosevelt had taken possession of what was to become the Panama Canal Zone. In the poem Darío provides a vivid contrast between the admiration that he feels for what the United States stands for—or at least what it had stood for until then—and the outrage that he feels for the annexation of Latin American land. He also expresses fear that this will only be the beginning of successive attempts to dominate—either directly or indirectly—the countries of the South. The poem opens as follows:

> It is with the voice of the Bible, or Walt Whitman's verse
> that I should reach you, Hunter,
> primitive and modern, simple and complex,
> with something of Washington, and four parts of Nimrod.
> You are the United States,
> the future invader
> of that naïve America with Indian blood
> that still prays to Jesus Christ and still speaks Spanish.[60]

Darío ends with the warning that it will not be so easy to dominate this region; there will be strong opposition, and short of the invader being God, it just would not happen: "Be careful, Spanish America lives! / There are a thousand cubs of the Spanish Lion wandering and free." Mexican historian Enrique Krauze has asserted that Augusto Sandino, Che Guevara, and Fidel Castro are the cubs that Darío alludes to.[61] But why stop there? New cubs named Hugo Chávez, Evo Morales, and Daniel Ortega are now roaming the Americas. What should be done about them? What will they do themselves? Will they self-destruct, as earlier cubs did, or will they find a way to transform their anger and outrage into good policies that will help their people get out of poverty and frustration? Though this is not the place for wagers, if I had to bet, I would bet on self-destruction.

But it is Chile's Pablo Neruda who, in his monumental *Canto General*, published in 1950, best captures the complex relationship that South America has had with the United States.[62] The *Canto* has 340 poems that sing to the Americas and their people, to their heroes and villains, to their happiness and sorrows. Canto 9, titled "Let the Woodcutter Awaken," begins with a celebration of the United Sates, its citizens, and its prowess. Neruda sings to "the machine that spins, the iron spoon that eats earth," and to the "farmer's little house" in the plains. He says, "You are beautiful and wide, North America. / You come from a humble cradle like the white woman who washes clothes / by your rivers." And then he says: "We love your city, your substance, / your light, your mechanisms . . ."

But not everything is celebration. Neruda also writes about an ugly side—about racism, poverty, and destitution. He writes about political persecution and Lincoln's assassination. And then, with fury, he turns to the United States' support for Latin American tyrants and despots, to its support for the Trujillos and the Somozas and the González Videlas. Like Rubén Darío before him, Neruda warns the giant of the North:

> [I]f you arm your hordes, North America,
> to destroy these pure borders
> . . . to govern the music and the order
> that we love, we will emerge from the air and the stones
> to bite you: we will get out through the last window
> to throw fire at you:
> we will emerge from the deepest waves . . .

And then, quite suddenly, he mellows, evokes Abraham Lincoln's spirit, and hopes that "nothing of the sort happens." The woodcutter (Lincoln), he says, should awaken: "Abraham should come, with his ax / and his wooden plate / and eat with the farmers." Lincoln should come back from the

> golden and green land of Illinois,
> and raise his ax
> against the new slave traffickers.

The canto closes:

> I don't come to solve anything.
> I come to sing,
> and for you to sing with me.

Neruda also writes about the economic relationship between the United States and South America, and he deplores the fact that multinationals take the region's natural resources, impoverishing it, leaving its earth barren. Canto 5, "The Sand Betrayed," the angriest of the nine cantos, includes three long poems on the Standard Oil Company, the Anaconda Copper Mining Company, and the United Fruit Company. Standard Oil, Neruda writes,

> buys countries, towns, seas,
> policemen, congressional delegations,
> faraway places where
> the poor hold on to their maize
> as tycoons hold on to their gold.

But it is perhaps his poem on the United Fruit Company that best encapsulates what several generations of Latin Americans have felt about the United States economic incursions in the region:

> United Fruit Inc.
> reserved for itself the juiciest part,
> the central coast of my land,
> the sweet waist of America.
> And it rebaptized its lands
> "Banana Republics" . . . ?

One of those strongly influenced by "Ariel" and by Rodó's views was Mexico's José de Vasconcelos, who as secretary of education during the second half of the 1920s helped define the official version the Mexican Revolution. One of Vasconcelos's greatest legacies is having commissioned many of the murals by Diego Rivera, David Alfaro Siqueiros, and José Clemente Orozco that adorn numerous public buildings. Vasconcelos thought that Latin America's confluence of races positioned it for achieving—sooner rather than later—Rodó's dream of a cultured, harmonious, and spiritually advanced cultural region. This dream was not very different from that of Simón Bolivar, a figure revered by most South Americans. As time passed, it became increasingly clear that Bolivar's dream was nothing more than that, a dream. But it was not just any dream; it is a dream that refuses to die, that reemerges with force from time to time, and whose most recent proponent is the president of Venezuela, Hugo Chávez.

Of course, Mexico's complex relations with its neighbor to the north were not born with the Mexican Revolution. The ambiguous relationship has always been there—since the colonial times and the days of the early independence; since the Mexican-American War of 1846, the Treaty of Guadalupe Hidalgo, and the loss of Texas, New Mexico, and Alta California. Porfirio Díaz's quip "Poor Mexico, so far from God and so close to the United States" came from Mexico's self-defined "modernizer," a man who admired the order and organizational power of the United States. It didn't come from a bandito-turned-revolutionary. But as Enrique Krauze has noted, during the second half of the twentieth century this anti–United States sentiment has been mostly confined to Mexico's intellectuals, many of whom believe that, historically, the United States has pursued expansionist policies aimed at gaining greater power south of its border. As Krauze has argued, the vast majority of the population, in particular the poor, look toward the North with admiration; for them the United Sates is not seen as an enemy but as a land of opportunity. And many of them risk their lives by crossing the Rio Grande in search of better standards of living for themselves and their families.[63]

The grievances, of course, are real. It is true that for some time the United States embarked on a land-grab strategy—gaining control of Cuba, Puerto Rico, and the Philippines after the Spanish-American War in 1898 and then of the Canal Zone in 1903—and that through the years it supported a succession of despots that enriched themselves and violated human rights as a matter of course. Then there were the decades of political and diplomatic neglect, with barely a nod to the impoverished neighbors to the south, neglect that was broken only rarely and for very short periods of time—such as seen under the Alliance for Progress in the early 1960s.

Enrique Krauze has argued that this neglect was compounded by a profound lack of interest and even disdain for Latin American culture.[64] I am not so sure, however. Clearly, there has been limited political and diplomatic concern, but culture is a different story. After all, Diego Rivera found powerful patrons in the United States—although, as the destruction of his mural in the Rockefeller Center shows, they didn't always understand his work—and his wife Frida Kahlo still has a cult following. Works by writers Gabriel García Márquez, Mario Vargas Llosa, Carlos Fuentes, and Isabel Allende have been extremely well received by North American readers and reviewers. Recently, the *New York Times* named Roberto Bolaño's monumental and critically acclaimed novel *2066* among its 10 Best Books of 2008. For a long time poet Octavio Paz has had an important place in literature curricula in U.S. colleges, and Pablo Neruda, a fierce critic of U.S. policies toward Latin America (in 1973 he published a book titled *Incitación al Nixonicidio*) has been a perennial best-selling author.[65] But that is not all: almost every major university in the United States has a Latin American center or program where men and women research different aspects of the region's history, arts, or culture. And of course there are many works on Latin America by North American authors—Oscar Lewis, Albert O. Hirschman, Herbert L. Matthews, Francis Fukuyama, and Alan Riding, to name just a few. Although not all of them are equally illuminating, they do reflect the interest that the region holds for large groups of intellectuals outside of its borders.

In the end, however, what really matters is that Latin Americans' grievances with their neighbors to the north have existed for decades and that they are at least partially if not fully justified. But the fact that the complaints about neglect and lack of interest may have some validity does not mean that Latin America's underdevelopment has been caused by the North; nor does it mean that being "so close to the United States" is a curse. The idea that Latin America's long-term decline is the result of a vast capitalistic Anglo-Saxon conspiracy from the North simply doesn't hold water. The causes of the region's mediocre economic performance should be looked for inside Latin America.

Chapter 3
From the Alliance for Progress to the Washington Consensus

Beginning in the late 1930s most Latin American nations followed an economic strategy based on protectionism, government controls, and a broad involvement of the state in economic activities. For some time this approach, which came to be known as import substitution industrialization, seemed to work: economic growth picked up in many countries, industrialization proceeded at a brisk pace, and wages in the manufacturing sector increased rapidly. During the early 1950s many observers were optimistic and thought that economic development, reduced poverty, and prosperity would come about in a matter of time. But underneath this veneer of success, deep problems and social tensions were simmering. The newly developed industrial sector, which included huge steel plants, petrochemical complexes, refineries, and auto plants of various sizes, was highly inefficient, and in order to survive it required higher and higher import barriers to keep foreign competition out of the country. Consumption goods were significantly more expensive than in the advanced and medium-income countries, and simple goods, such as bicycles—the preferred mode of transportation of blue-collar workers in third world nations—were out of reach for the poor. In Chile, for example, a bicycle cost four times more than in the United States, a basic radio appliance was more than three times more expensive than in a European nation, and a small heater was 90 percent dearer than in the international markets.[1] The comparison is even more dramatic when one takes into account how much lower incomes of Latin Americans are than those of Europeans and workers in the United States. In effect, with increased protectionism, producers of industrial products had a captive market and were benefiting at the expense of the average consumer. One of the collateral effects of protectionism was that the region's currencies became artificially strong. Stronger currencies, in turn, meant higher costs and greater difficulty competing internationally. This discouraged exports, hurt competitiveness in the agricultural sector—a sector subject to international competition from more efficient nations—and generated a widening political gulf between city dwellers and those who lived in the countryside. As the 1950s unfolded, massive poverty persisted in most Latin American nations, and inequality became more pronounced.

The Cuban Revolution and the Alliance for Progress

In the late 1940s the public in an increasing number of Latin American countries became frustrated by the lack of progress in social conditions and by the brutality of authoritarian and dictatorial regimes. The first signs that not everything was well south of the Rio Grande came in 1952 when Guatemalan president Jacobo Arbenz—only the second leader elected democratically in that Central American country—implemented an agrarian reform program aimed at redistributing landholdings and reducing poverty among Guatemala's indigenous population. These policies, however, were resisted by landowners and large multinationals and generated a serious diplomatic rift with the United States. In 1954, with the support of the CIA, the Guatemalan military staged a coup that put an end to Guatemala's incipient democracy and Arbenz's program.

But Guatemala was only the beginning. In the years to come small groups of armed men took to the jungles and mountains of Latin America in efforts to start revolutions aimed at toppling what they saw as illegitimate and corrupt governments. Senior officials at the U.S. State Department considered these developments minor nuisances and were convinced that in due course these groups would be defeated. But they were wrong. On January 1, 1959, Fidel Castro and his men triumphantly entered Havana. At first Castro and his new regime were looked at with sympathy by the Western democracies. After all, former strongman Fulgencio Batista might have been called at the time, as Franklin Delano Roosevelt had earlier called Anastasio Somoza of Nicaragua, "our son of a bitch." No one in Washington lamented his departure. Indeed, during their years in the mountains the guerrilla forces had gathered strong support among some of the most powerful media outlets and journalists in the United States, including Herbert L. Matthews, an editorial writer at the

New York Times and the first United Sates–based reporter to interview Castro in his Sierra Maestra hideaway, in 1957.[2]

However, things did not work out as most Fidel Castro supporters in New York, Washington, and Miami had expected. Instead of building the basis for a modern liberal democracy, Castro moved rapidly to the left and established close ties with the Soviet Union and the other members of the Warsaw Pact. It soon became clear that Castro was serious about creating a socialist republic ninety miles from the coast of Florida and that in order to do so he would rely on Moscow's support. But what was even more disturbing to Washington was that Fidel was extremely popular in the rest of Latin America. Guerrilla movements modeled on Cuba's 26th of July Movement quickly sprang up in country after country. Of course, Castro's regime was not fully tailored after the Soviet model, but as Herbert Matthews put it in his 1961 book, it "had borrowed its ideas and methods from Iron Curtain Europe."[3] Without any doubt, by 1960 the Cold War had arrived in earnest in Latin America.

The Kennedy administration decided to tackle the communist threat through a two-pronged strategy: First, military assistance was provided to the region's governments. The goal was to professionalize local armed forces, allowing them to successfully engage Marxist insurgents. Scores of Latin American military officers went through the Pentagon-sponsored School of the Americas in Panama. The most famous graduate of this academy is Manuel Noriega, the former Panamanian strongman who in 1992 was condemned by U.S. courts to forty years in prison for narcotics trafficking.

The second component of Kennedy's plan was a large economic assistance program called the Alliance for Progress. This was formally launched in August 1961 at the meeting of the Inter-American Economic and Social Council in Punta del Este, Uruguay. Paradoxically, it was at this same meeting that Ernesto Che Guevara announced Cuba's aggressive policy of nationalizing, without compensation, United States assets in the Caribbean island. Many years later, Richard Goodwin, a lawyer who was then a special counsel to President Kennedy, recalled meeting informally with Guevara in Montevideo. Che told Goodwin that the Alliance for Progress would fail because it came too late. In his own speech at the summit the guerrilla commander–turned–minister predicted that socialist revolutions would spread through Latin America and that by 1980 Cuba's income per capita would be higher than that of the United

States at the time of the meeting.[4] Although Guevara was already a romanticized international symbol of rebellion, no one expected that in less than four years he would resign his government positions to lead a guerrilla army engaged in a bloody civil war in the Congo or that in October 1967 he would be assassinated by the Bolivian military in the town of Vallegrande.

In a major speech announcing the Alliance for Progress, President John F. Kennedy recognized the extent of social conflict in the region. He said: "Throughout Latin America—a continent rich in resources and in spiritual and cultural achievements of its people—millions of men and women suffer the daily degradations of hunger and poverty. They lack decent shelter or protection from disease. Their children are deprived of the education or the jobs which are the gateway for a better life."[5] The Charter of Punta del Este set forth ambitious goals for the Alliance for Progress, including an income per capita growth rate of at least 2.5 percent per annum; more equitable distribution of income; diversification of regional exports; implementation of "programs of comprehensive agrarian reforms"; elimination of adult illiteracy and expansion of educational coverage; construction of massive housing facilities; low inflation and price stability; and establishment of policies that would reduce the occurrence of major currency crises. To achieve these goals the countries in the region were to develop consistent economic programs for the medium and long terms. The charter also stipulated that the United States would provide substantial aid—$2 billion per year for at least ten years. Interestingly, there was no call for drastically opening up Latin American economies by reducing import tariffs rates and dismantling other protectionist measures such as import quotas, licenses, and prohibitions.[6]

Implementing the policies of the Alliance for Progress was not easy, however. In the poorer countries there was very limited expertise in economics, and it was nearly impossible to design coherent economic programs to meet the alliance's goals. Moreover, in most countries the ruling class opposed many of the measures espoused by the alliance. Landowners were against any form of land reform, and there was great reluctance to implement the type of austere policies required to bring down inflation. In spite of these difficulties, immediately after the alliance was launched there was a ray of hope, and President Kennedy became a revered figure throughout the region. When he was assassinated in 1963, the poor of Latin America wept as if one of their own had died.

Protectionism and Social Conditions

By the late 1960s, almost a decade after the launching of the Alliance for Progress, Latin America was a region of contrasts.[7] In some countries, such as Brazil, Mexico, and Venezuela, growth had accelerated significantly and averaged more than 6 percent per year; in others (Argentina, Chile, Guatemala, Honduras and Uruguay) growth was modest at best. In some nations (Argentina, Chile) instability and high inflation were the norm, while in others (El Salvador, Guatemala, Honduras, Nicaragua) inflation was very low, indeed lower than in the United States.

Most countries, however, shared two interrelated characteristics: First, the degree of openness to international trade—both in goods and in financial capital—was very low. Indeed, the alliance program did not explicitly call for increasing openness or international competition. And second, in most countries social conditions failed to improve: poverty continued to be widespread, and income distribution remained extremely unequal. In 1970—three full decades after the initiation of the import substitution development strategy—40 percent of all Latin America's families still lived below the poverty line; in the rural sector the incidence of poverty was an astonishing 62 percent.[8]

The low degree of openness to international competition predated the Alliance for Progress and was the result of the increasingly protectionist policies implemented since the late 1930s as a way of encouraging industrialization. One of the most influential promoters of this policy was Argentina's Raúl Prebisch, who as head of the UN Economic Commission for Latin America—generally known by the acronym for its name in Spanish, Comisión Económica para América Latina (CEPAL)—led a small group of economists who argued that unless Latin America industrialized rapidly, it would be left behind. The reason for this, they pointed out, was that in the decades to come international prices for Latin America's exports—mostly commodities such as oil, copper, wheat, iron ore, and soybeans—would decline significantly, while prices of imported manufactured goods would increase steadily.

In most Latin American countries the industrialization process had gathered force during World War II, when imports of manufacturing goods from the United States and Europe dried up. During this time the region's nascent industrial sector expanded almost exclusively on the basis of substituting those imports that were not available due to the war effort. During the second half of the 1940s, as international economic relations began to normalize, Latin America's authorities faced a dilemma: Should industrialization continue to be based on the substitution of imports of consumer goods? Or should it be tied to an expansion of exports? The former strategy required protecting national industries through even higher import tariffs and other forms of trade restriction because domestic industries simply were not as efficient and thus not competitive with foreign producers. The latter involved adding value to commodity exports and keeping domestic currency at a highly competitive value. These two approaches differed in terms of the role given to foreign capital—the import substitution model restricted it, while the export-oriented alternative encouraged it—and had very different implications for the distribution of income. In most countries, the import substitution model implied transferring income from the countryside and the provinces, where most export activities were located, to the nascent industrial sector and the large cities. By contrast, export-oriented development would benefit the provinces.

During the second half of the 1940s and the early 1950s, in country after country the authorities opted for the import substitution model. This reflected a shift in political power that had occurred since the Crash of 1929 and the Great Depression. Exporters had lost influence, while the state—and with it, civil servants and bureaucrats—had gained considerable power, as had the new urban industrialist class and labor unions. The technical bases and underpinnings for the protectionist policy drive were provided by the new ideas developed by Raúl Prebisch and his CEPAL colleagues.[9]

Supporters of the import substitution strategy—most notably German-born economist Albert O. Hirschman—argued that in order for it to succeed, two conditions were required. First, protectionist measures had to be strictly temporary and had to be reduced over time. More generally, import tariffs and other restrictions on trade had to be high enough to protect the targeted industry and low enough to act as a "pressure mechanism" to force producers to improve productivity and become efficient.[10] And second, only selected industries should be protected. This recommendation was a result of Hirschman's conviction that a healthy and successful growth process was always "unbalanced" and that some industries and sectors were supposed to grow faster than others for prolonged periods of time. Hirschman contrasted his "unbalanced growth" view with what he considered blunt and unsophisticated efforts to implement huge development plans that would indiscriminately create large state-owned manufacturing firms and to generate industrialization through massive and blanket protection programs.

According to Hirschman's views—which became very popular in academic and policy circles—trade restrictions should be used to protect and encourage those sectors with strong "forward and backward linkages." That is, protection should be provided only to those industries whose expansion would feed into other promising economic sectors and demand large amounts of production from other industries. The goal was to encourage rapid and effective industrialization. At the time, steel was usually mentioned as an industry with significant forward and backward linkages. On one hand, steel mills required iron ore and coke coal, and on the other the finished product could be used in the manufacturing of automobiles and white goods and in construction.

Hirschman had come to these views after many years of working in the field as an economic advisor to governments and development agencies—in Europe with the Marshall Plan and in Colombia from 1952 through 1957. In spite of its appeal, the proper implementation of this protectionist model required a remarkable amount of fine tuning and very precise and detailed knowledge of the economy; indeed, it required the type of knowledge that no government official—not even the best trained, most cable, and well informed—was likely to have or ever acquire. Which industries had the greatest linkages? How much should they be protected and for how long? What combination of import tariffs, quotas, and licenses would provide the adequate "pressure mechanism" to force firms to become efficient? And more important than all of these questions was the challenge of preventing policy makers from being influenced by industrial lobbyists who claimed that their specific sectors had extremely high linkages and were utterly deserving of protection? As Columbia University professor Carlos F. Diaz-Alejandro put it, the problem with Hirschman's linkages approach was that its policy implications were extremely complex and were likely to become "dangerous in the sloppy hands of mediocre followers."[11]

And sloppy hands, indeed, they were. Instead of being selective, protection became general and massive. It rewarded industries with high degrees of linkages, with low linkages, and with no linkages at all. It took private manufacturing sector lobbyists no time to convince policy makers that their particular industries were exceptional, had great promise, contributed to the process of technological transfer from the advanced world, and deserved to be protected by tariffs, quotas, and even straight prohibitions. But that was not all. The maze of regulations became so intricate that it paid to obtain exemptions and permits to import otherwise protected goods at little or no tariff. Of course, those who managed to become sole importers with little or no import duties made fortunes in very short periods of time. Tariff books throughout Latin America became huge monsters that detailed import tariffs for tens of thousands of goods, described the extent of restrictions and regulations, presented sliding duties schedules, detailed the coverage of prior licenses and the levels of surcharges, and specified a number of exemptions.

Chile starkly illustrates excesses of protectionist policies during the years of the import substitution industrialization model. In the mid-1960s, after more than two decades of protection, import tariffs and duties continued to be extremely high in the manufacturing sector. This resulted in much higher domestic prices than Chilean consumers would have paid if they had freer access to the global marketplace. It also allowed Chilean producers to be less efficient than if forced to compete with foreign suppliers. In the mid-1960s, for instance, a Chilean consumer paid 52 percent more for a pair of pants than he would have paid in the international marketplace; wool coats were 23 percent more expensive and shoes 20 percent dearer. In 1965, as noted previously, bicycles cost 300 percent more than in the advanced nations. This basically put them out of reach of average blue-collar workers. Worse yet, the quality of locally produced goods was much lower than that of goods produced in other regions: shoes wore out more rapidly, white and electronic goods malfunctioned often, and bicycles broke down frequently—I know this firsthand because as a child I owned a bike made in Chile.[12]

There are more examples: Imported textiles were subject to duties ranging from 80 to 120 percent. Dyed textiles carried a 92 percent tariff, while those made of combed wool had 80 percent duties. Automobile tires were subject to a 125 percent import tariff, which increased their domestic cost to consumers by at least that much relative to global prices. Drills had a 75 percent tariff; heaters, 244 percent; electrical motors, 162 percent; radios, 340 percent; vacuum cleaners, 85 percent; and refrigerators, 136 percent. I could go on and on, but these examples are enough to illustrate clearly how surreal things had become under the protectionist industrial policy.[13]

Producers of these and other protected industrial products were the big winners of Chile's import substitution industrialization policy. The losers were exporters—wineries, mining companies, and fresh fruit producers to name just a few—who had to pay heavy tariffs on imported materials and on capital goods and machinery but received no government incentives when they sold their products abroad. A few examples illustrate this point: furniture manufacturers had to pay average import tariffs of 20 percent on their materials, wine producers paid 90 percent, wheat producers paid 32 percent, and corn farmers paid an average import duty on imported goods of 28 percent.

Exporters were additionally penalized because, as a result of the high degree of overall protection and the concomitant low degree of openness of the economy, the domestic currency strengthened significantly, and artificially, in value. This meant that for each dollar's worth of goods sold abroad, exporters received fewer units of domestic currency—escudos at that time—than they would have obtained under freer trade. It has been estimated that in the late 1960s the degree of currency overvaluation in Chile was equivalent to a tax on exports ranging from 24 to 32 percent of the value of the goods exported.[14]

From today's perspective the irrationality and arbitrariness of Chile's import tariffs in the 1960s is striking and difficult to understand. Indeed, these levels of protection hardly constituted what Hirschman had called a "pressure mechanism" to force producers to be efficient.

Instead of declining, as Raúl Prebisch, Albert O. Hirschman, and others had predicated, the degree of protectionism in Chile—and in most of Latin America—increased over time. For example, by late 1969 import duties on combed wool textiles had increased to 120 percent from 80 percent four years earlier, and tariffs on men's shirts, which had previously had no tariff, and coats, which had carried a tariff of 23 percent, had increased to 120 percent as well. Export sectors also continued to be penalized by high costs of materials and machinery and by the artificially high value of the local currency.

Chile's experience with protectionism during the import substitution industrialization era was hardly unique. In a 1971 study, Johns Hopkins professor Bela Balassa estimated that average Brazilian and Mexican import tariffs on manufacturing and consumer goods were as high as Chile's. According to his estimates, at that time import tariffs in Latin America were significantly higher that in Malaysia and other East Asian nations. In 1994, English economist Victor Bulmer-Thomas showed that in the 1960s average import tariffs were 131 percent in Argentina, 168 percent in Brazil, 138 percent in Chile, 112 percent in Colombia, and 61 percent in Mexico.[15] In contrast, average import tariffs in the European Economic Community stood at 13 percent. According to data compiled by the Fraser Institute, in 1980 Latin American was one of the most protectionist regions in the world; import tariffs across all countries and sectors—including those export sectors with no import tariffs—were on average 42 percent. By comparison, at that time average import tariffs were only 15 percent in the nations known as the Asian Tigers.[16]

Beginning in the mid-1940s, in most Latin American countries the state grew significantly. According to the prevailing views, it was not enough to encourage industrialization through massive protectionist policies; in order to build a substantial manufacturing base, it was also necessary to create large state-owned enterprises in what were defined as "strategic sectors," including sectors with considerable backward and forward linkages. Two interrelated ideas were behind this drive for an active role of the state in the production sphere: First, it was thought that the private sector would be unable to obtain the financial resources required for investing in very large companies in the steel, energy, mining, and oil sectors. This was not a completely unfounded point; what the proponents of the government-led development strategy failed to note, however, was that the private sector's inability to obtain the required financing was the direct consequence of poorly developed credit markets and of legislation that failed to protect the rights of minority owners and share holders. Second, these sectors were considered too important to be left to foreign investors because of geopolitical or strategic considerations. Indeed, since the expropriation of oil fields and the creation of the giant state-owned oil company Pemex in 1938, many nationalistic political leaders throughout the region argued that Mexico provided the right model to follow.

A number of state-owned companies were created across Latin America. These included CORFO (Corporación de Fomento de la Producción) in Chile, created in 1939; BNDES (Banco Nacional de Desenvolvimento Econômico e Social) in Brazil, founded in 1956; and Argentina's Banco Industrial, established 1944. In Mexico, Nacional Financiera was created in 1934 with the aim of financing large investment projects in infrastructure and basic industries. With time the number of state-owned enterprises grew significantly. Some, such as Petrobras in Brazil, were created from scratch; some were the result of nationalization processes—Petróleos de Venezuela S.A. (PDVSA) in Venezuela and Chile's copper giant Codelco are two prominent examples—and others were acquired by the state as a result of bailouts of private-sector enterprises that had been poorly managed and run into financial trouble. In the late 1970s, heavy industry, telecommunications, water supply, and mining, among other sectors, were dominated by the state throughout most of the region. In some countries the state also had a strong presence in the financial sector and owned or controlled banks, financial concerns, and insurance companies. Many of these firms were managed based on political criteria, developed a bloated payroll, and became highly inefficient. By the early 1980s the vast majority of them were losing money and contributed significantly to public-sector deficits and, thus, to inflationary pressure. In 1990 there were more than 300 state-owned enterprises in Argentina, more than 700 in Brazil, and more than a 1,100 in Mexico.[17]

Unemployment and Informality

In the late 1940s unemployment became a serious problem throughout Latin America. At that time an increasingly large number of people worked in the "gray economy," without proper labor contracts or formal attachment to employers. They did not receive benefits, were not enrolled in pension or retirement programs, and were often paid extremely low wages. This large group of workers constituted what came to be known as the "informal sector."

This state of affairs was the direct consequence of the development model based on protectionism, heavy government regulations, and artificially strong domestic currencies. These policies helped create dual labor markets. Some urban workers were able to get jobs in the modern, highly protected manufacturing sector. To the extent that these companies were sheltered by high barriers to international competition, they could pay relatively high salaries, as well as retirement and health benefits. However, an informal or unprotected sector coexisted side by side with this modern labor market. Informal workers often had the same skills as those employed in modern firms; they simply were not fortunate enough to obtain one of the highly coveted high-paying jobs. Informality was concentrated in very small firms, the service sector—repair shops, food stalls—and menial jobs.

As protectionism grew, so did the extent of informality. In 1950 informal workers represented on average 9 percent of the regional labor force. Informality was particularly high in Chile (14 percent), Venezuela (11 percent), and Guatemala (11 percent). Two decades later, in 1970, the overall degree of informality had climbed to 12 percent of Latin America's labor force. Peru now led the region with 17 percent of its workers in the informal sector, followed by Mexico and Bolivia with 15 percent. In 1989 more than half of nonagricultural jobs were in the informal sector (52 percent). Of those employed in the formal sector, one-third worked for the government and had dubious levels of productivity. This dismal situation starkly exemplified the severe limitations of the import substitution protectionist model followed by most Latin American countries without interruption since the late 1930s.[18]

Massive migration from the countryside into the cities was another consequence of the import substitution policies. The existence of high-paying jobs in the modern sector acted as a strong magnet. The fact that these jobs were few and hard to get did not dissuade poor rural families that could barely survive in a stagnated agricultural sector that was plagued by economic problems including unproductive land holdings and artificially strong domestic currencies that reduced crop prices and exports' competitiveness.

Those rural migrants who failed to find jobs in the modern and protected segment of the economy enlarged the army of the unemployed and of those toiling in the informal sector. They had no benefits, earned very low wages, and were trapped in a perpetual cycle of poverty and desperation. Like the family of Jesús Sánchez—the destitute Mexican family depicted in Oscar Lewis's *The Children of Sánchez*—they lived in slums, in *villas miserias, favelas, pueblos jóvenes*, and *poblaciones callampas*. They were the victims of violence and crime, and their children did not attend school—or if they were lucky enough, would barely complete two or three years of formal schooling—and would die if they became seriously ill.

With time these slums became cities in themselves. Dwellings that started as mere mud huts became sturdier. Slowly, and often with the help of relatives and neighbors, a cement floor was installed. Then there was a solid wall or two, and a few years later there might even be a dining room or a second story. Governments often tried to improve conditions; they would install electrical connections, and potable water and sewers would be made available. After a number of years—often a number of decades—some of these poor families had a small amount of capital invested in their houses. However, as Hernando de Soto has pointed out in his book *The Mystery of Capital*, there is tragedy and irony in this story. In spite of all the suffering and all the effort, these families lacked titles to their homes; without a title they were not eligible for small loans, and without financing they could not start a small business. It was just not possible; even if they wanted to do so, even if they had the ability and the entrepreneurial spirit, they just couldn't do it.

Fiscal Profligacy, Monetary Largesse, Instability, and Currency Crises

Protectionism and lack of social progress were only two of the economic problems encountered by Latin America between 1940 and 1989. During these years most countries in the region experienced rapid inflation, difficulties with balance of payment, and currency crises. Between 1960 and 1970 inflation in Latin America averaged 20 percent per year, while worldwide inflation was only 4 percent. During that time five Latin American countries—Argentina, Brazil, Chile, Colombia, and Uruguay—had double-digit inflation and were largely responsible for the region's high average.[19]

Macroeconomic conditions worsened in the late 1970s and early 1980s, when most Latin American countries experienced accelerating rates of inflation and more frequent currency crises and devaluations. Whereas inflation averaged 7 percent per annum in 1970–71, it was 49 percent in 1974–75. During the 1970s the number of Latin American countries with double-digit inflation increased from five to fourteen. By 1983–85 the average rate of inflation had increased to an astounding 300 percent per year. At that time one out of four Latin American countries had an annual rate of inflation in excess of 75 percent. This rapid increase in prices had a number of negative effects: credit virtually disappeared, uncertainty increased, investment declined, government controls became stricter, and the population at large—especially the poor—saw the purchasing power of its wages, pensions, and savings erode rapidly.

Two fundamental and interrelated factors were behind this state of affairs: First, government deficits increased significantly in the aftermath of the dramatic oil price hikes of 1973 and 1980. In 1970–71 the average public-sector deficit in Latin America amounted to a modest 2 percent of gross domestic product, not very different from deficits in the Asian Tiger countries. By 1983–85, however, average government imbalances in Latin America had climbed to 6 percent of gross domestic product; in the Asian Tiger nations, by contrast, government deficits remained on average below 2 percent of gross domestic product. And second, because of the political difficulties involved in raising taxes and reigning in expenditures, Latin American countries turned to money-printing by the central banks as a way of financing the deficit. After the oil shock of 1980, even traditionally conservative central bankers, such as those in Central America, were forced by politicians to grant very large loans to the government or to ailing state-owned enterprises. This excessive creation of liquidity resulted in additional pressure on prices and made already large trade deficits even larger. During the 1970s and 1980s the old principle that "inflation is the result of too much money chasing too few goods" was proven to be correct again and again.

One of the consequences of high inflation was that wages were adjusted frequently, as were other costs such as rent, insurance, and prices of intermediate industrial materials. This cost pressure was extremely detrimental for exporters, in particular in countries that fixed the value of their currency to the U.S. dollar. Because of the pegged exchange rates, the amount of domestic currency that exporters received per U.S. dollar remained constant while domestic production costs increased steadily. As a result, exports lost international competitiveness, imports became inexpensive, and large trade imbalances developed. These external deficits were initially financed through foreign borrowing. When external sources of finance began to dry up, local governments turned to international reserves held at their central banks to cover the imbalances. Eventually, however, country after country ran out of international reserves; when that happened, a bailout by the IMF and a large devaluation were the only options available.

Almost invariably, major devaluations and currency crises are followed by periods of economic retrenchment and adjustment. Government expenditures are cut, employment declines, wages collapse, and income contracts abruptly. As a result of currency devaluation, the domestic value of debts contracted abroad and denominated in foreign currency—U.S. dollars, yen, or other currencies from the advanced counties—increase dramatically, triggering financial dislocation and massive bankruptcies. This was indeed the case in Latin America between 1983 and 2003, when the region went through twenty-six external crises and devaluations. In the aftermath of eighteen of these currency crises, income distribution became more unequal, and the proportion of people living below the poverty line increased significantly.

But that is not all. As Harvard professor Richard Cooper documented more than three decades ago, most currency crises in emerging markets usually result in political upheaval and instability.[20] Historically, the economic costs of major currency crises have been staggering. Recent research that I conducted indicates that after twenty-five years—that is, after roughly one generation—a country that has experienced a currency crisis will have an income per capita 18 percent lower than one that has not. This means that after seventy-five years the gap in income per capita between two such hypothetical countries will be almost 50 percent; that is, the typical crisis country will have a level of income per person equal to half the income of the healthy nation.[21] Is it any wonder that Latin American countries continue to fall further behind both the developed countries and other developing countries that have not had currency crises?

Oil Shocks and Debt Crisis

In 1973 the international price of oil increased by more than 200 percent—from approximately $4 per barrel to a little over $12 per barrel—and in 1979 it increased by another 125 percent, to approximately $32 per barrel. These major price changes fundamentally shaped the path followed by the Latin American countries during the last quarter of the twentieth century.

The large increase in oil prices affected oil exporters and importers in very different ways. The former—particularly Mexico and Venezuela—embarked on ambitious development plans aimed at rapid industrialization; Mexico's president José López Portillo said, "[W]e will administer abundance." Most of this effort was led by the public sector and consisted of gigantic and, as it turned out, inefficient investment projects that were laden with corruption.[22] As a way of leveraging the oil monies, governments in the oil-exporting countries borrowed heavily from the rest of the world and rapidly accumulated very large external debts.

Oil-importing countries tried to cushion the sudden worsening in their terms of trade—or prices of exports relative to those of imports—by borrowing liberally from abroad. Like their oil-exporting neighbors, they accumulated foreign debt at a pace that proved unsustainable. Many countries that for decades had maintained price stability—mostly the countries of Central America—began to rely on printing money to finance rapidly increasing government expenditures. As a result, inflation increased, exports lost competitiveness, and international reserves held by the central banks declined rapidly.[23] Most countries responded to this situation by implementing exchange and capital controls and restricting the purchase of hard currency by local firms and individuals. Businessmen and families traveling abroad were allowed to obtain nominal amounts of foreign currency that did not cover the costs of hotels or subsistence. As trade deficits became larger, a number of countries adopted multiple exchange-rate regimes, whereby different transactions, including the exportation of different varieties of the same good, were subject to different exchange rates. These systems were highly inefficient, encouraged corruption and black markets, and eventually forced the countries that adopted them—including the Central American nations—to devalue their currencies and abandon their decades-long fixed exchange-rate regimes.

On the evening of August 12, 1982, Mexico's finance minister, Jesús Silva Herzog, a respected economist known for his charm and thunderous baritone voice, flew to Washington, D.C. The purpose of the trip was to inform his American counterparts that, in spite of the high price of oil, Mexico—one of the world's major oil exporters—would be unable to make interest payments on its debt that were due the following Monday.[24] His first meeting, on the morning of Friday the thirteenth, was with Jacques de Larosière, a Frenchman who at the time headed the IMF. Fund officials had recently returned from Mexico City and were already preparing a sizable loan that they hoped would help stabilize Mexico's finances. The meeting with de Larosière was short and to the point; the two officials agreed that the sooner the IMF funds were made available the better. They also concluded that Mexico would need additional financing and that some of it had to become available immediately. Silva Herzog's next stop was at the Federal Reserve, where chairman Paul Volcker rapidly grasped the impact that a Mexican default would have on world financial markets. He said that the Fed would work with other national and international institutions in an effort to find a solution to Mexico's problems. During the next few weeks Volcker would play a key role helping arrange a bridge loan from the Bank of International Settlements (an international institution headquartered in Basel, Switzerland, whose goal is to coordinate central banks from around the world) and organizing the G-7 response to this unexpected turn of events. In spite of Volcker's efforts and those of Secretary of the Treasury Donald Regan and other officials from the advanced countries, it was not possible to avoid the Mexican default.

The causes behind the 1982 Mexican crisis read like a catalog of Latin America's economic excesses and policy mistakes of the import substitution era. Byzantine government regulations and controls coupled with generalized protectionism had greatly distorted the price system. This in turn resulted in a significant misallocation of productive capital. Instead of financing capital projects in areas where the country had competitive advantages, huge investments were made in gigantic and inefficient initiatives with little or no economic return. Monies were also wasted on corruption and mammoth infrastructure projects that did not contribute to improving efficiency, making exports more competitive, or accelerating economic growth. Massive government expenditures put pressure on prices and inflation and resulted in rapid accumulation of foreign debt. The collapse of the Mexican peso, which lost almost 75 percent of its value in 1982, was a traumatic event that marked the beginning of Latin America's "lost decade."

During the next seven years income per capita in most Latin American countries barely grew, social conditions worsened quickly, and some countries suffered serious bouts of hyperinflation. In 1989 the rate of inflation in Argentina exceeded 3,000 percent; in Bolivia it was almost 12,000 percent in 1985, and in Brazil it climbed to almost 3,000 percent in 1990. Worse yet, during most of the "lost decade" many countries in the region were governed by military dictators who violated human rights, prohibited dissent, and persecuted political opponents.

The Lost Decade, Market Reforms, and the Washington Consensus

The 1980s were the culmination of Latin America's love affair with protectionism and a government-led economic strategy. These ten years were devastating for the people of the region, especially for the poor and the disadvantaged. For the region as a whole, income per capita *declined* at an average rate of almost 1 percent per year. Income per capita in Argentina contracted at an annual rate of 2.3 percent. The reduction of income per person was 2.2 percent per year in Bolivia, 1.6 percent in El Salvador, and 1.8 in Guatemala. In Mexico income per capita contracted at an average annual rate of 0.5 percent; the annual decline was 2.6 percent in Peru and 2.4 percent in Venezuela. During the 1980s income per person expanded in only five Latin American countries: Brazil, Chile, Colombia, Paraguay, and Uruguay. But even in these nations, performance was mediocre; their income per capita grew at a very mediocre average rate of 0.8 percent per year. Average wages (adjusted for inflation) also declined dramatically during this period. For example, in Mexico, average wages in 1988 were 27 percent below their 1980 level, in Costa Rica they were 11 percent below the level of 1980, in Peru wages were 20 percent lower than in 1980, and in Venezuela average wages declined by 8 percent between 1980 and 1988.[25] Labeling the 1980s the "lost decade" is definitely neither hyperbole nor exaggeration.

In the late 1980s it became increasingly apparent that a solution to the crisis would require coordinated action by the Latin American governments, advanced countries, creditors, and international multilateral institutions. A breakthrough was achieved in 1989 when the Brady Plan—named after U.S. treasury secretary Nicholas Brady—was announced. This initiative was based on two simple principles: First, Latin American debtors were de facto granted significant debt relief. Second, creditor banks and nations would provide fresh funds to participating countries to help them jump-start their economies, resume growth, and drive enough economic activity to return to a normal state of affairs. But the most important feature of the Brady Plan was that in order to be eligible for debt relief and new monies, governments had to make a commitment to initiating economic reforms aimed at controlling inflation, deregulating their economies, and fostering competition. Although these re-form conditions were set in rather vague terms, they provided an impetus to the strong economic transformation process that engulfed almost every coun-try in the region and came to be known as the Washington Consensus.[26]

In contrast with the Alliance for Progress, the Washington Consensus was not an officially sponsored economic program. It was rather a collection of loosely articulated ideas aimed at modernizing, deregulating, opening up, and reforming the Latin American economies. There has been considerable controversy about whether the name Washington Consensus correctly re-flects the origin of these ideas. I have argued elsewhere that the Washington institutions—the U.S. Treasury, the World Bank, and the International Mon-etary Fund—had little to do with the specifics of these reforms.[27] It is true that to participate in the Brady debt forgiveness program the Latin American countries had to show *some* commitment to modernizing their economies. However, there was no detailed list of reforms that had to be implemented. Clearly, the actual policies were not imposed or forced upon the Latin Ameri-can governments. The reform programs were largely homegrown and were Latin America's own response to more than a decade of crisis; they were developed by a group of foreign-trained economists who have been labeled "technopols."[28] In fact, the Washington institutions were skeptical—and in some cases openly opposed—to some of the most daring reform proposals. To be sure, as time passed, and more and more countries adopted these policies, Washington began to support the effort.

In a highly influential article published in 1989, English economist John Williamson summarized the main goals of the modernizing reforms that at the time were being implemented—or merely contemplated—in a number of Latin American nations. He also named this emerging approach toward economic policy the Washington Consensus. Williamson's list of ten policies may be summarized as follows:

- *Achieve fiscal balance as a means of reducing inflationary pressures and stabilizing prices.*
- *Target public expenditures on the poorer groups in the population.* Priority should be given to government expenditures aimed at improving social conditions and reducing poverty; generalized subsidies, which benefit mostly the middle class, were to be avoided.
- *Implement deep tax reforms in order to reduce evasion, increase government income, and eliminate perverse incentives to production and investment.*
- *Free interest rates and modernize the financial sector.* Interest rates had to be market determined, not set by government officials arbitrarily. A well-functioning capital market would help allocate scarce capital to the most productive uses, and market-determined interest rates would discourage capital flight.
- *Avoid artificially strong currencies that discouraged exports.* By staying away from currency overvaluation the probability of major and costly crises would be greatly reduced.
- *Reduce the extent of protectionism, and rationalize trade policy.* The irrational structure of protectionism that had evolved over half a century had to be dismantled and replaced by lower import tariffs.
- *Encourage foreign direct investment.* The region's lack of resources would benefit from investment by foreign companies, and these firms were likely to provide new technology and management techniques that would help increase productivity.
- *Privatize inefficient state-owned enterprises.* In particular, many of the companies that had found their way into state hands during the previ-

ous twenty years had to be sold to private investors—both domestic and foreign.

- *Deregulate business transactions, including investment decisions.* Red tape had to be cut, barriers to entry in key industries eliminated, and competition encouraged.
- *Improve legal protection of property rights in order to secure greater investment by both foreigners and nationals.*[29]

It is important to emphasize, once again, that these ten policy areas were not defined by the Washington bureaucracies at the IMF, World Bank, or U.S. Treasury. Williamson could have listed twelve policy areas—the "Washington Dozen," say—or fifteen or even twenty, but for ease of exposition he chose to synthesize what he believed was the core of the ongoing modernization reform movement in the ten propositions listed above. Interestingly, these ten policies—and the term "Washington Consensus" for that matter—acquired a life of their own and were soon considered some sort of official pronouncement on what the reform countries should do and not do. In many ways this is unfortunate, since a number of analysts have evaluated the reform effort through the lenses provided by this list, and thus have missed many of the subtleties and complexities of the actual stories of individual countries. Indeed, in the country-specific analyses presented in this book I provide detailed discussions that move away from the caricature of the "Washington Consensus Decalogue," as these points have come to be known by some.[30]

During the first half of the 1990s country after country began to implement a variety of modernization policies. Different nations proceeded at different speeds and emphasized different aspects of the reforms, but the vast majority made progress in four areas: fiscal deficits were reduced, tax reforms were implemented, import tariffs were lowered, and state-owned companies were privatized. In most countries the initial results were impressive. Inflation declined drastically and growth increased significantly: while in 1989–90 average inflation was 940 percent, in 1993–94 it was 129 percent; gross domestic product per capita fell by 0.5 percent in 1989–90 but grew by 2.2 percent in 1993–99.[31] And in most countries, after a decade of steep declines, wages recovered rapidly.[32] It is not an exaggeration to say that by 1994 there was heightened hope for the Latin American economies. Suddenly it appeared as if, after decades of frustration, the Latin American economies were ready to take off.

But behind these impressive early results hid important weaknesses. Many countries, including the three largest—Argentina, Brazil, and Mexico—continued to peg the values of their currencies to the U.S. dollar at artificially high levels, and during the first half of the 1990s they allowed this currency overvaluation to increase. This reduced exports' competitiveness in the global marketplace. Pegging currency values to the U.S. dollar also encouraged speculation; this was reflected in huge increases in short-term capital inflows. But currency overvaluation and the resulting decline in international competitiveness were not the only problems: in most countries privatization of public utilities—including energy, water, sanitation, and telecommunications—was implemented without first putting in place proper regulation and competition policies. As a result, in many countries state-owned monopolies were replaced by privately owned monopolies. In a number of countries privatization was accompanied by corruption and giveaways, allowing insiders—including government functionaries in charge of the public enterprises and the sales process—to buy large blocs of shares at conveniently low prices.[33] At the same time, most countries failed, or were unwilling, to move forward in the creation of strong and modern institutions that would encourage the rule of law, protect property rights, and reduce the extent of corruption. Although competitive exchange rates, policies designed to encourage competition, and protection of property rights through institutional reforms were part of the original Washington Consensus Decalogue, most countries paid only lip service to them. As a result, most countries were unable to move to the higher phases of growth transition discussed in chapter 1 and became increasingly vulnerable to changes in global economic conditions. During the second half of the 1990s and the early 2000s many of them succumbed to deep and costly crises that increased unemployment, wiped out savings, reduced wages, and generated disappointment and anger.

Part II

The Washington Consensus and the Recurrence of Crises, 1989–2002

Chapter 4

Fractured Liberalism

Latin America's Incomplete Reforms

By late 1992 every country in Latin America except Cuba and Haiti had initiated market-oriented reforms. Some countries—Bolivia, Chile, and Mexico—began earlier and some, such as Argentina, moved very fast.[1] But more important and impressive was that the quest for modernization was massive and regionwide. There was excitement and great expectations. Foreign observers were surprised to see that countries that for half a century had moved away from globalization, openness, international markets, and competition were suddenly embracing all of these. As always, there were those who reduced everything to a conspiracy theory: it was the United States and its peons—the IMF and the World Bank—that had imposed these models on the poor Latin American countries. More astute observers, however, considered other factors—some of them deep and historical—in an effort to understand what was going on throughout the region. Some looked as far back as the colonial times, others to the Baring Crisis in the late nineteenth century, while still others talked about the exhaustion of the "easy phase" of the import substitution and protectionist model in the 1970s. But whatever were the causes of the reforms, throughout the region and among observers of Latin America there was a sense of disbelief; some analysts even paraphrased Karl Marx and Friedrich Engels and said that a specter was haunting Latin America—the specter of liberalism, free markets, and competition.[2]

Almost two decades after the reforms were launched, the initial euphoria has died, and several crises have occurred; the time is ripe to make an assessment of how much progress has really been made in this modernization effort. The general sense in Latin America and among media analysts and academic observers from around the world is that the region has joined the ranks of modern capitalism; it is still, of course, a poor part of the world, but according to this view, it has made great strides in its quest to adopt market-oriented economic policies and modernize its institutions.

Reality, however, is different from perception. The economic reforms of the 1990s and 2000s were incomplete and stalled before transforming Latin America into a competitive region. In spite of all the hoopla and media attention, the Washington Consensus only scratched the surface of Latin America's policy environment. In fact, most Latin American economies are still among the most regulated, distorted, and protectionist in the world. In many of them it is difficult to start a business, regulations are stifling, and taxes are very high. With very few exceptions, institutions continue to be extremely weak: property rights are not protected sufficiently, the judiciary is inefficient, contracts are difficult to enforce, corruption is pervasive, and the rule of law is wanting. Moreover, throughout the region governments continue to be very large and highly inefficient and fail to provide basic services including quality education, infrastructure, and support for research and development. The Latin American economic reform process clearly remains fractured and incomplete.

This does not mean that no reforms have been implemented. Of course they have, and in some areas—from a historical perspective—they are significant. Indeed, during the 1990s most countries pared down controls, regulations, and red tape and made an effort to reduce corruption. In almost every nation import tariffs were lowered, business and financial regulations were relaxed, and a large number of state-owned enterprises were privatized. At the same time, value-added taxes were introduced, fiscal deficits were reduced and in some cases even eliminated, and inflation was gradually brought under control. In many countries central banks have been granted independence from day-to-day political pressures, and the budget process has been modernized. More importantly, in every country democracy has returned after decades of military rule and dictatorship. In that sense, it is fair to say, as Francis Fukuyama has, that in the past two decades Latin America made progress; it may even be argued that within Latin America there has been a silent revolution.[3]

There is, however, another way, and I would argue a more appropriate one, of looking at progress on the modernization and reform fronts. If one uses an international benchmark and compares the Latin American countries with more successful competitors—such as the Asian Tigers; the southern Euro-

pean nations of Greece, Portugal, and Spain, or the advanced commodity exporters Australia, Canada, and New Zealand—the picture that emerges is not
very satisfactory. In fact, it is disturbing, showing a region that continues to
lag behind significantly in the global economy.

Focusing on these somewhat demanding international comparisons is important because, in the end, what really matters is not whether distortions—
including protectionist tariffs and stifling regulations—are partially reduced
but whether the reforms are deep enough to fundamentally address the challenges faced by firms and individuals. What is important is whether the reforms substantially reduce what Nobel Prize winner Douglas C. North has
called "transaction costs" and create the basis for a modern market-oriented
system that encourages innovation and productivity growth and at the same
time provides the resources required to improve social conditions. The appropriate way of assessing how much progress Latin America has made is not
by comparing current Latin American policies with those of its own past—
say, the policies that led to the "lost decade" of the 1980s—but by comparing
them to those of successful countries including the Asian Tigers and the advanced commodity exporters. The result of such a comparison is crystal clear:
Latin America's revolution—if there ever was one—has not only been silent,
as Francis Fukuyama has claimed, but it has also been incomplete and has left
most countries in the region at a significant comparative disadvantage in the
quest to build modern, vibrant, resilient, innovative societies where social
conditions for the poor improve in a significant way.

Some may argue that using these international comparisons for assessing
progress in the region's modernization distorts the picture because the countries to which the region is compared are politically and culturally different
from the Latin American nations. For instance, the three advanced commodity
exporters—Australia, Canada, and New Zealand—are Anglo-Saxon countries
with parliamentary governments; every Latin American country considered in
this book, in contrast, has a presidential political system. The Asian Tiger nations also have different cultural influences and a different colonial experience
than the Latin American nations. And the southern European countries all
have parliamentary systems, belong to the European Union, have a past as great
global powers. Though all of this is true, it does not invalidate the comparisons
or make less dramatic the fact that in all of them the Latin American nations do
very poorly and lag behind in almost every policy or institutional category.

One should be careful, however, not to extract mechanical lessons from the comparisons such as "All we need to do is tweak this or that indicator and everything will be fine" or recipes that call for senselessly copying a particular country or region's development path. Be that as it may, the entrenched problems of Latin American countries have prevented growth and development. The fact that half-hearted and incomplete reforms have not provided the solution has had the ironic and unfortunate effect of decreasing popular support for needed changes. Latin American voters have blamed capitalism and the reforms for the poor economic performance of the 1990s and first decade of this century and have held the Washington Consensus and neoliberalism responsible for the costly currency crises of those years. This largely explains why, in country after country, voters have elected neopopulist leaders who promised to roll back the reforms and greatly increase the role of government in economic affairs. Given the institutional weaknesses in Latin American governments, that is akin to having the wolf guard the chicken coop.

Institutions and Economic Performance

For a long time economists have been aware of the importance of institutions. In *The Wealth of Nations* Adam Smith argued that institutions played the important role of protecting the free interaction of individuals in the marketplace. In his view the most important role of the state is protecting private property, providing a standing army and police, administering justice through an independent judiciary, providing infrastructure (roads, bridges, canals), and making sure that monopolies don't stifle competition.[4] Over time, however, the interest in institutions declined among economists. Indeed, in many theories developed during the first six decades of the twentieth century it was assumed that institutions were efficient and optimally designed. Explanations for poor performance—both at the national and corporate level—were sought elsewhere, in areas such as the failure of markets and lack of coordination between different market participants.

In the late 1960s and early 1970s Douglas C. North, a Washington University professor and winner of the 1993 Nobel Prize in economics, began to develop an approach to economic history that emphasized the fundamental role of the institutional setting. One of North's most important insights was to recognize that institutions were often inefficient and that there were political forces that favored keeping them that way. North defined institutions as "the rules of the game in a society, or more formally, the humanly devised constraints that shape human interaction."[5] Defined in this way, it is clear that institutions provide the incentives structure that governs human behavior and economic relations in a particular community. If these rules and regulations encourage innovation, capital accumulation, and skill improvements, both productivity and economic growth will tend to be high. On the contrary, if they favor the status quo and encourage rent-seeking activities, whereby income is obtained by taking advantage of regulations, entrepreneurial activity will be scant, productivity will stagnate, and growth will tend to be low.

At the center of North's approach is the concept of "transaction costs," or costs that individuals and firms have to pay in order to engage in economic exchange. Transaction costs include the cost of finding an honest partner, verifying the truthfulness of a provider, monitoring workers, protecting private property from the voracity of others, enforcing contracts, and dealing with government officials (who may be corrupt). Countries that have institutions that reduce transaction costs perform better than countries that don't. The reason for this is simple: with lower transaction costs, more time and effort can be devoted to innovation and improving productivity.[6] As a result of North's research and influence, during the last two decades an increasingly large number of scholars have analyzed the role of institutions to explain differences in long-term economic growth between countries. The role of institutions in long-term economic performance has been aptly summarized by James A. Robinson: "[S]ome societies are organized in a way that upholds the rule of law; encourages investment in machinery, human capital and better technologies; facilitates broad-based participation in economic and political life by the citizens; and supports market transactions. Others are not. The former prosper while the latter stagnate."[7]

Historical analyses of the increasingly large income gap between North America and South America suggest that institutional differences are at the heart of this long and painful story in divergence. The ineffective, centralized, and autocratic cabildos of the Spanish colonies provide a marked contrast to the vibrant, participatory, and inclusive North American townships discussed by Alexis de Tocqueville. Early tendencies toward corruption and lack of representation in local decision making are also important, as are the succession of plots, conspiracies, and coups d'état. Other important institutional issues include the poor provision of educational services, the structure of land tenure, and the lack of protection of property rights. All of these characteristics and institutional shortcomings of the Latin American nations have been well known to students of the region since at least the mid-nineteenth century, as seen in the writings of Domingo Faustino Sarmiento.[8] Indeed, the architects of the Latin American reforms in the 1990s and 2000s were well aware of the need to go beyond pure economic reforms and to introduce great changes in the institutional fabric of these countries.[9]

Recently some authors have argued that concepts such as strong institutions and the rule of law are rather vague concepts and difficult to measure. This view was aptly summarized by the *Economist* in 2008, when its editors pointed out that not everyone means the same thing when talking about the rule of law. For some it has to do with broadly defined governance and includes an ethical or moral dimension; for others, mostly economists, it is a narrower concept centered on the protection of property rights and the absence of corruption. But the fact that a concept is complex, multifaceted, and difficult to measure doesn't mean that it is unimportant.[10]

At the risk of antagonizing some economists, I would argue that the rule of law—the central component of strong institutions—is, indeed, a very broad concept that comprises several aspects of the way a society operates and behaves. The rule of law means that existing laws and regulations are enforced in a fair, effective, prompt, and unbiased way. This requires courts to be independent, free of corruption, and efficient. It also means that the police are ready, willing, and able to enforce court decisions. It further means that laws and regulations facilitate the signing, monitoring, and enforcement of contracts and that mechanisms for conflict resolution are available to the population at large—not only to large companies and a few wealthy individuals—and operate in an efficient, fair, and prompt way. Fairness is an important component of the rule of law. This means that the extent of democratic rule, the existence of clean elections, and the degree of respect for human and civil rights should be considered in any attempt to measure countries' adherence to the rule of law.

But there is more to it. The rule of law also implies a generalized attitude among individuals, businesses, and institutions—some may consider this an aspect of "culture"—that makes them abide by existing laws and regulations. That is, in countries where the rule of law operates effectively, behaving within the boundaries of the law is the norm rather than the exception. A powerful illustration of the weakness of the rule of law is the way in which labor conflicts are played out in many Latin American countries. It is not unusual for workers with grievances to take over highways and interrupt the flow of traffic for days at a time. The *piqueteros* in Argentina are legendary for their violence and for using force and intimidation to achieve their demands; similarly the *contratistas* in the copper industry in Chile have used strong-arm tactics that involve attacking other workers and cutting off supplies to the mines. And in Mexico there are the *manifestantes*, who block major traffic arteries in order to pressure the authorities to give in to their demands. Needless to say, these are illegal acts, but out of fear of political repercussions, the authorities, including the police, don't attempt to clear demonstrators who are impeding traffic or to enforce the law; more often than not, such actions are met with impunity.

The foregoing discussion suggests that when measuring and evaluating the strength of institutions, particularly the rule of law, it may be misleading to rely on a single indicator. Multifaceted and complex concepts should be measured using a series of indicators; the different dimensions of the rule of law should be made explicit, and countries' failings (or strengths) should emerge from this analysis. In analyzing the rule of law—and other indicators of institutional strength, for that matter—it is also important to avoid mechanical interpretations of the type "If such-and-such index of the rule of law improves by so much, the country's income per capita will increase by this much." More often than not these mechanical analyses miss the intricacies of the real world and result in misleading conclusions. In the analysis that follows I discuss many individual indicators of aspects of the rule of law and institutional strength in Latin America, and I compare them to those in other parts of the world. The picture that emerges from this broad analysis is as clear as it is disappointing: in the vast majority of these areas the Latin American nations fare poorly, and, contrary to widespread belief in the region and among some analysts, they have not experienced significant gains in the last two decades.

Institutions Interrupted: A Latin American Scorecard

In this section I show that in most Latin American countries the reforms since the 1990s have failed to modernize the institutional setting. Indeed, most institutional areas—including the degree of protection of property rights, contracts' enforceability, the rule of law, and the degree of independence of the judiciary—are weaker in Latin America countries than in the countries with which they are compared. Worse yet, a number of Latin American nations—

including Argentina, Bolivia, Ecuador, and Venezuela—have retrogressed in many of these areas during the last few years.

THE RULE OF LAW, THE PROTECTION OF PROPERTY RIGHTS, AND THE JUDICIARY

Academic researchers have found that the rule of law is closely related to economic performance. Countries with an independent judiciary that enforces the law, protects property rights and the rights of minorities, and solves conflict efficiently perform better than countries where judges are not independent and are controlled by special interests.[11]

According to a World Bank index on the rule of law, the countries of Latin America do very poorly in this area; indeed, they do significantly worse than emerging Asia, worse than the Asian Tigers, the advanced commodity exporters, and the group of southern European nations in our comparison group. This index, available since 1996, is defined as "the extent to which agents have confidence in and abide by the rules of society, and in particular the quality of contract enforcement, property rights, the police, and the courts, as well as the likelihood of crime and violence."[12] The index assigns values from negative 2.5 to positive 2.5, with lower numbers indicating a lower presence of the rule of law.

In 2007, the last year for which data are available, Latin America had an index value of −0.523 on average. This is significantly lower than those for emerging Asia (−0.169), the Asian Tigers (0.636), the southern European nations (0.907), and the advanced commodity exporters (1.853). Worse yet, according to these data the extent to which the rule of law is observed in Latin America has tended to deteriorate between 1996, when the index for the region averaged −0.277, and 2007, when it averaged −0.523. When alternative data sources such as the Fraser Institute index on law and order are considered, the results are very similar. Latin America does worse than any of the comparison groups, and its situation has deteriorated through time. Of course, as is the case with every indicator, there are significant differences between countries. In 2007, the World Bank index for the rule of law was positive in three of the Latin American nations: Chile scored 1.173; Uruguay, 0.486; and Costa Rica, 0.438. These figures are not very different from those for most of the Asian Tigers. At the other end of the spectrum, with extremely low rule of law indexes, are Ecuador, Guatemala, Paraguay, and Venezuela.

The Fraser Institute provides an index on the degree of independence of the judiciary, both from political pressure and from lobbying groups for private interests. Latin America is on average at the bottom of the scale among the groups of countries compared in this chapter. On a scale of 1 to 10, with 10 being best, Latin America's average score stood at 3.2 in 2006, the last year for which information is available; this is significantly worse than Asia generally (4.2), the Asian Tigers (6.4), the advanced commodity exporters (8.8), or the southern European countries (6.0).

Stories of political interference in judiciary appointments abound in Latin America. Some of the most egregious cases have taken place in Argentina. In the 1990s President Carlos Menem increased the number of members in the supreme court from five to nine and packed it with his supporters. A decade later, President Néstor Kirchner decided that the Menem court was not to his liking and forced out a number of its members. During the Kirchner administration judges were threatened with impeachment if they didn't rule on economic matters—particularly on issues related to the pesification of bank deposits—along the lines suggested by the government.[13] In 2004 Venezuelan president Hugo Chávez increased the number of members of the supreme court from twenty to thirty-two in order to gain control over the judiciary. The opposition also accused Chávez of stacking the Electoral Council to assure that his supporters would be elected to various posts. In the mid-2000s Human Rights Watch stated that these decisions were eroding democracy and individual rights in Venezuela.

Attempts by politicians to influence or control the courts are neither new nor unique to Latin America. A well-known case is U.S. president Franklin D. Roosevelt's attempt to add six justices to the U.S. Supreme Court in 1937.[14] The final outcome, however, was very different in the United States than in Argentina, Venezuela, or other Latin American nations. To Roosevelt's surprise, his proposal was criticized across the board. The media opposed it, as did citizens' groups, scholars, and opinion leaders, and members of his own Democratic Party opposed it in Congress. The system of checks and balances built into the U.S. Constitution worked, and the Roosevelt administration dropped the bill in June of 1937.

There are important differences between Latin American countries in terms of the quality of the judicial system. According to the World Bank, in 2007 Guatemala and Venezuela did particularly poorly with respect to the rule of law. Chile had the best rating; only two Asian countries (or territories) were ranked higher than Chile in 2007—Hong Kong and Singapore. The Fraser Institute data indicate that Nicaragua, Paraguay, and Venezuela fare worst in terms of independence of the judiciary; those with the most independent judiciaries are Costa Rica and Uruguay.

In Latin America the judiciary not only lacks independence but also tends to be highly inefficient. Commercial disputes take a long time to be resolved, and the enforcement of contracts is weak; bankruptcy procedures are cumbersome, and the courts take a long time to rule on complaints brought forward by minority stock owners. According to the World Bank's Doing Business data set, in 2008 it took an average of 701 days to enforce a contract in Latin American countries.[15] In contrast, it took an average of only 393 days to do so in the Asian Tiger countries, 637 days in the southern European nations, and 394 days in the advanced commodity exporters. The results are similar when other indicators of judicial efficiency are considered, including the number of years it takes to legally close a business.

In a series of influential works, Professor Andrei Shleifer of Harvard University and his associates have analyzed the connection between legal systems and economic efficiency and performance. With the assistance of teams of lawyers from around the world, Shleifer and his coauthors have compiled an impressive data set on various aspects of legal practices and procedures. Once again, the Latin American nations do poorly when compared with other parts of the world. Trials tend to last longer and be more expensive than in countries in Asia and the Anglo-Saxon world. Shleifer and his coauthors also found that it is more difficult to enforce contracts in Latin America than in many other regions. In an index ranging from 1 to 10, with 10 being best, the degree of "contract enforceability" in Latin America has a value of 4.8; in contrast, the Asian Tigers have an index of 5.8; the southern European nations, 5.5; and the advanced commodity exporters, 8.0.[16]

These findings are consistent with the data collected by the World Bank. According to the Doing Business survey, in 2008 the Latin American countries were ranked on average 100th among 181 countries in terms of contract enforceability. During the same year the Asian Tigers ranked 48th on average; the southern European countries, 58th; and the advanced commodity exporters, 30th. These indexes were computed by analyzing specific real-world situations that are common to all 181 nations in the sample. Specifically, the World

Bank experts considered a case involving two lawful businesses that have a commercial dispute amounting to twice the value of the country's income per capita. Two questions are considered by the contract enforceability index: how much time it takes for the courts to reach a decision and for it to be enforced, and how much it costs to go through this judicial process.

An important discovery made by Shleifer and his team is that the "legal origin" of the judicial system is an important determinant of its degree of efficiency and of the extent to which it protects property rights. According to their research, the most important difference is between systems whose origin is in civil law—specifically the Napoleonic civil code—and those based on common law. The main conclusion is that common law countries emphasize markets and contracts and give citizens the strongest protection of property rights, while French-based civil law countries rely more heavily on regulation and governments and provide the weakest protection to property. Since the early nineteenth century, when Napoleon invaded Spain, the countries of Latin America have had a legal system based on the French civil code.[17] Historically, however, the weak Latin American institutions predate Napoleon by a very long time. As I discuss in great detail in chapter 2, as early as the sixteenth century Spain imposed on its colonies a highly centralized administrative and political system, under which the Crown had tremendous discretion over all types of decisions. Property rights protection was weak, tax collection was concentrated on a few sources, and due process was almost nonexistent.[18]

The Latin American nations have also done poorly in protecting property rights. In fact, the region's history is replete with incidents of expropriation of foreign investments without appropriate compensation. Local investors have not fared much better. The rules of the game have been changed often, with contracts being repeatedly violated. The Argentine debt default of 2001 and the subsequent breach of international contracts regarding the prices that utilities and telecommunication companies could charge is perhaps one of the most patent recent violations of property rights. Other historical examples include the expropriation of oil investments in Mexico in 1938 and of foreign mining holdings in Chile under President Salvador Allende's administration in the early 1970s. More recently the expropriation of oil and gas investments in Venezuela and Bolivia has reminded investors that property rights protection continues to be tenuous in many Latin American nations. The nationalization of the international air carrier Aerolíneas Argentinas in 2009 with compensation to investors of one peso (approximately 30 cents of a dollar) has also reminded European investors that they are not safe from the violation of property rights and the risk of expropriation.

For many years the Fraser Institute has generated an index of degree of protection of property rights. The index ranges from 1 to 10, with 10 denoting the highest possible level of protection. According to these data, at the time the Washington Consensus reforms were being launched in the early and mid-1990s, the average level of protection in Latin American countries was 5.1. By 2006, when the Fraser Institute index stood at 4.9 for the Latin American countries, the degree of protection of property rights had slightly decreased. Moreover, according to the latest data available, Latin America has one of the lowest property rights protection indexes among our four comparison groups. In 2006 the index was 6.8 for the Asian Tigers, 8.7 for the commodity-exporting advanced nations, and 6.8 for the southern European countries. Of course the protection of property rights is not equally weak in all Latin American nations. The Fraser Institute data indicate that in 2006 Costa Rica and Chile did quite well, with index values of 6.8 and 7.0; at the other extreme of the scale are Paraguay and Venezuela, with dismal indexes of 3.4 and 3.2, respectively.

According to the Fraser Institute, eight out of eighteen Latin American nations experienced some deterioration in the degree of protection of property rights between 1990 and 2006. The largest declines occurred in Argentina, Ecuador, Mexico, and Venezuela. In Argentina and Venezuela this decline in property rights protection was concentrated in the last few years, when the administrations of presidents Néstor Kirchner, Cristina Fernandez de Kirchner, and Hugo Chávez breached contracts signed with foreign investors, expropriated property, criticized and harassed the business sector, and interfered with judiciary decisions.

Other indexes of the protection of property rights, including indexes generated by the World Bank on the degree of protection of minority investors, tell a similar story. In constructing this indicator the World Bank researchers considered a potential transaction between two domestic companies and assumed that the transaction benefits the majority owner at the expense of minority investors. It then used data for each country to analyze how easy it was for the majority to have the deal approved. The results were discouraging: most Latin American countries rank in the bottom half of a group of 181 nations. Venezuela, Costa Rica, and Honduras did particularly poorly and were ranked in the 170th, 165th, and 150th positions, respectively. Only four Latin American countries were ranked in the top 25 percent of the sample: Peru (18th), Colombia (24th), Chile (28th), and Mexico (38th).

CORRUPTION AND ECONOMIC PERFORMANCE

It is no surprise that more advanced nations have a lower degree of corruption than poorer countries. Indeed, most international rankings—including those by the highly respected nonprofit organization Transparency International— list countries such as the Scandinavian nations among the least corrupt in the world; on the other hand, very poor countries, often in Africa, are among the most corrupt. A more difficult question is whether a lower degree of corruption helps propel growth. This is not a trivial issue, since the countries that grow very quickly, such as China and India, are typically countries with relatively low income per capita and tend to do relatively poorly in corruption surveys. In order to answer this question in a useful way, the analysis should go beyond casual empiricism or simple correlations. The relevant question is, given other important factors such as the skills of the labor force and savings ratios, what is the effect of corruption on economic performance? In principle, corruption may affect economic growth in two opposing ways. On one hand, in an economy with massive regulations, red tape, and distortions, corruption may be an efficient way of getting things done. If this is the case, corruption—or at least a certain level of it—would "grease the wheels" of commerce and help achieve higher rates of growth. An alternative view is that corruption has a negative effect on trust, transparency, and credibility, negatively affecting productivity growth and investment. In reality, it is possible that both of hypotheses may hold true in any particular country at a given moment in time. If this is the case, an important economic question is which of them dominates.

During the last few years, a number of scholars have investigated these issues using complex and highly advanced statistical techniques and have found fairly conclusively that higher degrees of corruption reflect weaker institutions and have a negative effect on economic growth.[19]

According to the International Country Risk Guide, which evaluates the degree of international risk faced by investors, the Latin American countries have not done well with respect to corruption. According to the index—which ranges from 0 to 6, with higher values denoting lower corruption—in 1990 Latin America countries had an average rating of 2.9, worse than the Asian Tigers (3.1), the advanced commodity exporters (5.7), and the southern European nations (4.7). Almost fifteen years later, in 2004, Latin America's ratings were lower than in 1990 and still below those of the three aforementioned groups.

Other measures of corruption, including those calculated by the World Bank and Transparency International, tell a very similar story. Once again, however, there are important differences between countries. In the year 2008, for example, Transparency International ranked Venezuela as one of the countries perceived to have the highest corruption in the entire world. On the other hand, Chile and Uruguay, the two Latin American countries with the lowest perceived corruption, did as well as some of the more advanced nations; indeed, Chile's rating is similar to those of the United States and Belgium.

DEMOCRATIC RULE AND CIVIL LIBERTIES

The political system also affects long-term economic performance. Academics who have analyzed the determinants of economic growth over long periods of time have found that countries with a higher degree of political stability and civil liberties have done better, even after other factors have been taken into account, than unstable countries with poor civil liberties records. The main reason for this is that under democratic rule citizens' rights—including property rights—are protected broadly. Democratic countries also have more independent judiciaries and fewer corrupt judges and politicians. All of these factors have a positive effect on the incentives to innovate and therefore on productivity growth. Societies that are politically more inclusive and have fewer ethnic conflicts also provide greater incentives for investing in projects with a long gestation period.[20]

Between 1980 and 2000 the Latin American nations made remarkable progress on the political front. Whereas in the late 1970s most countries had de facto dictatorial regimes, by 2000 every country in the region with the exception of Cuba had a democratic system. To be sure, many countries traveled a bumpy road toward democracy, but by and large constitutional rule prevailed even in countries that saw heads of government resign, such as in Argentina, Bolivia, and Ecuador.

The Center for International Development and Conflict Management at the University of Maryland has developed an index that measures how well democratic institutions function around the world. The index, known as the Polity Index, ranges from 0 to 10, with 10 being best and indicating better-functioning democratic institutions. In 1980 its average for Latin America was only 3.5; Chile had an index of 0, reflecting the dictatorial nature of the military regime led by Augusto Pinochet. In 1980 Costa Rica was the only country with a perfect democratic score of 10; Ecuador and Venezuela had indexes of 9. By 2000, however, things had changed dramatically. The average democracy score for Latin America had climbed to 8.0; Costa Rica and Uruguay had perfect scores of 10, and Bolivia, Chile, and Panama had indexes of 9. By 2007, the average score for Latin America was still 8.0. Chile joined Costa Rica and Uruguay in the group that had indexes of 10, while Nicaragua, Panama, and Peru received indexes of 9.[21]

Since 2000, however, there has been a decline in the extent of democratic rule in a number of Latin American countries, including Bolivia, Ecuador, and Venezuela. The case of Venezuela is particularly telling: its democracy index declined from a level of 9 in 1990 to merely 5 in 2006. This downgrading reflects harassment of the press, attempts at controlling the judiciary, the packing of the supreme court, and attempts to repeatedly reelect the president among other factors.

What is of greater concern, perhaps, is that during most of the past decade support for democratic rule and institutions has declined in most Latin American countries. As reported by economist Eduardo Lora in an evaluation of state of reforms in Latin America, in 1996 a majority of voters in sixteen out of seventeen countries surveyed stated that "democracy is preferred to any form of government." Only a very small percentage of those surveyed—in no country did the percentage exceed 26 percent—stated that authoritarian and nondemocratic regimes were justified under exceptional circumstances. In 2006 the support for democratic rule had declined in a number of countries; indeed the only nations where public support for democratic systems had increased were Chile, El Salvador, Mexico, and Venezuela.[22] Ironically, in Venezuela the actual degree of democratization was moving in the opposite direction from what the people desired.

An index on the protection of civil liberties developed by Freedom House tells a similar story for Latin America, of a rapid improvement in civil liberties between 1985 and 2000 followed by a decline in the years since. The fact that the deterioration in democratic rule and civil liberties has taken place in some of the countries that have abandoned, at least partially, competition policies and have introduced populist measures suggests quite strongly that their economic performance is likely to suffer in the long run.

The message of the analysis presented here is unmistakable: institutions in most of Latin America are weak—indeed much weaker than in the comparison nation groups—and this weakness contributed significantly to the region's mediocre economic performance during most of the twentieth century. More important, perhaps, the reforms of the Washington Consensus have done very little to improve the region's institutions. In spite of all the talk of modernization, greater efficiency, and transformation, Latin America continues to be largely a region with weak institutions, limited rule of law, feeble protection of property rights, and inefficient mechanisms for conflict resolution.

Economic Policy Reform: A Decalogue Manqué

The goal of the Latin American reforms was to reignite growth and improve social conditions in a region that for almost two decades had been sliding down and that in the 1980s had lived through an economic catastrophe. The architects of the reforms—including the "Chicago Boys" in Chile and other technopols—were convinced that these objectives could be achieved by putting together a set of economic policies that encouraged competition, innovation, entrepreneurship, efficiency, and productivity growth. In this section I evaluate for the region as a whole how much progress has actually been achieved during the first two decades of the Washington Consensus. Although most of the analysis is at the regional level, I discuss the individual experiences of a number of countries, and I note exceptions to the regional trend. This discussion is amplified in the chapters that follow, where I analyze in great detail the experiences of Chile, El Salvador, Mexico, Colombia, Argentina, Venezuela, and Brazil.

EFFICIENCY, ENTREPRENEURSHIP AND PRODUCTIVITY

A number of think tanks, academics, and multilateral institutions have recently compiled impressive and detailed data sets to measure economic policies. Among the most useful and complete are the World Bank's Doing Business data set, which measures the extent of regulations and the costs of doing business in more than 180 countries, and the Fraser Institute's Economic Freedom of the World data set.[23]

The Fraser Institute data set provides detailed information on trade restrictions and economic regulations since 1980—including restrictions on credit, red tape and bureaucracy, and labor market regulations—for 141 countries. The Doing Business data set provides information on the number of hours a businessperson spends paying taxes and registering a property, the number of documents required to import intermediate goods, the number of years it takes to close a business, how difficult it is to formally hire an employee, how costly it is to dismiss a worker, and many other data. The World Bank summarizes data in the following eight categories related to competition policies and the investment climate:[24]

- how easy it is to start a business legally
- how easy it is to deal with licenses
- ease of employing workers
- how easy it is to register property
- how easy it is for small and medium size firms to get credit
- how easy it is to pay taxes
- the ease of trading across the border
- the ease of closing a business

These data provide a detailed picture of how much a country's policies encourage—or discourage—competition and entrepreneurship. It is important to notice, however, that these categories do not constitute a checklist of policies to be implemented, nor do they provide a mechanical blueprint for success. Moreover, it is highly unlikely that slightly improving a country's standing in one of these categories without implementing additional supporting measures will result in higher growth over the medium term. These caveats notwithstanding, there is persuasive evidence to suggest that countries whose policies strongly support competition as measured by this set of indicators perform better economically than those with weaker policies in these areas.

An analysis of these data shows a troublesome picture: the Latin American countries do poorly in terms of economic policies. In fact, they do worse on average in every single one of the eight Doing Business categories than the Asian Tigers and the advanced commodity exporters. The southern European countries do better than the Latin American countries in every category except the ease of employing workers. Other surveys including the data sets collected by academics such as Harvard's Andrei Shleifer and his colleagues and by the KOF Swiss Economic Institute provide a very similar picture and show that the Latin American countries are dominated by the comparison nation groups in almost every category of competition policies.[25]

Consider the following examples: In Latin America it takes an average of 3.3 years to legally close a business; in the Asian Tigers it takes 2.3 years, and it takes 1.7 years in southern Europe and only 1 year in the advanced commodity exporters. A businessperson in Latin America spends 219 days dealing with licenses, regulations, and red tape; in contrast, she would spend 140 days doing the same chores in the Asian Tigers, 143 days in Southern Europe, and only 120 days in the advanced commodity exporters. In Latin America it is significantly more difficult to hire workers formally than in the comparison groups excepting the southern European countries. Moreover, in Latin America the nonwage component of labor costs—withholding taxes and other contributions—is much higher than in many of the other regions: it is 16.9 percent of labor costs in the Latin countries, 10.7 percent in the Asian Tigers, and 11.3 percent in the advanced commodity exporters.[26] In Latin America it takes 47 days to register property; it only takes 38 days in the Asian Tigers, 8 days in the advanced exporters, and 27 days in the southern European nations.

In the countries of Latin America it is more difficult on average for a small a firm to obtain credit than in other regions except emerging Asia and southern Europe. As Peruvian economist Hernando de Soto has emphasized in his book *The Mystery of Capital*, in Latin America it is particularly difficult for the poor to pledge collateral for loans. The reason for this is that in many countries registries are fragmented and often incomplete, and many among the poor don't have legal rights over the small houses they live in.[27]

The costs of trading across borders in Latin America—measured either in the number of days spent obtaining import and export permits or in monetary terms—is higher than in the comparison nation groups. Paying taxes in Latin America is a cumbersome process that takes many more steps and more time than it does almost anywhere in the world, and tax rates are higher on average in Latin America than in our comparison groups. The number of different taxes that businesses have to pay is greater in Latin America than in any other region; the overall tax rate in Latin America is 55 percent, while it is only 33 percent in the Asian Tigers, 52 percent in southern Europe, and 44 percent in the advanced commodity exporters.

Not surprisingly, these excessive regulations have encouraged a large underground economy throughout most of Latin America. As discussed in chapter 3, informality is rampant—according to the UN Economic Commission for Latin America and the Caribbean, in the mid-2000s more than 40 percent of Latin American urban workers were not part of the formal sector and did not participate in the social security system—and many businesses use cash as a way of avoiding taxes and the transaction costs involved in dealing with the banking system. Indeed, cash transactions were so common that in July 2007 the equivalent of $60,000 was found stashed in Argentina's economic minister Felisa Miceli's private bathroom at the Ministry of the Economy. Her explanation was that she needed the cash to purchase a property.[28]

The World Bank's Doing Business data, as well as those from alternative sources, provide a strong refutation to the notion that the Latin American countries on the whole have put in place a set of aggressive policies that have transformed them into modern capitalist nations. Indeed, when compared with other regions and groups of countries, the opposite picture emerges: Latin America has lagged behind in the vast majority of competition categories.

Averages, however, tend to hide a rich and textured reality. Not surprisingly, an analysis of the country-specific data shows that some Latin American countries do relatively well in individual categories, while others do well overall. However, there are very few Latin American countries ranked in the top twenty-five positions in any of the eight broad categories of the Doing Business data. Peru is ranked twelfth in ease of getting credit and Mexico is ranked twenty-third in ease of closing a business. Panama is ranked eighth in trading across borders. And that's it: no other Latin country—not even Chile—ranks in the top twenty-five in any of the World Bank data set categories for 2008.[29] According to the Fraser Institute's latest ranking, for 2006, three Latin American countries are in the top twenty-five nations: Chile (6th), Costa Rica (21st) and El Salvador (25th). Brazil is ranked 96th; Ecuador, 113th; Argentina, 114th; Colombia, 115th; and Venezuela, 136th. The Heritage Foundation has computed an index of economic freedom for a number of years and has reached a similar conclusion. In its 2009 index only one Latin American country is ranked in the top twenty-five—Chile in the 11th position—and only four others are in the top fifty—El Salvador (33rd), Uruguay (38th), Costa Rica (46th), and Mexico (49th). According to the KOF Swiss Economic Institute Index on Globalization for 2009, Chile, Panama ,and Uruguay are the most globalized Latin American countries, ranked in the 37th, 42nd, and 50th positions, respectively, among 158 countries. According to this index the five least global-ized Latin American countries, all between the 90th and 100th positions, are Bolivia, Colombia, Nicaragua, Paraguay, and Venezuela.[30]

Chile has been a clear outlier among the Latin American nations in terms of both the quality of its competition policies and its institutions. In many of the policy categories in the Doing Business data set Chile does better than the Asian Tigers, and in all but one it outperforms Emerging Asia as a group. Interestingly, in spite of its good showing, Chile is the highest-ranked Latin American country in only one of the eight competition policy categories con-sidered by the World Bank: ease of paying taxes. In the other seven categories it does well, but it is not the top country in the region. This supports the notion that in order to perform well a country needs to follow a holistic approach, making sure that its overall policies provide the right incentive to innovate, expand the stock of productive capital, and improve workers' skills.

What makes Chile stand out is that its policies have been pragmatic, co-herent, and uniformly procompetition and that it has made progress on all fronts—institutional setting and economic policies—in a balanced way. In addition, since the mid-1980s the country has avoided major policy mistakes and has stayed away from policies that interfere with competition and ef-ficiency. Particularly important is the fact that Chile has avoided currency crises or upheavals similar to those that have plagued many countries, includ-ing Mexico and Argentina.

However, when Chile's policies and institutions are compared with the advanced commodity exporters—Australia, Canada, and New Zealand—the results are less than spectacular. Indeed, Chile is behind the advanced com-modity exporter nations in every single one of the eight Doing Business policy categories. For instance, while Chile is ranked 55th in ease of starting a busi-ness, the commodity exporters are ranked 2nd on average; Chile is 62nd in ease of dealing with licenses, and the commodity exporters' average ranking is 29th; Chile is 39th in ease of registering property, while the advanced ex-porters average 23rd; in ease of obtaining credit Chile is ranked 68th, and the exporters average 13th.

It is possible to argue that progress in some of these indicators is achieved only after a country has become a successful and advanced nation. Although this is possible, it is unlikely. In any case, it is beside the point, as the purpose of the present comparison is to illustrate the gap in terms of policy efficiency between Chile and the countries it would like to emulate and not to determine strict causality. And when one focuses on the gap, it is clear that in spite of significant progress in the last thirty years there is still much to be done.

TRADE OPENNESS AND ECONOMIC PERFORMANCE

As noted previously, beginning in the 1940s Latin American countries adopted increasingly protectionist policies as a way of encouraging industrialization. Contrary to what the proponents of these policies had predicted, productivity in the protected sectors did not increase, and import duties, licenses, and prohibitions became a permanent feature of the Latin American economic landscape. By the mid-1980s Latin America was one of the most protectionist regions in the world. In 1985, for example, average import tariffs were 51 percent in South America and 66 percent in Central America; in contrast, they were 40 percent in North Africa and 25 percent in East Asia. In the same year import licenses and quotas—the preferred form of protectionism in many countries—covered on average 60 percent of imports in South America and 100 percent of imports in Central America, compared with 85 percent in North Africa and only 21 percent in East Asia.[31]

Import duties were not only high; they were also very different across import categories. This encouraged corruption and smuggling. Indeed, when import duties are different for different products, there is an incentive to misclassify high-duty goods as low-duty imports. This practice, which requires the complicity of customs officials, was widespread in Latin America until the early 1990s.

As pointed out in the preceding chapters, one of the consequences of protectionist policies was that local currencies became artificially strong and exports lost competitiveness in the global marketplace. From 1950 through the late 1980s the majority of the Latin American countries developed a strong antiexport bias.

An important objective of the reforms of the 1990s was to eliminate this bias against exports. Most countries reduced their import duties significantly, eased import restrictions, and eliminated most import prohibitions. There is a voluminous economic literature that argues that freer trade promotes greater efficiency and improvements in productivity growth. Nobel laureate Edward C. Prescott and his coauthor Stephen L. Parente have made the point strongly. According to them "governments should foster free trade. . . . International trade matters for development precisely because it is an important source of competition."[32]

Exhaustive research undertaken by a number of economists during the last two decades has indeed established that there is a strong relationship between trade openness and economic performance. Some of this work has relied on studies of individual countries, some has focused on the comparative experience of many countries over long periods of time, and some has combined cross-country analyses with analysis of the evolution of economic behavior over time. These works have painstakingly addressed a large number of technical and statistical issues and have dealt with criticisms raised by skeptics. This significant effort has paid off, and it is possible to state that at this time the empirical evidence strongly indicates that economic growth of countries that are more open to international trade have tended to outperform that of countries that have adopted more protectionist policies.[33]

The extent of the Latin American trade reforms during the 1990s was quite remarkable, especially when compared with the region's own protectionist history. In 1985 import duties in Latin America averaged over 42 percent; they averaged 11 percent in 2000, and by 2006 they had been lowered to 9 percent on average. In addition, and perhaps more important, import licenses and quotas were reduced significantly during this period. This trade liberalization process also lowered the dispersion of import duties across goods, thus reducing the potential for corruption and abuse. As in other areas, Chile was the pioneer country in terms of openness and trade liberalization: in 1979 Chile instituted a uniform import tariff of 10 percent, and by 2003 the average import tariff was a low 6 percent.[34]

Some critics of the Washington Consensus and the Latin American reforms have argued that trade liberalization—including lowering import tariffs—is not a required or even an important component of a procompetition policy package. These critics point out that some of the most successful countries in the world—particularly the Asian Tigers—have been able to achieve an impressive growth record without low import tariffs or free trade. It is true, these authors have argued, that the Asian Tigers encouraged exports through a number of incentives, including procompetition policies such as those that encourage abundant credit and maintaining a competitive value for local currencies, but they did not lower import tariffs significantly. The critics have also argued that by emphasizing trade openness, the Washington Consensus encouraged the wrong policy path for Latin America and generated a highly fragile economic structure that made the region vulnerable to external crises.[35]

These arguments, however, do not reflect reality fully and are flawed in several respects. First, import tariffs in the Asian Tiger countries have historically been relatively low, indeed much lower than in the Latin American nations. In 1980, for example, average import tariffs were 42 percent in Latin America and only 15 percent in the East Asian Tigers. By 1990 import duties averaged 25 percent in Latin America and only 16 percent in the Asian Tigers. A decade later, average tariffs in Latin America were 11 percent and in the East Asian Tigers, 9 percent. In addition, in the Tiger countries import duties have been more uniform across goods than in the Latin American nations.[36]

A second reason these criticisms are flawed is that lower import tariffs have historically gone hand in hand with other procompetition policies. That is, as economist Stephen Parente and Nobel laureate Edward C. Prescott, among others, have argued, economic policies have tended to be more supportive of competition and innovation in countries that are more open to international trade. Indeed, a detailed analysis of the World Bank's Doing Business data set shows clearly that countries with higher import tariffs have weaker competition policies than countries with lower restrictions on international trade. This is the case across the spectrum of the forty-two indexes, subindexes, and policy measures considered in this data set. This indicates that trade openness is a very good summary indicator of countries' overall policy stance with respect to competition, efficiency, and productivity incentives.

One might be tempted to argue that averages hide very different realities in different countries and that the large and important Tiger countries such as South Korea maintained relatively high import tariffs throughout the 1980s and 1990s. The data, however, do not support this claim. In 1980 the average import tariff in the Republic of Korea was 20 percent, while in that year the average tariff was 42 percent in Latin America. In 1990 South Korea's average tariff was 13 percent; it was reduced to 11 percent in 1995 and to 9 percent in 2000. It is true that these tariff averages don't constitute strict free trade, but they definitely don't indicate an overly protectionist policy stance; indeed throughout these years South Korea was significantly more open to trade than almost every Latin American country.

The foregoing discussion shows that in spite of the progress made in trade policy, both the Latin American countries and the Asian Tiger nations still have some way to go. This is particularly the case for Latin American countries that have chosen to participate in regional trade agreements with relatively high import tariffs with respect to the rest of the world. The most important of these is Mercosur, a trading bloc formed by Argentina, Brazil, Paraguay, and Uruguay.

In recent years there has been considerable debate on whether emerging countries should open up their economies to the free mobility of financial capital. Some authors have argued that limiting the extent of international financial integration reduces speculation and helps countries withstand external shocks without suffering massive crises. According to this view, countries that control and limit capital mobility are less likely to suffer contagion from abroad. In his criticism of the IMF, Joseph Stiglitz argues that the fundamental reason why India and China were spared from substantial currency crises—and were not subject to contagion from the East Asian or other crises of the 1990s and early 2000s—is that they did not allow free capital mobility. He goes so far as to argue that the easing of controls on capital mobility was at the center of most modern currency crises in the emerging markets—in Mexico in 1994, East Asia in 1997, Russia in 1998, Brazil in 1999, Turkey in 2001, and Argentina in 2002. According to other authors, however, restrictions on capital mobility are ineffective (the private sector always finds ways of circumventing them), introduce costly microeconomic distortions, and encourage corruption.[37] I address this issue in further detail in the chapters that follow on individual countries' experiences.

INEFFICIENT POLICIES AND EFFICIENT COMPANIES

In spite of policy deficiencies and weak institutions, there are a number of large, well-run and profitable global firms in Latin America. Brazil's Embraer, a successful manufacturer of regional and executive jets as well as military aircraft, is a premier example of this new type of Latin American multinational. The company was founded in the 1940s by the Brazilian government, and for almost fifty years it manufactured midsize planes for military use and small commercial airplanes. Although from early on the quality of its aircraft was considered to be high—indeed comparable to that of its international competitors—the company's productivity and efficiency were subpar, and Embraer struggled financially. During the early decades it survived thanks to government subsidies. In 1990, during the presidency of Fernando Collor de Mello, Embraer and other state-owned enterprises were privatized. In the years that followed, international partnerships were forged and investments in new technologies were made in an effort to improve productivity. In 1995 a new regional jet, the now legendary ERJ 145, was launched. This aircraft, which has capacity for fifty passengers and a cabin layout with a three-abreast seat configuration, became "a runaway sales success."[38] Since 2000, new models have rolled off the assembly line, the company has gained an increasing global market share, and its stock has outperformed that of other aeronautics companies, including Boeing and Bombardier. Some may argue that Embraer's success was possible precisely because for years it received government subsidies and was protected from foreign competition. There is no doubt that government support allowed the company to survive during its first four decades. This, however, does not invalidate the point that the company only took off when it became subject to the demands of the market and international competition; indeed, it is possible to argue that if it had been privatized and forced to sink or swim on its own ten or fifteen years earlier, it would have flourished even earlier than it did.

Embraer's story is not unique, however. Other Brazilian companies that have grown rapidly and positioned themselves as world-class players during the last fifteen years include Vale (formerly known as Companhia Vale do Rio Doce, or CVRD), the fifth-largest mining company by revenue in the world, and Petrobras, the giant oil company partially owned by the Brazilian government. In the period 2001–8 Petrobras's stock price outperformed that of its international rivals by an order of magnitude. In 2007 Petrobras announced the discovery of significant reserves in the Tupi oil field off the coast of Rio de Janeiro, and a few months later it announced that it had discovered another major offshore field. Although these deposits are at great depths in the subsalt cluster, some experts believe that they are commercially viable and are likely to make Brazil an important player in the international oil market in a decade or so.[39] Many Brazilian global companies are not only efficient and expanding at a rapid pace, they are also very big. For example, in mid-2008, before the subprime crisis and the collapse of the global stock markets, Petrobras's market capitalization was larger than that of Royal Shell, Total, and British Petroleum; Bradesco—Brazil's largest bank—had a higher market capitalization than Deutsche Bank; and Banco Itaú's market capitalization exceeded that of Goldman Sachs.

During the last few years a number of companies from other Latin American countries have also taken advantage of globalization and have become up-and-coming players in their industries. Examples include LAN airlines in Chile, a company that in 2007 captured 10 percent of profits in the international airline industry in spite of carrying less than 1 percent of passengers; Chile's wineries Santa Rita and Concha y Toro, two companies that have expanded exports at a neckbreaking pace while at the same time improving overall profitability; Argentina's food processors Arcor and Molinos Río de la Plata, which managed to grow global operations and maintain profitability during the late 1990s and early 2000s despite the country's economic turmoil; and Chile's copper producer Antofagasta PLC, whose Pelambres mine is one of the best run in the world.[40]

Of course, this is only a partial list of Latin American companies that have recently succeeded in the international market place; there are others. However, these competitive firms are the exception. Most companies in the region—particularly most small and medium-sized firms—are mired by inefficiencies, have a labor force with inadequate skills, and are held back by the scores of regulations and distortions documented in this chapter. It is precisely the existence of this great mass of inefficient firms that explains the low rate of overall productivity growth experienced by the vast majority of the counties in the region during the last few years. In fact, the very high costs of starting a business and making it grow in most countries have stood in the way of massive entrepreneurial initiatives. These costs include the difficulty in finding financing, the weak protection of minority investors, and the maze of regulations and red tape that discourage many new investors.

What the well-managed and successful Latin American companies have in common is their heavy involvement in international trade. Indeed, all of the firms mentioned above are subject to the rigors and demands of international competition, export most of their output, and compete for talent internationally. In addition, all of these firms have a transparent and open governance system. They are also relatively large companies with access to international financial markets. This allows them to access capital at a lower cost than smaller companies—including most startups—and eschew the red tape and bureaucracy that in most countries surrounds local capital markets.

The case of Brazil's Petrobras, a company that is partially owned by the state, is particularly interesting. In contrast with Mexican state-owned oil giant

Pemex, it doesn't have a monopoly inside Brazil; since 1997 private companies have been allowed to operate in the country side by side with Petrobras. Although the Brazilian government owns 56 percent of the voting shares in the company, its stock is traded on the São Paulo and New York stock exchanges. That is, Petrobras subjects itself to the same type of market exigencies as any large company in the world. This sets it apart from other large state-owned companies in Latin America. Neither Venezuela's PDVSA, nor Mexico's Pemex or giant electricity producer CFE, nor Chile's copper producer Codelco are publicly traded; these giant corporations are not subject to the public scrutiny of stockholders or the strict requirements that large publicly traded companies face, and none of them have exhibited the profitability, rate of expansion, or innovation shown by Petrobras. In fact, these four giants are largely inefficient and fare poorly in international comparisons and rankings.[41]

THE IMPORTANCE OF LABOR MARKET LEGISLATION

Globalization is like Alice's world in *Through the Looking Glass*: it takes all the running you can do to keep in the same place. If you want to go somewhere else, you must run at least twice as fast as that. In order to take full advantage of the opportunities offered by the world economy—and not to succumb to international competition—countries need a lean and dynamic labor market. Companies should be able to adjust their payrolls quickly and at a low cost. This means that employment laws should be flexible and that hiring and dismissal costs should be kept as low as possible. This, of course, does not mean that there should be no social protection or that workers' rights should be ignored. What it does mean, however, is that labor legislation should be modern and allow for the coexistence of flexibility and effective unemployment insurance plans. Security should take the form of a safety net, unemployment insurance, cooperation between firms and labor unions, and an efficient and dynamic educational system that helps retrain displaced workers.

To be sure, issues related to labor market flexibility are not unique to Latin America or other emerging markets. Indeed, debates on labor market flexibility were at the center of the highly disputed 2007 French presidential election, which pitted socialist candidate Ségolène Royal against promarket conservative candidate Nicolas Sarkozy.

Over the last fifteen years the Latin American nations have made very little progress in deregulating labor markets. Labor laws in the region resemble those of the older social welfare era in Europe. According to the Fraser Institute, Latin America ranks lower on average than most of the comparison nation groups in terms of labor market flexibility. The only group with more regulated labor markets is the southern European nations—Greece, Portugal, and Spain.

The World Bank's Doing Business survey indicates that the average Latin American country ranks 125th in the ease of employing new workers category (out of 181 nations). Argentina is in the 130th position, Brazil ranks 121st, Chile 74th, and Mexico is ranked 141st. In contrast, the East Asian Tigers are ranked 85th on average, and the advanced commodity exporters rank 13th on average.

In every Latin American country—including Chile, the most reform-oriented of them all—it is cumbersome to hire new workers, and dismissing them is difficult and costly. Consider the case of Argentina, where in 2007 it took an average of 95 weeks for a firm to legally dismiss an employee. On average it takes 69 weeks to do so in the Asian Tigers, only 11 weeks in the advanced commodity exporters, and in the highly regulated southern European economies it takes an average of 58 weeks. These difficulties for hiring workers legally have had a very simple and predictable consequence: small and medium-sized firms often hire workers informally, without paying taxes or making social security contributions. Needless to say, informality contributes to the region's dismal social indicators.

Nobel laureate James J. Heckman and Spanish economist Carmen Pages have studied the functioning of labor markets in Latin America in great detail. Their main conclusion is that labor market regulations in Latin America tend to encourage inefficient production techniques and promote inequality.[42] Their findings indicate that costs associated with job security are significantly higher in the Latin American nations than in many of the advanced countries of the Organisation for Economic Co-operation and Development (OECD). Within Latin America and the Caribbean, Heckman and Pages found that in the late 1990s the costs of severance payments were highest in Peru, Colombia, and Ecuador and lowest in the Caribbean countries. The average (expected) cost of severance payments in Latin America is equivalent to 2.46 months' wages; in contrast, in the advanced OECD countries this cost is 0.8 months' wages.[43]

The reluctance to reform labor markets has had a number of negative consequences in Latin America. Strict regulations have kept many potential foreign direct investors away. Indeed, the prospect of having to keep unproductive workers on the payrolls, independently of how the business performs, are not particularly attractive. Also, the size of the informal, or underground, labor market is much larger in Latin America than in the comparison groups of countries.[44] According to a recent World Bank study more than 50 percent of Latin America's labor force works in the informal market; figures range from 32 percent in Chile to 70 percent in Bolivia and Peru.[45] The global crash of 2008 has also suggested that those nations with more flexible economic structures—particularly more flexible labor markets—are better able to withstand major shocks and disturbances. It is precisely in these flexible countries—Chile being a good example within the Latin American region—where the crash has had a less profound effect.

CURRENCIES AND EXCHANGE-RATE POLICIES

There is one policy area, however, where there has been significant progress in many Latin American countries: most have implemented policies aimed at avoiding currency overvaluation and inflationary imbalances, and as a result there is some indication that in the future the region will experience a decline in the number of currency crises. Specifically, most Latin American countries have reduced their fiscal deficits and public debt. They have also pared down their foreign indebtedness, and in the past few years, the majority have run current account surpluses.

But undoubtedly the most important development is that most countries have adopted flexible exchange rates and have allowed market forces to be the predominant determinants of their currency values. Gone are the times when governments would defend tooth and nail an artificially high currency value. Historically, attempts at maintaining fixed currency values ended badly, with large devaluations, wage declines, output contractions, and increased unemployment.[46]

In many countries the creation of independent central banks in recent years has also helped maintain overall macroeconomic policies geared toward stability and low inflation. The global financial crisis of 2008 has shown that these advances in macroeconomic management have paid off throughout Latin America: in contrast to other historical episodes of global financial upheaval, there have been no major currency crises in the region during the last two years. To be sure, in some countries—Venezuela and Argentina—

inflationary pressures have increased significantly, but unlike in previous cycles, no currency collapses have been observed—at least not yet.

Summing Up: Mediocre Policies and Weak Institutions

The indicators discussed in this chapter unequivocally show that in spite of the reforms of the Washington Consensus the vast majority of the Latin American countries continue to be highly inefficient at almost every conceivable level. Some may argue that the indicators computed by various think tanks and analyzed here reflect the legal (or de jure) as opposed to the actual (or de facto) requirements to get something done—start a business, expand a plant, hire someone, or litigate some problem in the courts. Yes, this argument would go, if one were to legally start a new business, obtaining all the licenses and permits would take more than a year, but there are ways of cutting corners: if one pays the appropriate bribes, things can be accomplished much faster. And, our interlocutor would say, everyone does it; paying a small and well-established bribe when necessary is indeed the preferred way of doing things. And, of course, there is always the alternative of operating without the required licenses or permits; this is not uncommon, especially in the poorer neighborhoods and among microenterprises. This argument, however, seriously misses the point. As discussed earlier, a society that abides by the rule of law—one that lives within the boundaries set by laws, legal requirements, rules, and regulations—has a lower cost of doing business, or what Douglass North has called transaction cost, than countries that mostly ignore the law. Strength in the rule of law translates into more time available to pursue innovative activities and ultimately into greater economic growth and prosperity. Countries with a very large informal economy also have lower wages, collect lower taxes, and have a higher incidence of poverty and inequality than countries that abide by the rule of law. Avoiding the rules, taking shortcuts, and promoting bribes and corruption are definitely not the best ways of achieving prosperity or improving social conditions.

Chapter 5
Chile, Latin America's Brightest Star

On December 6, 1976, Milton Friedman arrived in Stockholm to receive the Nobel Prize in Economics. At the airport he was greeted by a large crowd of protesters accusing him of supporting Chile's military junta and its violations of human rights. During the next week Friedman and his wife Rose were under constant police protection; everywhere they went they were accompanied by two bodyguards. At the awards ceremony a demonstrator dressed in white tie and tails shouted slogans against the junta, capitalism, and Friedman and had to be expelled from concert hall. As the prizes were being awarded by King Carl, ten thousand people demonstrated outside the hall and shouted slogans against Friedman and his policy recommendations. A few months earlier, when Friedman's Nobel Prize was announced, a number of former winners, including scientific luminaries Linus Pauling and David Baltimore, wrote letters to the *New York Times* protesting the award.[1]

In March 1975 Friedman had visited Chile to lecture on economic policy, including how to fight inflation and reignite growth. At the time, Chile faced economic stagnation, triple-digit inflation, and very high unemployment. During this short trip Friedman met with senior economic authorities and had a forty-five-minute meeting with Chile's strongman General Augusto Pinochet. Friedman summarized his views on the Chilean economy in a long letter to the general, in which he recommended a drastic cut in the public-sector deficit as the only way of eliminating inflation.

Soon after Friedman's visit the junta implemented what the media called a "shock treatment" to tackle a vicious circle of government imbalances, high inflation, currency depreciation, wage hikes, and further inflation.[2] At the center of this program was a steep reduction in public-sector expenditures. The historical record, however, suggests that Friedman's visit to Pinochet had little to do with the implementation of this "shock" policy. Sergio de Castro, the most senior of the Chicago Boys, who is often referred to as "the architect of the Chilean reforms," has said that Friedman had no influence on Pinochet in this or other matters. Similarly, in his account of the launching of the 1975 program, journalist Arturo Fontaine Aldunate does not mention Friedman or his letter as having played any role; according to Fontaine Aldunate the draconian fiscal policies of 1975—under which expenditures in every ministry and government department were cut between 15 and 25 percent—were devised by recently appointed minister of finance Jorge Cauas and his team.[3] Moreover, in other regards, the junta's economic program of the mid-1970s differed significantly from Friedman's recommendations: import tariffs were reduced gradually— Friedman had suggested a very rapid reduction—and a fixed exchange rate between the Chilean peso and the U.S. dollar was adopted instead of a flexible one as Friedman had recommended.[4] As will be seen below, pegging the value of the currency to the U.S. dollar turned out to be a serious mistake.

Years after his death, Milton Friedman is still criticized for his involvement in Chile's economic reforms.[5] These criticisms, however, are off the mark and reflect a poor understanding of the evolution of Chile's history over the last four decades.

Chile under President Salvador Allende, 1970–73

On September 11, 1973, Chile's president Salvador Allende was overthrown in a bloody military coup led by his army chief of staff, General Augusto Pinochet. For three years Allende's Unidad Popular coalition had tried to move Chile toward socialism. However, things did not work as the president and his advisers expected. Allende had gained power in 1970 with only a 39 percent plurality of the popular vote, and the government was unable to broaden its political support significantly. Political relations with the opposition parties—the centrist Christian Democrats and the conservative National Party—rapidly became strained; legislation was blocked, and several members of Allende's cabinet were impeached. The country became deeply polarized, and violent demonstrations from both sides became increasingly common.[6]

Allende's economic program had several objectives, including nationalization of the large copper mines, the banking sector, and a number of large monopolistic companies and implementation of a deep agrarian reform under which large land holdings (latifundia) would be replaced by a combination of small holdings, cooperatives, and state-owned farms. In addition, a system based on socialist-style planning was to replace the market system at least partially as the main mechanism for making economic decisions. In the short run, the Unidad Popular sought to increase production and incomes—particularly the incomes of the poor—by stimulating demand. This was to be achieved through a massive increase in government spending, higher salaries (in the first year alone minimum wages were raised by over 50 percent), and liberal credit creation by the central bank.

At first the new approach to economic policy appeared to work. A year after Allende took office average wages (adjusted for inflation) had increased by 25 percent, the overall rate of economic growth had shot up to an impressive annual rate of 8 percent, and inflation was contained at 22 percent. However, behind these rosy figures, major imbalances were mounting; investment in equipment and machinery had all but disappeared, a substantial trade deficit developed, and prices began to increase at a ferocious pace. In 1972 overall economic growth stagnated, official inflation was 260 percent—this greatly underestimated true inflation, as many goods were unavailable at the officially controlled prices—and wages (adjusted for inflation) fell below their 1970 levels. In addition, shortages of all sort of products became pervasive, and a generalized black market for goods and foreign exchange developed. An important factor behind the decline in overall production was an increase in labor unrest accompanied by a succession of national strikes called by the opposition parties. Particularly serious was a national work stoppage organized by the trucking industry in October of 1972.

Government officials were shocked by the economic developments of 1972. With a mixture of naïveté and stubbornness they insisted that theirs was a recipe for income expansion, redistribution, growth, and success. Right-wing politicians and the United States were blamed for the explosion in inflation and for the massive shortages. Even in the face of a dismal economic picture no corrections were made to economic policy, and the government ploughed ahead with great determination. In 1973—partially as a result of even greater political instability—the economic conditions worsened significantly. During the first three quarters of that year—that is, until the time of the coup d'état—inflation-adjusted wages experienced significant declines, ranging from 33 to 50 percent; inflation for the year was over 600 percent, and overall income contracted by more than 4 percent.

In September of 1973, when the military overthrew President Allende, the Chilean economy was in chaos. Ever since that time analysts, scholars, and the media have wondered whether the United States was involved in Pinochet's coup and in the subsequent implementation of market-oriented reforms. There is little doubt that the election of Allende was not welcomed by the Nixon administration. In his memoirs Henry Kissinger wrote: "Allende's election was a challenge to our national interest. We did not find it easy to reconcile ourselves to a second Communist state in the Western hemisphere. We were persuaded that it would soon be inciting anti-American policies, attacking hemisphere solidarity, making common cause with Cuba, and sooner or later establishing close relations with the Soviet Union."[7]

According to information declassified by the U.S. government, over the next three years Washington provided financial assistance to Chile's opposition political parties and organizations, and according to a report by a U.S. Senate committee that investigated covert actions in Chile, known as the Church Committee, the CIA was involved in an early attempt to keep Salvador Allende from becoming president.

After extensively reviewing thousands of confidential documents and cables, the Church Committee concluded that there was no evidence supporting the view that the CIA was behind the September 11 coup. Even if doubts remain about the extent of CIA support to Pinochet and his conspirators, it is clear is that Allende's economic policy was a failure. It was based on a deeply flawed diagnosis of the country's economic problems, and it relied on policy measures that had failed time and again in a number of populist experiments. As with many populist movements, significant short-run benefits—such as the spurt in growth and wages during 1971—were obtained at the cost of mortgaging the future and creating significant inflationary trends. Austrian-born economist Paul Rosenstein-Rodan—one of the pioneers of economic development as an academic discipline and a staunch supporter of the welfare state—had these harsh words regarding Chile's Unidad Popular experience during the early 1970s: "Salvador Allende died not because he was a socialist, but because he was an incompetent."[8]

The Chicago Boys and Chile's Trip to the Market

The Chicago Boys have become a legend of sorts—a legend and a myth. It has been said that they worked for the CIA, that they helped commit genocide, and that their policies responded to ideology and dogma; they have been praised for anticipating the global trend toward markets that swept the world in the 1990s, and they have been blamed for tainting the concept of reform by working with a repressive dictatorship. The real story of the Chicago Boys, however, is significantly more complex than what is suggested by crass caricatures and crude renditions. In fact, the Chicago Boys were not part of the Pinochet conspiracy that overthrew President Allende. During the early years of the dictatorship not a single Chicago Boy had an executive position in the military government; they were relegated to the windowless basement offices where advisors and consultants usually toil. With time, however, they gained influence and eventually joined the cabinet and worked to implement the early stages of what became Chile's economic miracle; interestingly, the miracle itself—and there is no doubt that what has happened to Chile over the last thirty years is nothing short of miraculous—was consolidated under the aegis of center-left democratically elected governments whose leaders once despised the economic advice provided by the boys from Chicago.

Contrary to what some critics have argued, the Chicago Boys' policies were not dogmatic, rigidly implemented, and ultimately rejected by the population at large.[9] It is also incorrect to claim that the Chicago Boys were the natural allies of the military government that seized power in 1973. In reality, the Chicago Boys had to work hard at persuading Pinochet and his colleagues that they should adopt a market system. According to Sergio de Castro, who held several positions in the regime, the problem was that "the military preferred a control economy" to a market-oriented one.[10] Furthermore, the actual reform program implemented by the Chicago Boys had important elements of pragmatism and flexibility. Among other things, Chile did not privatize all state-owned enterprises, nor did it eliminate all government controls and restrictions. For more than two decades the government intervened actively in the foreign-exchange market, and in the mid-1980s—still under the Pinochet dictatorship—the government put in place a Keynesian economic program that played an important role in the country's takeoff. Moreover, throughout most of the early years of the reform there were strict controls on the international mobility of capital.

More important, however, is that the reforms of the Chicago Boys were not undone by the democratically elected governments that came to power after 1990. Indeed, market-oriented modernization and free trade policies have been embraced by two successive socialist governments led by Ricardo

Lagos and Michelle Bachelet, as well as the administrations of Social Democrat presidents Patricio Aylwin and Eduardo Frei. The fact that many of the high-level officials in the two Socialist administrations—including the presidents themselves—were persecuted or sent into exile by the Pinochet regime is not a minor point and should not be belittled by critics trying to score easy points in the globalization debate.

The administrations of presidents Ricardo Lagos and Michelle Bachelet furthered modernization and market orientation not because of a deep conservative ideological bias, nor because they were bewitched by Milton Friedman and his followers. Market orientation has been a hallmark of Chile's return to democratic rule because it has worked; economic growth has been impressive—indeed the highest in Latin America—inflation has virtually disappeared, poverty has been massively reduced, and a solid middle class has emerged. Of course, this doesn't mean that everything in Chile is perfect; it does mean, however, that Chile's policies since the mid-1970s have transformed a backward country plagued by runaway inflation, stagnation, and widespread poverty into a modern nation solidly moving toward prosperity.

It is tempting to argue that the new democratic governments of the 1990s maintained market-oriented policies because they had no alternative. According to this view, before the return to democracy the military put in place institutional reforms that made policy changes very difficult. These included the creation of an independent central bank whose board members serve for ten-year periods, a senate with appointed senators (after stepping down, Pinochet served briefly in the senate), and budget rules that made it difficult for members of congress to add programs that were not fully funded. The problem with this view, however, is that over time these political and institutional constraints ceased to be binding. For some years now the board of the central bank has been dominated by economists who support the Concertación coalition, appointed senators have been eliminated, and by controlling the presidency, the government has been able to pass, every year, the budget it has deemed appropriate. And yet, under these circumstances, the left-of-center, democratically elected governments of Chile have decided to expand the market-oriented policies that many associate with the Chicago Boys and the Washington Consensus. These policies have not been furthered because the center-left had no alternative but because, as I have noted, they have succeeded.

The Chicago Boys' initial participation in the military government was restricted to advisory roles. During its first months in office the military government gravitated toward more conventional views and appointed traditional industrialists to senior government positions. These appointees believed in implementing gradual corrections to economic policies and in maintaining a prominent role for the state and a relatively high level of protection. As political scientist Juan Gabriel Valdés has pointed out, it was only slowly that the Chicago Boys' views became dominant.[11] This gain in influence was the result of two factors: first, the original gradualist approach to solving the Unidad Popular imbalances—and especially to eliminating inflation—did not work out as anticipated, and second, in the midst of the crisis, the Chicago Boys' proposed policies appeared to be internally consistent, based on serious thinking, and rooted in empirical and statistical studies of Chile's economic history.

In April 1975 a breakthrough occurred when Jorge Cauas, a prestigious economist who had been director of the World Bank's Research Department and was in many ways an honorary Chicago Boy, was named minister of finance. He was instrumental in the decision to shift gears and accelerate implementation of the new economic program. After an initial difficult period, his approach to taming inflation, based on major across-the-board cuts in government expenditures, proved successful. In a matter of two years inflation was reduced significantly, the economy was opened to international competition, and a major privatization program was put into place. Most banks and more than five hundred state-owned enterprises—many of which had been expropriated during the Allende years—were privatized. Also, many regulations were eliminated and red tape was reduced. By 1977 the Chilean economy was growing at almost 10 percent per annum, and the Chicago Boys had seen their views vindicated. The boom years lasted until 1981, when as a result of an artificially strong currency, extremely high real interest rates, and an unfriendly external environment the economy entered a profound crisis.

Although in the mid-1970s the reform program of the Chicago Boys was seen as truly revolutionary, it looks rather timid from today's perspective. The trade policy recommendations clearly illustrate the gradualist and moderate nature of the original Chicago Boys' economic program: in order to have a competitive and healthy trade sector it was fundamentally important to avoid an artificial strengthening of the currency and to lower import tariffs gradually and eliminate other trade restrictions in a step-by-step fashion. According to the Chicago Boys' original program the new, postreform import tariffs should have averaged 30 percent—hardly free trade. Indeed, it is interesting to note that in 2009, after two socialist governments, Chile's average import tariff is close to 3 percent, one-tenth of what the Chicago Boys had proposed, which would seem scandalous to most old Latin American hands in the mid-1970s. By early 1975 Chile had eliminated import licenses and had already gone through four rounds of import tariff reductions. The maximum tariff stood at 140 percent and the average tariff was 67 percent, down from over 120 percent in September 1973. In August of 1977 the average import tariff was 20 percent, and by June 1979 Chile had a uniform import tariff of 10 percent and no other forms of trade restriction.[12]

The Chicago Boys, Politics, and Labor Unions

The implementation of the Chicago Boys' economic program was neither easy nor straightforward. In particular, industrialists who had benefited from decades of protectionist and preferred treatment by governments of different persuasions and stripes strongly opposed opening up the economy and deregulating business. Their goal was to return to the status quo ante, to go back to the golden era of protectionism in which, protected by the high walls of import tariffs, quotas, and prohibitions, they could do as they pleased; they wanted to return to the times when there was no need to compete, produce quality goods, or do research and development—times when they had millions of captive consumers who had no alternative but to buy products from them. The most prominent representatives of this sector had powerful connections with senior officers in the armed forces and did not hesitate to use them in an effort to stall and even reverse the reforms. The Chicago Boys were called unpatriotic and derided for being ivory tower academics. It was argued that a heavy industry—even one that was inefficient and protected by all sorts of barriers—was needed for the survival of the nation and that without it Chile would become easy prey for its neighbors with expansionist ambitions. There was talk of Argentina's interest in having access to the Pacific Ocean and of Peru's and Bolivia's quests to recover the vast extensions of land that they had ceded to Chile at the end of the War of the Pacific in 1881. A number of senior armed forces officers agreed with this view and tried to alter the course of economic policy. Chile's future, it was said, depended on it, and the Chicago Boys had to be ousted and their program brought to an end.[13]

The disagreements within the armed forces and the government reached a climax in mid-1978 when one of the four members of the junta, air force general Gustavo Leigh, became increasingly skeptical about the reform program and voiced his disagreements in public. Although he didn't quite say it, he intimated that the government's economic policy was leading the country toward destruction and that this was General Pinochet's fault. The power struggle was resolved on July 24, when after obtaining the support of the other junta members and senior officers, Pinochet ousted General Leigh. He was replaced by General Fernando Matthei, who was much more sympathetic toward the modernization project and was personally involved in many of the reforms of the years to come.

After the coup, most labor leaders were imprisoned or sent into exile, and all labor union activities were banned. In July 1974, the International Labor Office in Geneva released a critical report on Chile, and the military decided to enact new rules on labor relations. Tripartite commissions made up of representatives of management, the government, and labor were put in place to negotiate wages. Unions, however, continued to be restricted, as were strikes and other traditional negotiating tactics used by labor to pressure management. Workers responded to this situation by organizing in unofficial groups and associations and voicing their discontent in any way they could. In 1979, under pressure from the Carter administration, which had threatened to impose economic sanctions if unions were not allowed to operate, Pinochet decided to put in place a completely new set of labor laws. Harvard-trained José Piñera was appointed minister of labor, and a new code was proposed. This established that union affiliation within each firm was voluntary and forbade industrywide labor negotiations. It also allowed companies to replace striking workers after a brief period of time and mandated severance payments for dismissed workers.

Once again senior officers in the armed forces disagreed. To the hard core, the new code was too flexible and gave too much power to unions. A substantial group of senior generals, however, had the opposite view. They believed the proposed legislation was too restrictive and ran the risk of alienating workers and creating antimilitary sentiment in the long run. To them, restricting union activities made sense in the immediate wake of the coup but was not something they wanted as a permanent feature of Chile's economic system.

Contrary to skeptics, Piñera argued that his proposal would create a modern, dynamic, flexible, and prolabor regime. In particular, he pointed to a provision in the code that assured that inflation-adjusted wages could never decline. No matter what happened in the economy, how the economic circumstances of the country might change, or how the international prices of Chile's exports might evolve, the law mandated that private-sector companies periodically adjust wages for inflation. In making his case Piñera was professorial and charming, articulate and vehement, passionate and charismatic. It didn't take too long for him to gain the support of the senior echelons of the military. What he had not done, however, was find out what his colleagues on the economic team thought about the proposal. As it turned out, they had serious reservations about it.

In his memoirs, Sergio de Castro, the leader of the Chicago Boys and a minister of economics and finance during the Pinochet regime, argues that this legislation was extremely detrimental to the functioning of the Chilean economy. In particular, he points out that by impeding downward movements in inflation-adjusted wages, the new labor law made it impossible for Chile to maintain full employment when international economic conditions—including the prices of Chile's exports—deteriorated. De Castro goes so far as to say that the crisis and deep slump of 1982 were direct consequences of this provision of the labor law. According to de Castro, he confronted Piñera in front of Pinochet and urged him to modify his proposal. The young Harvard economist refused and asked the general to make a decision. After some deliberation within the junta, the new labor code was approved as the minister of labor and his team had drafted it. This squabble between de Castro and Piñera—two of Pinochet's most senior ministers—illustrates clearly that, although it was enacted under a dictatorial regime, the passage of reform legislation was neither automatic nor easy.

Chile: A Case of a Successful Growth Transition

For the last three decades Chile has been by far the most economically successful Latin American country and provides a fascinating case study of a successful growth transition encompassing the three phases discussed in chapter 1. In 1975 Chile's income per person was 25 percent that of the United States; in 1990 it was 28 percent, and in 2006 it had climbed to 40 percent of U.S. income per capita. This contrasts sharply with the region as a whole: while in 1975 average income per capita in Latin America was 24 percent that of the United States, by 2006 it had declined to 19 percent.

As noted previously, in an effort to accelerate the reduction of inflation, the Chilean authorities pegged the value of the peso to the U.S. dollar in 1979. This proved to be a serious mistake. The story is by now familiar: since inflation was not eliminated, domestic prices and costs continued to rise, squeezing exporters' profit margins. As the peso became artificially strong, a very large trade deficit developed. At first this was financed with foreign funds, but in 1982 international investors became concerned about the country's ability to pay its debts. A profound crisis erupted in June 1982 when the peso lost half of its value, the economy contracted by 14 percent, and unemployment exceeded the astonishing level of 20 percent.

The years that followed were painful, but the authorities decided to maintain the market-oriented policies. Furthermore, a round of institutional reforms aimed at improving the protection of property rights, enhancing the rule of law, and avoiding the capture of the State by interest groups was initiated: social security was reformed, and a system based on individual retirement accounts that eventually became famous around the world was introduced. A mining code that protected investors against expropriation was passed, and the labor market was modernized by reducing the costs of both hiring and dismissing workers. The judiciary was reformed, and the central bank was granted independence from partisan pressure groups.

By 1984 Chile had recovered from the currency collapse of two years earlier. As a result of the combination of a competitive currency and increased productivity stemming from the reforms, Chile's real gross domestic product grew by almost 7 percent per annum between 1984 and 1989. Consistent with phase one of growth transitions, this very rapid economic growth was accompanied by a rather low rate of investment in equipment, machinery, and infrastructure; measured as a proportion of gross domestic product, investment was a mediocre 18 percent. To put things in perspective, most of the Asian Tigers achieved their fabled 7 percent growth rates while investing more than 30 percent of their gross domestic product. During these early years the engine of Chile's growth was a very rapid improvement in efficiency and productivity. Calculations made by the World Bank indicate that during that period total factor productivity growth in Chile was among the fastest ever recorded in Latin America's history.[14]

In the early 1990s, after more than six years of very solid growth, investment in capital, machinery, equipment, and infrastructure began to grow quickly. This was mostly the result of a perceived increase in investment profitability and of the institutional strengthening implemented since the mid-1980s, including improvements in the protection of property rights, strengthening of mechanisms for conflict resolution, and creation of an independent central bank that was free from short-term political pressures and interferences.

During this period there was a remarkable acceleration in foreign investment, which doubled from 2 percent of the country's gross domestic product in 1984–89 to more than 4 percent in 1990–97. Many of the new investment projects were in the export sector, including investments in mining, agribusiness, wineries, and production of fresh and canned fruits and vegetables, salmon, and other foods. In addition, there were significant investments in banking and finance and in infrastructure, including ports, telecommunications, and toll roads.

By 1990 there was little doubt that Chile's new approach to economic policy—at a time when market orientation was new in Latin America—had produced an export boom, an acceleration in productivity gains, rapid overall growth, and a reduction in poverty. That year, after seventeen years of dictatorship, Chile returned to democratic rule. The majority of the senior members of the new democratic government had been severe critics of the military regime and its pro–free market economic policies. In spite of this the new government of President Patricio Aylwin decided to deepen both the economic and institutional reforms pursued by the military.[15] Between 1990 and 2007 import duties were reduced further, to an average of 3 percent; a new round of privatization was implemented; free trade agreements were signed with the United States, the European Union, and other advanced countries; modern procompetition regulatory bodies were created; a "fiscal rule" that assured public-sector solvency over the long run was implemented; and far-reaching judiciary reform was put in place. In addition, an ambitious infrastructure program based on concessions, under which the private sector built roads and ports and charged users' fees, was put into action. This private sector–led infrastructure program resulted in a significant improvement in exports' international competitiveness and helped the country sustain a rapid rate of growth. In a 1990 *Newsweek* interview, newly appointed finance minister Alejandro Foxley was asked whether the new administration would introduce changes to the military's economic policy. His answer was straight-forward: "[We will] maintain an open economy fully integrated into world markets, dynamic exports' growth, and a private sector fully committed to the task of economic development."[16]

Of course, there were some areas of disagreement with the outgoing military regime. In particular, the Concertación coalition was determined to increase government expenditure on social programs. In the *Newsweek* interview Foxley talked about recapturing the balance between economic conditions and social policies aimed at improving the standard of living of the poor. Equally central to the democratic project, he said, was making sure that macroeconomic stability would be maintained; in particular, he mentioned "avoiding at all costs the typical cycle of populist economic policies in Latin America."

An important political decision made by the new government was to address two critical economic reforms during its first year: a tax package aimed at funding the new social programs was implemented, and a reform of the labor law that had been criticized by union leaders and political commentators was put in place. Government officials were careful to explain that these two pieces of legislation constituted the only important modifications to the economic model established by Pinochet. By tackling these issues in this way early on, the government sought to minimize possible negative effects on private investment that might result from policy uncertainty.[17] Since 1990 the center-left Concertación coalition has continued to implement policies that combine openness, fiscal stability, market orientation, competition, and social programs targeted to the poor. This pragmatic policy stance has been at the heart of Chile's solid performance and explains why the country stands out in every policy and institutional ranking.

While pursuing additional rounds of reforms, Chile's democratically elected governments have maintained an important element of pragmatism: not every state-owned enterprise has been privatized—in particular the state has retained ownership of some important copper mines—and for a number of years the country has relied on market-based controls on capital inflows as a way of keeping international speculation at bay (as discussed below). One could of course question the wisdom of maintaining 100 percent state ownership of large mining companies, but that is beside the point. What is clear is that Chile has followed a flexible approach to reform and hasn't rushed to mechanically implement every single policy prescribed by the so-called Washington Consensus. Chile's policy makers have understood that this decalogue—or similar lists, for that matter—provides general guidelines on a development strategy and is not a rigid "to-do" list.

By the mid-1990s the rate of investment in machinery, equipment, and infrastructure had jumped to 26 percent of gross domestic product, up from 18 percent in 1989. By deepening reforms Chile was able to move to the second phase of growth transition, in which the most important sources of growth are productivity improvements and an increase in productive capacity through the accumulation of capital. Educational reform aimed at improving the skills of the labor force were also put in place. The average rate of economic growth during this second phase of the growth transition (1990–97) was an impressive 7.7 percent per annum.

The surge in capital investment helped sustain growth in the late 1990s and early 2000s. During the first half of the 2000s Chile entered the third phase of its growth transition, as productivity growth declined from the breakneck pace of earlier years. As a result of institutional strengthening, capital accumulation—bolstered by a continuing high rate of foreign direct investment—remained high, and overall growth was a respectable 4.5 percent on average.

Pragmatism, Markets, and Success

The overall results of Chile's reforms are impressive: for more than two decades Chile's exports grew at double-digit rates.[18] Social conditions also improved markedly during this period. The number of people living below the World Bank's poverty line declined from 24 percent of the population in 1989 to 5 percent in 2003. There was also some progress in reducing income inequality, although the pace at which this took place was rather slow: the Gini coefficient—which, as explained in chapter 2, measures inequality on a scale from 0 to 1—declined from 0.59 in 1989 to 0.55 in 2003. The safety net was widened, and transfers to the poor and the elderly increased substantially. In the second half of the past decade efforts were made to provide preschool education to the poor and to increase the number of university scholarships to low-income students.

The fact that the Chilean reforms were pragmatic has been misinterpreted by some authors, who have attempted to minimize the role played by market orientation and have claimed that Chile's success is largely the result of public policies aimed at promoting specific sectors and industries through subsidies, tax holidays, and other forms of preferential treatment.[19] This is not so. What is true is that, like every modern market-oriented nation, Chile established a network of commercial offices around the world that help advertise Chilean products and assist exporters in penetrating new markets. The government also helped develop a modern food safety system that assures foreign buyers that Chilean products comply with international cleanliness, safety, and health standards.[20] And as in every market-oriented nation, the government supported applied research—through universities and other institutions—that helped launch new export products and improve international competitiveness of existing goods. But none of this amounts to an active industrial policy by which government officials "pick winners," make key decisions on what to produce and export, or favor one industry over another one.

Fundación Chile, a nonprofit organization partially funded by the government, provides a good illustration of these policies.[21] Over the years it has encouraged research and provided seed capital that has helped develop some successful nontraditional exports, including salmon and berries. But providing this type of technological support is a far cry from subsidizing specific industries or "picking winners" in the tradition of old-fashioned industrial policies.[22] Indeed, Fundación Chile has been successful precisely because it is not a public institution and operates under a clear and transparent budget constraint; its total budget in 2007 was merely US$30 million, a miniscule amount in a country with total production in excess of $140 billion and exports of more than $40 billion.

What a succession of Chilean governments have done over the last thirty years to help the export sector is simple and yet very powerful: they have kept inflation low and the fiscal accounts in check; they have encouraged competition by opening the economy and creating modern and well-functioning regulatory bodies; they have improved the protection of property rights, improved the rule of law, and reduced the costs—in terms of time, bureaucracy, and red tape—of signing and enforcing contracts; they have avoided artificial strengthening of the currency; and they have improved safety and security for the population at large and for foreign investors.[23]

Chile has also made a major effort to enhance competition through the creation of autonomous institutions that protect consumers' rights. For instance, in 2003 the Tribunal for the Defense of Free Competition was created as an independent government body. Its members are highly trained specialists (lawyers and economists), two of whom are appointed by the supreme court, two by the board of directors of the central bank, and one by the president. In 2008 the tribunal surprised most observers by rejecting the proposed merger of the country's two largest supermarket chains. The merger, the tribunal ruled, would have reduced competition at the retail level, stifling innovation and hurting consumers.

Restricting Speculative Capital Flows

After the 1982 currency crisis, Chilean authorities were committed to avoiding, at almost any cost, an artificial strengthening or overvaluation of the currency. Starting in 1990, large volumes of capital began flowing into Chile, attracted by economic success, a peaceful transition to democratic rule, and high interest rates. It rapidly became apparent that these inflows were strengthening the peso and negatively affecting exports' competitiveness. In an effort to avoid the mistakes of a decade earlier, in 1991 Chile put in place controls on capital inflows. This policy worked in a simple way: 20 percent of financial capital entering the country had to be deposited for one year in the central bank. During this period these monies did not earn any interest. From a financial point of view this unremunerated deposit worked as a tax, whose rate was proportional to the interest income forgone during that year. The rate of the implicit tax was higher for short-term investments than for longer-term ones.

As a result of the imposition of controls, volatile and speculative capital inflows declined precipitously, as the authorities had anticipated, while longer-term capital inflows, including foreign direct investment, increased. A number of studies have found that the controls had some effect in slowing down the strengthening of the peso.[24] As the years passed, several modifications were introduced to the scheme; for example, in an effort to discourage financial inflows further in the mid-1990s, the rate of the deposit requirement was raised to 30 percent. In June 1998, in the aftermath of the East Asian crises, the rate of the reserve requirement was lowered to 10 percent, and in September of that year—immediately after the Russian crisis—the deposit rate was reduced to zero. At that point the authorities believed that the economy was mature enough to fully open the nation's financial sector to the rest of the world.

Chile was not the only country that used controls on inflows to influence currency values in the 1990s. Similar schemes were used by other nations, including Brazil and Colombia. These policies have been generally supported by reform skeptics. In a 1998 *New York Times* article Nobel laureate Joseph E. Stiglitz said, "You want to look for policies that discourage hot money but facilitate the flow of long-term loans, and there is evidence that the Chilean approach or some version of it, does this."[25]

The currency crises of the 1990s and 2000s in Latin America and other regions made clear that the costs of major currency collapses can be extremely high. This suggests that the emerging nations should become financially integrated with the rest of the world gradually and establish ways of avoiding unnecessary strengthening of their currencies and development of large and unsustainable trade deficits. In a 1995 article, Nobel laureate Robert A. Mundell, not precisely a supporter of generalized government intervention, aptly recognized the risks associated to a rapid lifting of capital controls in the emerging nations.[26]

The question of how to move toward greater capital mobility is highly complex and requires additional research. Transparent mechanisms based on price signals, such as the flexible tax on short-term inflows used by Chile during much of the 1990s, work relatively well as transitional devices. Such mechanisms allow some capital mobility and discourage short-term speculative investments; at the same time, they prevent arbitrary decisions by government bureaucrats. But as I have argued elsewhere, even Chilean-style capital controls have costs, and these should be taken into account when designing a specific country's policy. In two detailed articles, MIT professor Kristin Forbes has shown that by restricting access to external funding, the controls increased the cost of capital to small and medium-sized firms, reducing their investment and, thus, negatively affecting growth.[27]

The Key Role of Institutions and the Failure of Copycats

Between 1987 and 2007 Chile put in place important institutional reforms. In fact, in institutional terms Chile looks more like a southern European country than a Latin American one. For instance, according to an index constructed by the World Bank, in 2007 the rule of law was stronger in Chile than in the southern European nations: 1.17 vs. 0.91 (the higher value in the index being better). Chile also did somewhat better in controlling corruption (1.35 vs. 0.86) and in terms of regulatory quality (1.45 vs. 1.01). When it came to protecting property rights, the World Bank ranked Chile at the same level as the southern European countries.[28]

The failure to move decisively in the institutional sphere explains why most other Latin American countries have failed to go through the three phases of successful growth transition discussed in chapter 1. This is true even in countries that have attempted to copy almost every detail of Chile's economic reforms. A case in point is El Salvador. In 1992, the opposing parties in El Salvador's civil war reached a peace agreement. The end of this armed conflict greatly increased the quality of life in El Salvador: families that had been separated and displaced could be reunited and return to their homes, and young people who had only known violence and war could finally have normal lives.[29] Peace also had important economic consequences. Suddenly the Salvadoran people were freed from the concerns of war and could focus on investment and production and devote their efforts to improving social conditions and achieving prosperity. In many ways El Salvador was uniquely positioned for taking off economically. Its proximity to the United States, the largest consumer market in the world, was and continues to be a blessing. Indeed, its geographical location made El Salvador very different from many Latin American nations, including those in the Southern Cone (Argentina, Chile, Uruguay)—and Brazil.

What makes El Salvador's case particularly interesting is that even before the peace agreement was signed, President Alfredo Cristiani's government had been putting in place a reform package very similar to that implemented in Chile a decade earlier. In fact, many of El Salvador's economic advisors were Chilean economists who had actively participated in their country's economic reform. Many of them were members of the fabled Chicago Boys. The fact that the Salvadoran reforms took place a decade after Chile's own reforms had been launched was also important, since some of the mistakes made in the Southern Cone country were avoided by El Salvador's policy makers.

In 1991 El Salvador entered the first phase of the growth transition process. From 1992 through 1995, as a result of the peace agreement and of the reform package put in place by the Cristiani administration—which included deregulation and measures aimed at opening up international competition—the rate of economic growth increased to a very rapid 6.8 percent on average. This is particularly impressive compared with the meager average for the previous five years (1987–91) of 2.5 percent per year or the average growth of the other Central American countries. That 1992–95 comprised phase one of the growth transition process in El Salvador is further confirmed by the extremely high pace of productivity growth—indeed more than half of the country's average growth during the period is explained by productivity improvements. As had been the case in Chile years earlier, during this first phase in El Salvador investment in machinery and equipment played a very minor role as a source of growth, remaining at a very low 17 percent of gross domestic product.[30]

By 1996 El Salvador's future looked bright. Not only had growth been very high during the previous four years, but the economic reform process was moving ahead at full speed. According to the Heritage Foundation El Salvador's policy stance was as strongly promarket as Chile's. Indeed, that year both nations were ranked thirtieth in the foundation's annual economic freedom ranking. In the years that followed, El Salvador continued to move forward in economic reforms: trade liberalization was stepped up, free trade agreements with the United States and Mexico were signed, business was further deregulated, and the local currency was replaced by the U.S. dollar as a way of reducing the probability of currency crises. This rapid progress in economic reform was duly recognized by the Heritage Foundation; in 2001 El Salvador had moved up to the twelfth spot in its Index of Economic Freedom, ahead of Chile and all other Latin American countries.

Yet in spite of its advances in economic modernization, and in contrast with Chile, El Salvador failed to implement institutional reforms and thus to move to the second phase of the growth transition process. Weak institutions—including the judiciary's lack of independence, scant rule of law, and weak protection of property rights—discouraged investment in capital, equipment, and machinery at a time when the country needed to establish the virtuous cycle that characterizes the higher phases of growth transitions. In fact, during 1997–2001 aggregate investment declined to 16 percent of gross domestic product (from 17 percent in 1992–95), and foreign investment was a low 2 percent of national income.

As a result of this inability to advance to phase two of the growth transition process, during the first half of the past decade the rate of growth in El

Salvador dropped to barely 2 percent per annum. Moreover, and in contrast with Chile, the extent of inequality increased—the Gini coefficient was 0.52 in 2003, up from 0.49 in 1990. On the other hand, the proportion of the population living below the poverty line declined slightly: in 2003 it was 41 percent, down from 43 percent in 1989. However, compared with the extent of poverty decline in Chile, where poverty fell from 24 percent of the population in 1989 to 5 percent in 2003, these results don't look particularly impressive.

In contrast to those of Chile, institutions in El Salvador have remained weak; in fact, no visible progress was achieved after 1995. By the year 2000, the control of corruption was weak, and the rule of law was wanting. Moreover, according to the Fraser Institute's index the degree of protection of property rights was significantly lower in El Salvador than in Chile—4.5 vs. 6.5 on a scale from 1 to 10. In almost every institutional category, El Salvador was doing worse in the mid-2000s than it had a decade earlier.

Safety and security were major problems in El Salvador even in the mid-2000s. According to the U.S. State Department's human rights report, in 2006 there were still significant abuses and criminal kidnappings in El Salvador; it was not unusual for businesspeople to be abducted and held for ransom. In fact, in 2006 the number of kidnappings increased by 50 percent over the previous year.[31] This insecurity coupled with low credibility and an absence of the rule of law discouraged foreign investors. In 2001–5 foreign direct investment in El Salvador barely amounted to 2 percent of gross domestic product; during the same period foreign investment in Chile reached the equivalent to 6 percent of gross domestic product.

Although critically important, institutional differences are not the only explanation for the stark contrast in economic performance between Chile and El Salvador during the last decade and a half. Two additional factors are geography and the emergence of China as a global economic powerhouse. While Chile is endowed with abundant natural resources—including minerals, fertile land, and an extensive coast line—El Salvador is a resource-poor nation. On the other hand, El Salvador has traditionally had two important assets: its proximity to the United States and its abundant and relatively inexpensive labor force. In the early to mid-1990s these geographical differences determined the production patterns of the two countries. Chile expanded commodity and natural resources–based exports such as wine, fresh produce, canned food, salmon, and minerals; El Salvador on the other hand saw an expansion of light manufacturing of items such as apparel and footwear in special export zones—the so-called *maquilas*. The economic emergence of China in the late 1990s and early twenty-first century—and to a lesser extent the emergence of India—affected Chile and El Salvador in very different ways. China's increasing appetite for raw materials has had a tremendous impact on commodity prices. The price of copper, for instance, quadrupled between 2004 and 2008. This has had a very positive effect on Chile's economy. At the same time, China has become a formidable producer of low-priced light-manufacturing goods, squeezing El Salvador out of the global marketplace.

Chile's Legacy

Over the last three decades Chile has become Latin America's brightest—and one could argue, only—star. The political and economic crisis of the mid-1970s allowed a band of technocrats to change the status quo and implement a set of policies and reforms that hurt the interests of what until then had been powerful groups. Traditionally powerful families that for decades had enjoyed rents and privileges were suddenly threatened by newcomers who espoused efficiency and were highly productive. Industrial barons who had become accustomed to protectionism were forced to compete and innovate. Public-sector bureaucrats who were used to receiving a paycheck for almost no effort and who systematically mistreated the public were suddenly held accountable for their actions. All of this resulted in an increase in productivity and efficiency, a spurt of entrepreneurship, the birth of an innovative private sector, and a move toward prosperity.

A long process of reflection and analysis by the left was fundamental in forging Chile's miracle. During the long and painful exile years, leftist politicians became convinced of the need to have an economy open to the rest of the world, an economy that encouraged efficiency and innovation and relied on productivity improvements as the main engine of growth. They became convinced that democracy, inclusiveness, social improvements, productivity improvements, and respect for the rule of law were not contradictory. Quite the contrary, the key to success was to promote all of these goals through a combination of policies that encouraged innovation and competition and provided an effective safety net to those less fortunate.

Chapter 6
So Far from God
Mexico's Tequila Crisis of 1994

In late October 1993, Mexico's trade minister Jaime Serra Puche addressed the Wall Street Journal Conference on the Americas at the Waldorf Astoria Hotel in New York City. The audience was captivated by Serra's charm and command of the stage. The sense among the conference participants—CEOs of large corporations, investment bankers, journalists, and pundits of various kinds—was that in spite of a campaign against the North America Free Trade Agreement (NAFTA) led by businessman Ross Perot, Mexico was the brightest star in the Latin American firmament. The mood was one of euphoria and complacency; the calls for caution made by some of the speakers were brushed aside as signs of unjustified gloom. The future looked brilliant, and virtually everyone expected that after the enactment of NAFTA, Mexico would rapidly join the ranks of the more advanced countries, with solid growth, stability, and prosperity. That evening, in a surprise visit to the conference, President Bill Clinton delivered a speech that basically supported this optimistic perspective.

Very few of the participants—if any—suspected that as this event was taking place in the venerable Waldorf Astoria, in Mexico's southern state of Chiapas hundreds of Indians and left-wing activists were going through the final stages of their military training to stage a major uprising that would shock the Mexican establishment, institutional investors, and the U.S. administration. Thus, a tale of two Mexicos was being forged: on one hand, that of modern Mexico, on the verge of entering the first world—or so the optimists thought—and on the other, that of quasi-feudal Mexico, with its poverty, destitution, sorrows, and frustrations. Throughout 1994 these two Mexicos coexisted, and while most international investors dismissed the Chiapas events as the work of a handful of adventurers in the style of El Zorro, the obstacles on the Mexican road to the free market became more and more apparent to perceptive analysts.

In December 1994 the international financial community had to face what most pundits had deemed impossible: for the third time in eighteen years Mexico's currency—the once strong and proud peso—collapsed. In a few months the peso lost more than two-thirds of its value, interest rates skyrocketed, unemployment increased significantly—with the concomitant increase in Mexican migration to the United States—many firms went bankrupt, and most banks were on the verge of insolvency. In 1995 income per capita declined by almost 8 percent, and Mexico was only able to avoid a default on its debt thanks to a multibillion-dollar loan from the U.S. government.

The Mexican crisis raised a number of questions throughout the world regarding the sustainability and the merits of the market-oriented reform process in Latin America and other regions. If Mexico was one of the best examples of a successful reformer, some observers asked, what could be expected of others? Across Latin America critics urged political leaders to move away from globalization and embrace once again the import substitution policies of the previous decades.

What made the Mexican crisis of 1994 particularly important was that it represented the first major setback encountered by the reform movement. It was a clear indication that, contrary to the rosy expectations and what was promised to the public by overly optimistic politicians, the road to modernity and efficiency was neither easy nor fast. It showed that even if a sincere effort were made to manage political opposition, serious setbacks could occur. The Mexican crisis also showed that, as some analysts already knew from Chile's experience almost a decade earlier, the exchange rate was a key variable that had to be monitored carefully and permanently in order to avoid the explosion of a major and devastating crisis.

The most important forces behind what Michel Camdessus, then managing director of the IMF, called the first crisis of the twenty-first century were the result of a series of macroeconomic policy mistakes that were amplified by a succession of political shocks, including the assassination of Luis Donaldo Colosio, the presidential candidate of the ruling party, the PRI.[1] These policy mistakes—including pegging the value of the currency to the U.S. dollar and allowing a very large external imbalance to develop—were not directly related to the reforms, but nevertheless the Mexican crisis affected the public's perception of market orientation, capitalism, and globalization throughout Latin America and the rest of the world.[2]

The Mexican Miracle: A Mirage?

In 1988 President Carlos Salinas de Gortari launched a major economic reform program aimed at modernizing Mexico's economy. The program, which was one of the templates that was used for developing the Washington Consensus two years later, consisted of four broad components:

- The opening of the economy to international competition through a deep reduction of import tariffs and an eventual free trade agreement with the United States.
- A privatization and deregulation process that would cover most economics sectors except oil, gas, and energy.
- A stabilization program aimed at controlling inflation. This program was based on maintaining a strict link between the value of the peso and the U.S. dollar. Specifically, the peso-dollar exchange rate was allowed to move daily at a slow and predetermined pace. During 1994 the peso–U.S. dollar rate was allowed to fluctuate within a very narrow band. Indeed the band was so slim that for all practical purposes Mexico's exchange-rate policy consisted of a very rigid rate relation between the peso and the dollar.
- A broad social and economic agreement between the government, the private sector, and labor unions—known as the Pacto de Solidaridad Económica, or Pacto—aimed at controlling the rate of increase of wages and prices. This agreement was supported by prudent fiscal and monetary policies that kept overall inflationary pressures in check.

The reliance on the Pacto was a key element of the Mexican program and distinguished it from those followed, for example, in Argentina and Chile. The yearly renewal of the Pacto became a major political event, surrounded by anticipation and at times by anxiety.[3] The Pacto's main objective was to ensure that the reforms had the political support of the Mexican public. In particular, the involvement of Fidel Velázquez, the legendary union leader who headed the Confederation of Mexican Workers (Confederación de Trabajadores de México), in the annual deliberations and decisions gave the Mexican reform process a degree of political legitimacy that the reforms in other Latin American countries did not have.

The use of the exchange rate as an anti-inflationary tool deserves particular attention. Since 1976 the Mexican public had associated exchange-rate changes with inflation. When the peso was depreciated, prices of imported goods increased. In response, labor unions asked for higher wages, putting additional pressure on prices. This in turn generated further depreciations of the peso, expectations of higher inflation, and yet further increases in wages and prices. As a way of breaking this vicious circle, in 1988 the Mexican authorities decided to link the peso to the U.S. dollar. The thought behind this policy was that when the extent to which the value of the peso could fall was restricted, inflationary expectations would decline and inflation would eventually reach a level similar to that of U.S. inflation.

In spite of the Salinas administration's reforms, the performance of the Mexican economy was rather modest between 1988 and 1994. Real growth averaged 2.8 percent—significantly lower than Chile's (7.1 percent) and Colombia's (4.1 percent)—productivity growth was almost flat, export expansion was positive but not impressive, real wages hovered around their 1980 level, private savings experienced a major decline, the incidence of poverty continued to be very high, and income distribution remained as skewed as in the past. On the positive side, fiscal balance was attained in 1992, inflation was reduced to the high single digits, and layers of protectionism were dismantled.

Despite the lack of major economic results, the Mexican reforms were consistently praised by financial experts, academics, the World Bank, and the IMF as a major success. In a way, a "Mexican miracle" was invented by these institutions. This enthusiasm and optimism were the result of a number of factors, including the tremendous faith that many analysts had in the reforms themselves; if results were not there, many argued, they were around the corner. A few months after the Mexican crisis, economist Paul Krugman argued that much of this enthusiasm represented a "leap of faith, rather than a conclusion based on hard evidence."[4]

The Clinton administration's efforts to persuade the public and Congress of the benefits of NAFTA also contributed to the popular notion that there was a Mexican miracle in the making. After NAFTA was approved, a large number of observers argued that the free trade pact would significantly accelerate investment and exports growth and that the success of the reforms would then become evident for everyone to see.

Furthermore, supporters of the reforms often cited the Mexican experience as an example of the possibility of undertaking successful structural reforms within a democratic regime. Mexico, in fact, was often contrasted with Chile, where many of the successful reforms had been initiated under a military dictatorship. It is possible to speculate, then, that the desire—especially among

U.S. officials—to find an example of successful market-oriented reforms under a democratic regime contributed to the creation of the notion that Mexico was a superior performer. However, one could question the notion that Mexico under the PRI was a true democracy. Novelist Mario Vargas Llosa famously said in 1990 that Mexico was "a perfect dictatorship."[5]

The World Bank, the IMF, and the U.S. Treasury were not the only institutions promoting the image of a super successful Mexican experiment, or even the most vocal. Investment bankers, mutual fund managers, and financial reporters were even more enthusiastic.[6] A forceful illustration of the private-sector enthusiasm came from the investment firm Bear Stearns, which in early November 1994—just a few weeks before the collapse of the peso—argued in one of its newsletters to investors: "[W]e expect a *strengthening* of the peso in the coming months, creating very high dollar returns on Cetes [peso-denominated government securities]."[7]

A compilation of major investment banks' views on Mexico during November and the first half of December 1994 indicates that most analysts continued to be optimistic up to the day of the collapse of the currency. Out of twenty written analyses released by major institutions during that period, twelve dismissed the possibility of currency devaluation. Of these, two predicted a strengthening of the peso, two urged an upgrade of Mexico's investment rating, and eight argued that although the trade deficit was very high, there would be no devaluation.[8]

This optimism was captured by a rapid improvement in the country's position in international risk tables. For example, in *Euromoney*'s country risk ratings, Mexico was upgraded from seventy-seventh position in 1985 to forty-fourth in 1994. Astonishingly, Mexico's *Euromoney* country risk ranking improved between March and September 1994; its perceived riskiness reached its lowest historical level barely ten weeks before the massive collapse of the peso. As a result of this perception and the sharp decline in interest rates in the U.S. between 1989 and early 1992, Mexico received massive amounts of foreign funds, many of a short-term and speculative nature.

The Exchange Rate, Capital Flows, and External Imbalances

In mid-1992, a few months before the collapse of the peso, Finance Minister Pedro Aspe delivered the prestigious Lionel Robbins Lecture at the London

School of Economics. The published version of this lecture provides one of the most comprehensive explanations for the rationale behind Mexico's anti-inflationary program. According to the view prevailing in the Mexican government at that time, a fixed value of the peso would rapidly eliminate the degree of "inertial inflation" and "place an upward boundary on ... prices."[9]

The Mexican stabilization program succeeded in reducing inflationary inertia but not in eliminating it. As a result, inflation declined slowly, and throughout the early 1990s local prices and costs increased at a faster pace than international prices. With the value of the currency almost fixed relative to the U.S. dollar, Mexico's international competitiveness gradually declined: while the number of pesos exporters received per U.S. dollar for exported goods remained virtually constant, domestic costs, including wages, rents, taxes, and insurance, continued to climb, squeezing exporters' profit margins.

In 1989 the Brady agreement that restructured Latin American debts from the "lost decade" was signed, and Mexico's external debt was reduced significantly. At that time Mexico opened up its financial sectors to foreign investors and began to privatize state-owned banks. As a result of these policies and the perception that an economic miracle of sorts was taking place, the international capital market rediscovered Mexico and began investing heavily in securities issued by the Mexican government and government firms. The resulting surge in capital inflows allowed the country to finance an increasingly large current account deficit, the broadest measure of a country's external transactions. From 1992 through 1994 this deficit averaged almost 7 percent of gross domestic product, a level that many economists would find dangerously high. Because government finances were under control and the incoming funds were of a private nature, a number of analysts, especially senior Mexican officials, were persuaded that although these flows were very large, they were not a cause for concern.

For a long time economists have argued about the appropriate sequencing of economic reform and have asked which markets should be liberalized first and which should be deregulated later and more slowly. In the mid-1990s most experts agreed that the most effective sequence of liberalization called for controls on international capital movements to be lifted gradually and in a way that avoided massive capital inflows that would suddenly increase liquidity and result in an artificial strengthening of the local currency. Contrary to this conventional wisdom, Mexico opted for eliminating restrictions on international capital mobility in 1989, very early in the reform process.[10] The adoption of this sequence of reform was a response to a series of factors, including Mexico's long tradition of free capital mobility and the country's desire to join the OECD, a rich countries' club that required that its members allow capital to move without impediments. This strategy contrasted with that followed by other Latin reformers, including Chile, which maintained some form of restrictions to the free mobility of capital in an effort to avoid a loss in international competitiveness.

In the absence of restrictions, international financial managers were free to move even larger volumes of funds in and out of Mexico. In 1993 alone net capital flowing into Mexico surpassed 8 percent of gross domestic product, an enormous figure compared with capital moving into other countries and relative to Mexico's own historical experience. Most of these funds were short-term, speculative investments in the stock market, private-sector instruments, and government securities.

In 1992 a number of observers began to argue that the strengthening of the inflation-adjusted value of the currency—or what economists call the "real exchange rate"—posed a serious threat for the sustainability of the reforms. Rudi Dornbusch, the MIT professor and old Latin American hand, pointed out that "[t]he current problem of the Mexican economy is the overvalued exchange rate."[11] In a public document issued in November of 1992 the World Bank noted with a tragic sense of premonition that "[o]pening its capital account also exposes Mexico to the volatility of short-term capital movements that can transmit destabilizing external shocks to the economy even if domestic policies are right." This report went on to say that Mexico could "adjust to these risks through higher interest rates and, possibly, depreciating the peso."[12]

The Mexican authorities responded to these apprehensions by once again arguing that, since capital inflows were largely private and the government's fiscal accounts were in balance, there was nothing to worry about. This position was based on a three-part argument: First, Mexican officials pointed out that the system had enough built-in flexibility—in the form of flexible interest rates and the narrow exchange rate band—to deal with eventual shocks and surprises. Second, it was argued that a rapid increase in productivity was about to take place and would generate a major export expansion that would help close the current account and trade gaps. And third, it was claimed that the long-term economic growth fundamentals remained healthy, especially in light of NAFTA's ratification.[13]

In January 1994 Miguel Mancera, the governor of the Banco de México, told the *Economist* that the trade imbalance was not a problem because it was associated with the inflow of foreign funds and not with expansionary fiscal or monetary policy.[14] Moreover, the authorities generated their own calculations that suggested that when properly measured the inflation-adjusted value of the currency had not strengthened as much as independent observers had argued.

What these analyses failed to recognize, however, was that the rate at which capital was flowing into Mexico—at levels exceeding 8 percent of the nation's aggregate output—was not sustainable in the long run and that at some point it would either slow down or come to a sudden stop. Although there are no mechanical rules for determining the volume of capital inflow that can be maintained in the long term, there are some helpful guidelines that analysts can follow to detect departures from sustainability; generally speaking, most of these guidelines call for keeping the current account deficit below 4 percent of gross domestic product, a level greatly exceeded by Mexico from 1992 to 1994.[15]

1994: A Recurrent Nightmare

On January 1, 1994, the Zapatista army staged an uprising in the southern state of Chiapas, reminding the financial world that, in spite of the reforms, Mexico continued to be a country with pressing social problems and tremendous inequalities.

As a result of the Chiapas events and of increased political uncertainty, in late February the value of the peso dropped to the lowest value allowed by the exchange-rate band. Surprisingly, perhaps, interest rates on peso-denominated government securities—twenty-eight-day cetes, for example—did not increase substantially, and international reserves held by the central bank did not fall. In fact, according to information provided by Mexican authorities, from January to mid-February there was a record inflow of foreign capital into the country.

By mid-March it seemed that things were at least partially under control. After the initial scare of the Chiapas uprising, the financial community was once again betting on Mexico. Then on March 23 fate struck again. The presidential candidate of the ruling PRI party, Luis Donaldo Colosio, was assassinated while greeting the crowd at a political rally in Lomas Taurinas, a poor suburb of Tijuana. This time the financial community reacted in panic, and both foreign and domestic investors reduced their purchases of Mexican bonds and other Mexican securities.

As a result, there was a rapid increase in interest rates; rates on twenty-eight-day cetes increased from around 10 percent in February to more than 16 percent in April. With the peso already at the weakest level allowed by the exchange-rate band, further depreciation was not an option within the prevailing system. Under the impression that this was a shock of a temporary nature, the authorities decided to spend more than US$10 billion in international reserves to shore up the currency.

The U.S. authorities reacted to these events with alarm, and on March 24 Treasury Secretary Lloyd Bentsen and Federal Reserve Board chairman Alan Greenspan announced that the United States was extending a $6 billion credit line to Mexico, to be used when and if needed.

In spite of the recurrence of negative shocks, the financial community still appeared to be confident that a collapse of the peso was not in the offing. This view was neatly reflected in a front-page article in London's *Financial Times* on March 25, 1994, that read: "[E]ven with Mexico's dependence on foreign capital to cover a current account deficit of over Dollars 20 billion, a crisis is eminently avoidable."[16]

Mexico, however, had difficulties rolling over its rapidly maturing public-sector debt. The authorities faced a dilemma: On one hand they could allow interest rates to increase further as a way of attracting buyers of government debt. The drawback of this option was that higher interest rates could lead to a recession during an election year. An alternative was to issue debt that was attractive in other dimensions and thus did not require higher interest rates to attract buyers. Government officials decided that investors would be willing to buy U.S. dollar–denominated debt at a lower interest rate. Thus, an increasing number of dollar-linked securities, known as *tesobonos*, were sold to investors. It was true that the interest rate paid on these bonds was significantly lower than that paid on peso-denominated government securities, the cetes. However, if the peso were to collapse, the cost of this new debt would skyrocket, as the government would have to cough up additional pesos for each dollar of debt.

At the same time as the government capped interest rates on peso-denominated public debt, the central bank continued to pump pesos into the economy through an active public-sector credit program. The problem, of course, was that more pesos were being made available at a time when nobody wanted to hold them, out of fear of a possible devaluation. In addition, fiscal policy was relaxed and government expenditures were increased in response to a political campaign that turned out to be unexpectedly difficult for the PRI, the longtime governing party.

During the first half of 1994 concerns about the sustainability of Mexico's external debt situation grew among some international analysts—though not the majority of them. This apprehension became particularly serious after presidential candidate Luis Donaldo Colosio's assassination. At the spring meetings of the Brookings Institution Economics Panel in Washington, D.C., Rudi Dornbusch once again sounded the alarm. He argued that the Mexican peso was overvalued by at least 30 percent and that the authorities should rapidly find a way to solve the problem. At the same meeting Argentine economist Guillermo Calvo pointed out that, because of the Mexican government's lack of credibility, any exchange-rate adjustment was likely to generate a financial panic and a flight away from Mexican securities and investments. Under these circumstances, he said, the cure for devaluation was likely to be worse than the disease.[17]

Internal U.S. government communications released to the Senate Banking Committee during a 1995 investigation on the causes of the Mexican crisis also reflect a mounting concern among U.S. officials. Several staff members of the Federal Reserve Bank of New York, for example, argued that a devaluation of the peso could not be ruled out. However, on May 2, 1994, in contrast to the view that was emerging in academic circles, Undersecretary of the Treasury Larry Summers stated in a memorandum to Secretary Bentsen that "[i]n our view, Mexico's current exchange rate policy is sustainable."[18]

In what proved in retrospect to be a serious mistake that greatly eroded credibility, the Mexican authorities decided against general disclosure of information. Instead, they only released financial figures at certain times of the year. This lack of transparency was increasingly becoming a source of concern among a handful of perceptive analysts of the Mexican situation, and was even commented upon in some articles in the specialized press.[19] In January 1994, for example, *Institutional Investor* ran an article on the subject titled "Transition to Transparency," in which several investors commented on the lack of readily available data in Mexico.[20]

In August 1994 Ernesto Zedillo, a young technocrat with a Ph.D. in economics from Yale University, was elected Mexico's president by one of the smallest margins in the country's modern history. In September, the annual accord between unions, private businesses representatives, and the government—the Pacto—was once again renewed, and after an active debate within the government, no major policy changes were introduced. In particular, exchange-rate, monetary, and fiscal policies were maintained, and the policy of substituting dollar-linked tesobonos for maturing peso-denominated cetes was continued. Mexico had an unusually long transition period between the presidential election and the inauguration of the new president (from August to December), and during that time economic policy was still being run by President Carlos Salinas de Gortari and his team, who decided to continue defending the value of the peso: a devaluation was to be avoided at all costs.

The decision to stay the policy course was the result of a combination of factors. First, there was still a sense of optimism among Mexican officials; they genuinely believed that the situation was basically under control. It was thought that with time investors would understand that the heightened turbulence was temporary and that inflow of additional funds would resume once the new president took office. Second, as already noted, there was great reluctance to allow interest rates to increase further. With the presidential elections already won by the PRI, the overriding concern was that higher interest rates would adversely affect the banking system, which was experiencing a rapid increase in nonperforming loans.

The policy stance remained firm even in late September, after José Francisco Ruiz Massieu, secretary general of the governing PRI party, was assassinated. As the cycle of assassinations, violence, and uncertainty grew, investors became even more nervous, and the authorities intensified the substitution of U.S. dollar–denominated tesobonos for peso-denominated cetes. On October 21 Governor Miguel Mancera announced that the Banco de México's reserve holdings exceeded US$17 billion. However, many analysts—including some in the U.S. government—believed that the bank had obtained a short-term loan, possibly from state-owned oil giant Pemex, to bolster its international assets.

In mid-October the U.S. Treasury debated how the United States should react if the Mexican government decided to draw on the $6 billion credit line approved a few months earlier. In a note to Secretary Bentsen, Undersecretary Larry Summers said that he "would be very uncomfortable agreeing to a drawing . . . and would like to discourage consideration of any request." And in a memo to Chairman Greenspan dated October 18, 1994, the Federal Reserve's staff suggested that he communicate to the Mexicans that "they should not count on financial support via the Federal Reserve and Treasury lines to sustain an inappropriate exchange rate. The swap lines are intended to deal with what are viewed as transitory market disturbances, not to buttress an unsustainable exchange rate regime."[21]

In November some international investors opted to reduce their exposure in Mexico, largely as a result of uncertainties linked to the inauguration of a new administration in December. By the end of the month Mexico's international reserves stood at $12.5 billion; short-term public debt, on the other hand, exceeded $27 billion, around 70 percent of it in short-term dollar-denominated tesobonos. The situation had gone beyond the trade-deficit and exchange-rate spheres and had all the characteristics of a major financial crisis. Funds in the coffers of the central bank had clearly become insufficient backing for short-term domestic public debt.

According to a *Wall Street Journal* story, on the night of November 20 President Carlos Salinas de Gortari met with President-Elect Ernesto Zedillo and a group of advisors. After a long discussion the majority of those present concurred that a preemptive devaluation of the peso was necessary to calm the markets. Apparently, Finance Secretary Pedro Aspe threatened to resign if the tight link between the peso and the dollar were abandoned, and the idea had to be shelved.[22]

The new administration took over on December 1, and Pedro Aspe was replaced by Jaime Serra Puche as secretary of finance. Although the new team had broad international experience—Serra had successfully negotiated NAFTA—it had not worked closely with the international financial community. Moreover, declassified U.S. Treasury documents suggest that when the decision to devalue the peso was made, the new Mexican authorities had not established official contact with their U.S. counterparts at the Treasury or at the Federal Reserve.[23]

The decline in international reserves accelerated during early December, and the lack of information on Mexico's reserves played an important role in magnifying the crisis as investors began to expect the worst. The fact that the level of international reserves was disclosed only three times a year by the Banco de México had for some time been particularly disturbing to a number of Wall Street analysts.[24] The U.S. Treasury was well aware of the speed at which reserves were being depleted. On November 18 Assistant Secretary Jeffrey Shafer informed the secretary of the treasury that "reserves have now fallen below $14 million," and a December 5 memo to Undersecretary Larry Summers said that "reserves are now only slightly above the critical $10 billion threshold. . . . [T]hey seem to have used up all the easy ways to boost reserves."[25]

With international reserves reaching dangerously low levels, on December 20 the Mexican authorities opted for a change in policy. The exchange-rate band was widened to allow for a potential 15 percent devaluation of the peso. Surprisingly, the announcement of the new band was not accompanied by a supporting program that dealt with the growing fiscal deficit, the dwindling international reserves, or the massive withdrawal of bank deposits caused by the heightened political and economic uncertainty. In disbelief, investors—foreign and domestic—fled, rendering the change in policy ineffective: in one day the Banco de México lost US$4 billion. At that time the authorities realized that they had no alternative but to allow the peso to float freely in the marketplace so that it could find its fair value. Six months later it had lost half of its value.

The Aftermath of the Tequila Crisis

The years 1995 and 1996 were difficult for Mexico. Output collapsed, the rate of unemployment almost doubled, many companies went bankrupt, inflation accelerated, the banking sector was on the brink of insolvency, and individual borrowers—mostly from the middle and lower classes—were unable to service their mortgages. In the years following the crisis the number of Mexicans living below the World Bank's poverty line of two dollars a day grew significantly, and income disparities increased significantly. Demonstrations by the unemployed and mortgage debtors became daily events. The Chiapas insurgence and the demands by the indigenous population made things even more pressing.

The disappointment among the Mexican people was deep. They had been promised that NAFTA, the reforms, and globalization would provide a sure and rapid path to prosperity. But instead of closing the income gap with its giant neighbor to the north and the countries of the OECD, Mexico was falling further behind. Not surprisingly, support for the reforms declined abruptly, and it became politically difficult to argue that what the country needed was a stronger dose of the same medicine. Populist rhetoric became common, and there were calls to reverse some of the reforms and once again embrace protectionism and a government-led development strategy.

The fact that the collapse occurred during the first weeks of a new administration made a huge difference, as there were six years to recover from the crisis. During this period President Zedillo refused to give in to the demands for reform backtracking. At the same time, however, his administration was politically too weak for him to push for major reforms, and no new initiatives were undertaken. Moreover, a strong undercurrent of criticism, frustration, and resentment developed. Many Mexicans moved to the left and supported antireform political leaders.

Many of the reforms' detractors were particularly critical of the way in which the PRI, which had dominated Mexican politics for more than seventy years, had exercised power. They accused it of corruption, authoritarianism, lack of transparency, and electoral fraud. In August 2000, after a hard-fought three-way election, more than seventy years of rule by the PRI came to an end when Vicente Fox, a former Coca-Cola executive from the conservative Partido de Acción Nacional (PAN), was elected president. Although he was a supporter of market orientation and modernization reforms, during his administration modest progress was made. In many ways President Fox was trapped between a rock and a hard place. On one hand he had to distance himself from the PRI and its legacy of corruption, authoritarianism, and failed management of the economy; on the other, he had to support, at least rhetorically, the market-oriented reforms initiated by his political adversaries.

In 2006 another three-way presidential election took place. At first it appeared that Andrés Manuel López Obrador, the populist mayor of Mexico City and a ferocious critic of globalization, neoliberalism, and the reforms, would win the contest. His speeches and campaign literature followed the populist script closely. He promised to tackle inequality and poverty in short order through a program based on taxing the rich, increasing expenditure, and renegotiating NAFTA. Not a word was said about strengthening institutions, increasing efficiency, or accelerating productivity growth. López Obrador's popularity began to decline when he received the open support of Venezuelan president Hugo Chávez. In the end, Felipe Calderón, a former cabinet member in Vicente Fox's administration and a supporter of markets and modernization, won the election by a slim margin.

By 2008 Mexico was stuck in the middle in most international rankings on competitiveness and strength of institutions, including the World Bank's Doing Business index, the Fraser Institute indexes, and the Heritage Foundation Index of Economic Freedom. In terms of the discussion presented in chapter 1, Mexico has failed to move past the first phase of the growth transition process. As a consequence, productivity improvements have remained low and overall economic growth continues to be mediocre; between 2000 and 2008, Mexico's growth in income per capita was a disappointing 1.9 percent.

The World Bank ranks Mexico 33rd out of 181 countries in ease of dealing with licenses, and the country is fairly well ranked in ease of legally closing a business (23rd). Its overall rankings, however, are still far from those of the Asian Tiger countries or the advanced commodity exporters referred to in chapter 4.

Paradoxically, perhaps, Mexico does quite poorly in the ease of trading across borders category, in which it is ranked 87th. One would expect that a country that has made the signing of free trade agreements a hallmark of its foreign policy would excel in this area. The problem, however, is not trade restrictions, import quotas, or import duties; the problem is that Mexico's customs offices and its ports and border passes—including those at the border with the United States—are extremely inefficient. Consider the average cost of exporting a twenty-foot container in 2008: it was $1,472 in Mexico, $1,240 in Brazil, and only $745 in Chile.

As in most Latin American countries, a particularly serious shortcoming of the reforms in Mexico is that privatization of state-owned enterprises proceeded without implementation of an appropriate procompetition regulatory framework. The case of telecommunications is perhaps the best known. Protected by barriers to entry, the telephone giant Telmex has been able to keep potential competitors at bay in most of its markets.[26] As a result Mexicans pay some of the highest prices for long-distance calls and Internet services, and technological advances such as Internet protocol (IP) telephony have not developed in Mexico as quickly as in other countries.

Lessons from the Mexican Crisis

The Mexican meltdown of 1994–95 was followed by abundant postmortems and a few mea culpas. The IMF and the World Bank tried to explain their involvement in the episode, the financial sector convened commissions of wise men, and the U.S. Senate investigated the role played by the U.S. Treasury in unleashing the crisis. Grandiose phrases were uttered, and everyone agreed that a greater degree of vigilance was needed in the future.

In retrospect it is tempting to argue that most of this was lip service and that international bureaucrats and Wall Street professionals went on about their business, leaving the Mexican crisis behind as a bitter experience that had affected that year's bonuses and had somewhat bruised their reputations but that would not be repeated in the foreseeable future. They were wrong. Merely thirty months later the Asian Tigers began to crumble in a way that, in more than one respect, resembled the Mexican saga.

In spite of some differences of opinion, by the late 1990s and early 2000s a number of lessons from the mistakes made by Mexico had emerged. Although not every author and analyst subscribed to every one of them, and not every country tried to avoid them—in particular, Argentina fell into some of the same traps as Mexico—I would argue that as a consequence of the Mexican crisis a new consensus on macroeconomic policies began to emerge. The following are the most important elements of this new consensus.

- Pegged (or very rigid) exchange rates are dangerous; an artificial strengthening of the inflation-adjusted value of the currency may be lethal. As the experiences of Mexico, Chile, Colombia, and Argentina among other countries have shown, allowing an artificial strengthening of the currency—or currency overvaluation—has negative economic as well as political effects. In particular, it alienates exporters, which during the early years of the reform process are the natural allies of a reformist government, and is likely to end up in a major crisis with huge unemployment costs.
- Very large external deficits—that is, trade and current account deficits—matter, even when they are financed with private funds and when the public accounts are under control.
- Short-term capital flows may be highly destabilizing.
- Issuing foreign-currency-denominated debt to defend the currency may prove to be extremely costly in the event that the exchange-rate peg has to be abandoned. Moreover, central banks should avoid sterilizing international reserve losses in the context of rigid exchange rates.

- Banks should be supervised closely; weak banks invite contagion. The existence of weak banks will reduce the authorities' ability to use interest rates as a macroeconomic tool and is likely to amplify a currency crisis.
- Transparency in financial operations is important to build confidence among investors. Timely and accurate information is of the essence.

The morals of this story were aptly summarized by MIT's Rudi Dornbusch, who in a postmortem said:

> Just a while back, Mexico was everybody's darling and now it's anyone's goat. All fine reforms notwithstanding, Mexico made the critical mistake of overvaluing its currency and hanging on and on. To offer apprehensive lenders the impression of reduced currency risk and increased liquidity, public debt was indexed in dollars and maturities shortened. Major Mexican companies and banks were encouraged to speculate by borrowing dollars to bypass high Mexican interest rates on peso loans. Income policies [the Pacto] perpetuated inflation and stood in the way of competition and employment. The newly "independent" Central Bank expanded credit at a vigorous rate, financing rather than stemming the capital flight.[27]

Pegging the Currency: A Recurrent Latin American Mistake

Mexico was not the only Latin American country that pegged its currency to the U.S. dollar at an artificially high value during the reform period. Other countries that made the same mistake include Argentina, Brazil, Colombia, the Dominican Republic, Uruguay, and Venezuela. Pegging the currency value at the wrong level was in fact a recurrent mistake throughout Latin America during the 1990s and early 2000s. In many ways, clinging to the notion of fixed exchange rates in the 1990s was similar to the obsession with the gold standard during the interwar period. As Liaquat Ahamed has pointed out in his 2009 book *Lords of Finance*, the religious and dogmatic attachment to fixed currency values during the interwar period—in those years currencies were fixed to gold—was at the heart of the economic maladies of the time, including the triggering of the Crash of 1929 and its magnification into the Great Depression.[28]

In the case of Latin America during the 1990s and early 2000s, what make this recurrent currency mistake surprising is that a number of prominent economists argued that pegging the exchange rate in order to reduce inflation was a policy fraught with dangers that more often than not ended in crisis. For example, Rudi Dornbusch wrote:

> Exchange rate–based stabilization goes through three phases: The first one is very useful. . . . [It] helps bring under way a stabilization. . . . In the second phase increasing real [currency] appreciation becomes apparent, it is increasingly recognized, but it is inconvenient to do something. . . . Finally, in the third phase, it is too late to do something. Real [currency] appreciation has come to a point where a major devaluation is necessary. But the politics will not allow that. Some more time is spent in denial, and then—sometime—enough bad news piles up to cause the crash.[29]

One could argue that Mexican and other Latin American policy makers should have been aware of the dangers of fixed exchange rates during a disinflation effort. After all, during the early 1980s Chile had a traumatic experience with that policy. In 1979 the Chicago Boys tackled Chile's stubborn inflation—which at the time lingered at about 35 percent per year—by pegging the value of the currency at 39 pesos per U.S. dollar. Over the next twenty-four months the country went through the three phases laid down by Rudi Dornbusch above. Inflation declined slowly, capital inflows skyrocketed, exports struggled, the inflation-adjusted value of the currency strengthened significantly, and a huge trade deficit developed. This assault on competitiveness was compounded by labor legislation passed in 1981 that literally outlawed reductions in inflation-adjusted wages. In early 1982, partially in response to a slowdown of the global economy, international investors abruptly reduced their exposure in Chile. This sudden interruption of capital inflows was followed by major currency devaluation, negative growth, a significant increase in unemployment—in 1983 the rate of unemployment exceeded 20 percent—and massive bankruptcies. The three key lessons from this episode were that an artificial strengthening of the currency had to be avoided, that rigidly fixed exchange rates were dangerous during a disinflation process, and that this danger was extreme if wages were mandated to increase at an unsustainable pace. Over the next twenty-five years these lessons were not forgotten by Chilean policy makers; indeed, as pointed out in chapter 5, maintaining relative exchange-rate flexibility and avoiding currency overvaluations became hallmarks of Chile's success after 1982.

Chile's experience from the early 1980s, however, was ignored by the rest of Latin America. Technopols from around the region claimed that their countries were different or that productivity growth would compensate for the strengthening of their currencies. Warnings by experts from other parts of the world were dismissed as irrelevant and esoteric. For instance, in 1995 Michael Bruno, then the influential chief economist at the World Bank said: "The choice of the exchange rate as the nominal anchor only relates to the initial phase of stabilization."[30] He went on to argue that after this initial phase—and after inflationary expectations were broken—exchange-rate flexibility had to be introduced. This was precisely to avoid the artificial strengthening of the currency and the resulting speculative capital inflows. Bruno's position was greatly influenced by his own experience as a policy maker in Israel, where in order to avoid the overvaluation syndrome a pegged exchange rate had been replaced by an exchange-rate band in 1989.[31]

In retrospect it is clear that the IMF was partially responsible for the use of rigid exchange rates during the reform process by countries as different as Mexico, Brazil, Argentina, and Uruguay. Indeed, IMF officials had repeatedly argued the emerging markets in general, and the Latin American countries in particular, could not successfully adopt flexible, market-based exchange-rate regimes. In a 1998 document the IMF said: "[I]t is questionable whether a freely floating exchange rate and an inflation target objective for monetary policy are feasible, advisable or fully credible for many developing and transition economies."[32]

This fear, however, was unfounded. In the first decade of the twenty-first century an increasing number of emerging nations, including most of the Latin American countries, moved from pegging their currencies to allowing their value to be determined by market forces. Contrary to what skeptics predicted, currency values did not become overly erratic, nor did speculators take over the foreign exchange market. In fact, during the last few years flexible exchange rates in the emerging markets have behaved similarly to those in the advanced nations. By allowing the exchange rate to respond to market forces, the emerging countries have been better able to absorb shocks stemming from the world economy, including changes in international prices and interest rates.

Why did well-trained and sophisticated policy makers ignore Chile's lessons and insist on clinging to pegged exchange rates? And, while insisting on these policies, why didn't they make sure that labor markets became flexible and wages stayed roughly in line with currency values? Why did policy makers ignore the need to maintain the political support of exporters, a group that was greatly hurt by currency overvaluation?

The answer to these questions lies in two general faults: hubris and political miscalculation. Many of the young technopols believed in certain economic propositions with religious zeal and labeled those who disagreed with them old-fashioned or ignorant. One of these ideas was that fixed exchange rates provided an effective and credible anchor for inflation. Evidence that contradicted this quasi dogma was dismissed as irrelevant for Latin America or was simply ignored. Impatience also played a role, as many policy makers were convinced that pegging the value of the currency would generate a rapid adjustment and that single-digit inflation would be achieved in short order—in two years at most.

Once again, Rudi Dornbusch provides an illuminating clue. In 1996 he argued that the transition from moderate to low inflation—from 15 percent to 3–4 percent per year, say—should be a gradual process, taking five or more years. By rushing this process, he warned, policy makers risked creating a situation of currency overvaluation and eventually a currency collapse. In Mexico, he explained, an "exaggerated urgency to 2 percent [inflation] . . . led year after year to mounting real appreciation [of the currency]. . . . The cumulative real appreciation in the end amounted to more than 40 percent! The Mexican currency crisis was not surprising; in fact, it had long been predicted. The surprise was the extent of the meltdown."[33]

Short-term politics were also behind the use of fixed exchange rates. The fact of the matter is that reducing inflation when currency values are allowed to fluctuate is politically difficult and costly. It requires strict fiscal and monetary discipline and tight control over public-sector wages. From a political point of view, the easier route to reducing inflation is to take a shortcut and generate short-term relief by pegging the currency value. Many governments that rely on fixed rates hope that when the day of reckoning comes a different administration will be in office and that the blame and political costs will be paid by others. What they often forget is that the real costs—in terms of unemployment, lower wages, higher poverty, and rapid inflation—are paid by the people, especially by the poor. By scoring short-term political points on the inflation front, the technopols fatally affected long-term support for the reform effort. This negative political effect over the long run manifested itself through two channels: the first was the aforementioned effect on exporters' support for the reforms; the second was that often the currency overvaluation ended in a major crisis that negatively affected popular support for the modernization effort.

In the end, what is particularly ironic—even tragic—about this story is that pegging the exchange rate was neither a central component of the reforms nor a necessary condition for market orientation. The advanced market democracies, including the advanced commodity exporters, have for decades had flexible exchange rates that respond to market forces. The enormous costs of the Latin American currency crises of the 1990s and 2000s were the result of wrongheaded policies that partially responded to political considerations and were pushed with arrogance and dogmatic zeal.

In the story of Latin American economic reform, then, one variable more than any other plays a crucial role. It is not inflation, wages, or economic growth; it is not privatization or the extent of openness and globalization; it is not even foreign debt. The key variable is the exchange rate, or the value of the local currency—the peso, the bolivar, the quetzal, the real, or the córdoba—in relation to the United States dollar. Repeated mistakes in exchange-rate policy will be singled out as the most important cause behind the region's economic travails, the waning support for modernizing reforms, and the eventual revival of populism during the twenty-first century.

Chapter 7
The Mother of All Crises
Argentina, 2001–2002

On December 20, 2001, after a week of riots and political unrest, Fernando de la Rúa, Argentina's constitutional president, resigned from office. A few weeks later Argentina defaulted on its foreign debt and went through one of the most traumatic currency crises in modern history. In little over two months the peso, which for more than a decade had been pegged to the U.S. dollar at a rate of one peso to one dollar, lost two-thirds of its value. The depth and political ramifications of the crisis were such that in a period of four weeks the country went through five presidents. The consequences of the crisis were profound: the proportion of households living below the poverty line in greater Buenos Aires jumped from 12 percent in 1994 to more than 40 percent in late 2002, and income disparity increased significantly.

In many ways, Argentina epitomizes Latin America's historical proclivity toward macroeconomic instability, trade imbalances, and costly crises. The implosion of the Argentine economy in 2001–2 has become one of the most important arguments against globalization, market reforms, and so-called neoliberalism. Critics such as Nobel laureate Joseph E. Stiglitz have argued that the policies of the Washington Consensus were at the center of these events and that the IMF has a major responsibility in what happened.[1]

The main forces behind Argentina's deep economic problems at the turn of the new century were highly complex and at times seemed reminiscent of a Greek tragedy. Paraphrasing novelist Gabriel García Márquez, if there were ever a death foretold in Latin America, it was the Argentine collapse of 2001–2. As will be seen in the pages that follow, the pegging of the currency was—as it had been in Chile in the late 1970s, in Colombia, and in Mexico—at the center of this drama.[2] In particular, the decision to peg the peso to the U.S. dollar in April 1991—and to maintain the peg even in the absence of supporting fiscal and other key policies—was made by Argentine politicians and not by IMF officials, U.S. Treasury functionaries, or academics and scholars who supported the Latin American modernization reforms. The fact that Argentina's own policy mistakes were the main cause of the events of 2001 was recognized by President Eduardo Duhalde, who was appointed to the presidency in January 2002 by the Argentine congress. In a 2002 opinion piece in the Financial Times he wrote: "In the case of Argentina, *no one bears more of the blame for the crisis than Argentina itself.*"[3]

A Long History of Instability and High Inflation

The 2001–2 crisis is only the latest in a series of crises, currency collapses, and debt defaults in Argentina. As discussed in chapter 2, during the nineteenth and twentieth centuries Argentina was plagued by repeated currency failures. In the second half of the twentieth century, Argentina implemented a number of stabilization programs aimed at eliminating inflation; all of them failed. Some important historical highlights include the stabilization program of Minister Adalbert Krieger Vasena in 1967 and the so-called Rodrigazo in 1975, which eventually generated a flare-up in the annual rate of inflation to 182 percent. In the early 1980s a major anti-inflation effort was put in place by Minister José Martínez de Hoz. The program attempted to guide inflation down by controlling the rate of change in the exchange rate between the peso and the U.S. dollar. This attempt ended in a serious crisis and heightened political instability. In 1986, a heterodox stabilization program known as the Austral Plan was put in place, but once again it failed due to the government's inability and unwillingness to control fiscal imbalances.

This inflationary saga rooted in fiscal profligacy culminated in hyperinflation in 1989, when the annual rate of price increase exceeded 3,000 percent per year. In Argentina, as in other developing countries that experienced hyperinflation, constant revisions to prices and nearly instantaneous erosion of the purchasing power of the domestic currency were extremely disruptive and eventually led to a collapse in economic activity. Worse yet, hyperinflation eroded the value of wages and incomes of the poor and the middle classes.[4]

Inflation was the most visible manifestation of Argentina's economic malaise. Problems, however, ran deeper and affected all spheres of the economy. For instance, Argentina had serious difficulties keeping its external debt payments current. According to MIT professor Kristin Forbes, Argentina was in a state of debt default or debt restructuring in 26 percent of the years between 1824 and 1999.[5] This resulted in a high degree of perceived (and real) risk and a reluctance by foreign investors to become involved in Argentina. From 1975 to 1990, foreign direct investment was very low in comparison with East Asian and other Latin American nations, including Chile and Mexico. National savings were also low; productivity gains were minimal, and overall economic growth was meager. Protectionism was generalized, and economic distortions affected every sector of the economy, including labor and financial markets. The extent of Argentina's economic malaise is reflected in the fact that gross domestic product growth per capita was *negative* from 1975 to 1990; during these years the average annual rate of growth per capita income was an astounding −1.4 percent.

Please, Tie My Hands!

In April 1991, as a way of dealing with more than a decade of negative growth and an almost complete lack of credibility in the government, President Carlos Menem enacted the so-called Convertibility Law. Its central feature was pegging the value of the domestic currency—originally the Austral and later the peso—to the U.S. dollar.[6] The initial peg was 10,000 australes per U.S. dollar; once the new peso was issued in 1992, the peg was one peso to one dollar. The Convertibility Law, which was the brainchild of Harvard-trained economist Domingo F. Cavallo, mandated that the central bank use monetary policy strictly to defend this currency peg. This was to be done by limiting the supply of local currency and strictly avoiding inflation. Thus, according to this legislation the central bank could not make any loans to the government and could only expand liquidity if the expansion was fully backed by foreign exchange reserves. For all practical purposes, the Convertibility Law created a currency board system.[7]

From a political perspective the Convertibility Law was a legal mechanism that forced the government to tie its own hands with strict legal limitations on central bank policies. After decades of economic mismanagement the Argentine authorities had come to a sober conclusion: the only way to avoid repeating the traumatic crises of the past was to renounce an independent monetary policy. Only by taking away this tool, which had been systematically abused, would stability be achieved. That Argentina had already had failed experiences with a currency board system in the late nineteenth and early twentieth centuries (see chapter 2) and that these failures had been the consequence of fiscal profligacy did not deter Cavallo, the architect of the Convertibility Law. Years later, a number of observers asked whether the main flaw of the Convertibility Law was that it only went halfway. In retaining a national currency and thus the option to change the law and liberally print money, a certain amount of risk and uncertainty remained. Some of these analysts argued that a better course of action would have been for Argentina to give up on its currency altogether and adopt the U.S. dollar as legal tender.[8]

In conjunction with the Convertibility Law, Argentina introduced a package of reforms aimed at modernizing financial markets and the productive side of the economy; many of these corresponded to the policies of the Washington Consensus. State-owned enterprises were privatized, regulations on business and investment were partially relaxed, and the economy was somewhat opened to international competition when the country signed a trade pact with Brazil, Paraguay, and Uruguay to form the customs union Mercosur. In addition, a tax reform was implemented, the social security system was partially privatized, and export taxes were eliminated.

A key objective of the Convertibility Law and related economic reforms—including the Law of Reform of the State and the Economic Emergency Law of 1989—was to attract foreign capital.[9] In the early 1990s, after fifteen years of negative per-capita growth, Argentina urgently needed to draw on foreign financing to jump-start the economy and generate positive and sustainable growth. Foreign investment was particularly important to develop Argentina's infrastructure, which had been neglected through the years of successive currency crises in the 1970s and 1980s, and to expand exports. As a way to increase credibility further, during the 1990s Argentina signed more than forty bilateral investment treaties with its most important trading partners. These treaties legally protected foreign investors and established clear arbitration processes in case any dispute might arise in the future.

In the years immediately following the adoption of the currency board and the fixed exchange-rate regime, Argentina's annual inflation rate declined rapidly, from more than 2,000 percent in 1990 to barely 3 percent by 1995. With inflation under control, output experienced a spectacular recovery: gross domestic product growth was 11 percent in 1991, 10 percent in 1992, 6 percent in 1993, and 8 percent in 1994.[10]

Initially the reforms received ample political support from the population. Those hurt by them—including the traditional manufacturing sector—were placated by progress made in other areas that also affected them, including the elimination of inflation, the increased availability of credit, and the creation of the trade pact Mercosur, which allowed them to access the very large Brazilian market. As with all of the Latin American reforms, producers of export goods—in Argentina these were mostly agricultural commodity producers in the provinces—were initially the staunchest supporters of the modernization effort. On the other hand, the most vocal opponents of the reforms were public-sector employees and workers in the scores of state-owned companies that were being privatized, including most of the country's utilities. In 1995, as a consequence of the Mexican crisis, gross domestic product declined slightly. Growth picked up in 1996, when gross domestic product increased at a 5 percent annual rate. Economic expansion continued at 8 percent in 1997 and 4 percent in 1998. In 1999, however, Argentina entered a recession.

The Mexican Crisis and the Weaknesses of the Convertibility Law

Mexico's Tequila Crisis of 1994–95 unveiled some important weaknesses of Argentina's fixed exchange-rate system and its currency board regime. Economists at the World Bank and the IMF as well as independent analysts and observers identified three areas of policy weaknesses in Argentina: large fiscal deficits, especially in the provinces; rigid labor legislation that made both the hiring and dismissal of workers very costly, and thus made the economy's response to foreign shocks such as decline in the country's export prices more costly; and a trade policy that emphasized regional trade through Mercosur and kept Argentina relatively closed to the rest of the global economy.[11]

For a currency board to succeed, fiscal discipline is essential. What is needed is a system that assures the public that, on average, the country will have a balanced public-sector budget. Argentina, however, did not maintain a prudent fiscal policy during 1991–2001. When all sources of expenditures are considered—including those that were kept off the books by the government—the average fiscal deficit during 1991–2000 was a very large 4.1 percent of gross domestic product. This would be a high number even in a country with a flexible exchange rate; for a country with a strictly fixed exchange rate and a currency board, this type of fiscal policy was clearly dangerous.

Countries with fixed exchange rates—especially countries with currency boards—are supposed to run fiscal surpluses during good years when growth is strong. These surpluses should then be used to build up a fiscal reserve fund that can be utilized during lean years. Argentina did not follow this simple countercyclical rule for fiscal policy. During the good years when gross domestic product growth was strong, the country still ran very large deficits. Argentina's rate of economic growth exceeded 5 percent in 1991, 1992, 1993, 1994, 1996, and 1997. The average deficit during these "boom" years was 3.4 percent of gross domestic product, a figure that many would consider excessive for any country at any moment in time, let alone for a currency board country during expansionary years.[12]

A particularly weak aspect of the Argentine economy was the so-called Coparticipation Law, which required the federal government to make large revenue transfers to the provinces. The provinces, however, had no incentive to balance their budgets; indeed, during the Convertibility Law years— 1991 to 2001—there were persistent provincial deficits. At the center of the Coparticipation Law—and of the inability to reform it—was an old dispute between the federal government and the provinces. This problem had been identified as early as 1845 by Domingo Faustino Sarmiento as one of the most serious impediments to Argentina's joining the ranks of the civilized nations.[13]

As former *Washington Post* reporter Paul Blustein has noted, officials from the IMF and the World Bank repeatedly told the Argentine authorities that a lax fiscal policy was almost suicidal in a country with a rigid exchange rate. The authorities acknowledged the problem and time after time said that they would address it. Little of substance was done, however; the measures taken were mostly window dressing and did not attack the sources of the fiscal imbalance with sufficient vigor. The reasons for this lack of serious action were mostly political, as any policies geared toward reducing the fiscal deficit would alienate provincial governors and result in a drop in the national government's popularity.[14] This inability to implement fiscal adjustment and build reserves during the good years became particularly serious in light of the reform of social security implemented in 1994. This reform created a hybrid system that combined private accounts with government-supported pensions. After the reform was implemented, a fraction of workers' contributions were deposited in their own personal accounts and were no longer available for financing existing pension obligations. This resulted in a deficit that should have been covered by general revenues, but the Argentine authorities decided, mostly for political reasons, to cover it by assuming additional debt.[15] It was expected that the cost of paying off that debt would be borne by future administrations.

During most of 1999 the upcoming presidential elections dominated government policy, including budgetary decisions. By then the popularity of the reforms had begun to wane. In particular, exporters, most of whom are in the provinces and who until then had been the major supporters of the modernization effort, were increasingly disappointed. As in other nations, one of the most severe problems had to do with the exchange rate: when measured relative to various other currencies and not just the U.S. dollar, and after properly adjusting for inflation, the Argentine peso had artificially strengthened, which negatively affected exports' competitiveness. In addition, international prices of Argentine exports—including oil, soybeans, and beef—had declined significantly after 1998. Problems, however, were not confined to producers of export goods. Overall unemployment continued to be stubbornly high, and interest rates, which responded to the global market's perception of Argentina's degree of riskiness, had increased substantially.

In an attempt to keep power in the hands of the Peronist Party, as the elections drew near the government of President Carlos Menem increased expenditures significantly, and the fiscal deficit jumped by 71 percent. In 1999 the public-sector debt increased by 6.1 percent of national income, and by the end of that year the government debt reached 51 percent of gross domestic product, up from 33 percent in 1993.[16]

The Fixed Exchange Rate Becomes a Straitjacket

In the early 1950s British economist and eventual Nobel laureate James E. Meade pointed out that countries that gave up exchange-rate flexibility and opted to peg the value of their currency to that of another country had to have very flexible labor markets. This flexibility would allow the economy to redeploy its labor force across sectors and industries in response to changing international prices without creating unemployment. Another way of stating Meade's dictum is that in countries with pegged currency values, labor market flexibility and dynamism are needed as a substitute for exchange-rate flexibility.[17]

Labor markets in Argentina, however, were extremely rigid. According to Nobel laureate James Heckman, the country had one of the most regulated labor markets in the world in the late 1990s.[18] A study sponsored by the World

Bank and published in 2001 reached a similar conclusion: Argentina's labor markets were among the most rigid and inflexible in Latin America.[19] In addition, Argentina's international competitiveness was dragged down by a highly inefficient and overly regulated health care system run by the unions—the so-called *obras sociales*—which significantly increased labor costs.

The de la Rúa government attempted to modernize labor legislation by taking some power away from labor unions and reducing the costs of hiring and dismissing workers. The measures, however, were rather timid and did not change regulations significantly. In addition, a major political scandal erupted in 2000 when the minister of labor was accused of bribing a number of senior senators in order to get enough votes to approve the labor reform.

In the early 2000s, as a result of its inability to introduce policy changes, Argentina continued to have a highly vulnerable economy. At the heart of this vulnerability was the lethal combination of (1) a currency that had strengthened to the point of severely limiting exports' competitiveness, (2) large and expanding fiscal deficits, (3) inflexible labor market legislation, and (4) a relatively small degree of economic openness.

The Inability to Withstand External Shocks in 1999–2001

Beginning in late 1998 Argentina, like the rest of the Latin American countries, was affected by a series of international shocks that slowed down growth, increased unemployment, and negatively affected credibility. On the heels of a recession in the United States that reduced global demand, along with a strengthening of the U.S. dollar in international currency markets, an increase in international interest rates, and the devaluation of Brazil's currency in January of 1999, Argentina experienced a decline in export prices (since the Argentine peso was pegged to the US. dollar, its peso strengthened relative to other major currencies) and a drop in the volume of foreign capital flowing into the country.

Most critics of the Washington Consensus and the IMF have argued that these external shocks were at the heart of the Argentine crisis. For instance, Nobel laureate Joseph E. Stiglitz noted that "suddenly Argentina's fortunes changed. The precipitating event was the East Asian crisis of 1997, which by 1998 had become a global financial crisis. Global interest rates to emerging markets soared. . . . These problems were compounded by the strong dollar; since the Argentine peso was tied to the dollar, it was increasingly overvalued."[20]

What Stiglitz and other critics failed to acknowledge, however, was that these external shocks were not unique to Argentina—they affected all of Latin America—nor were they unexpected or unusual from Argentina's own historical perspective. Moreover, they were temporary shocks that after some time reversed themselves. Indeed, the price of exports fully recovered to historical levels by 2000, the U.S. dollar began to weaken in international markets in 2001, world interest rates started to decline toward record lows in January 2001, the U.S. recession was over by November 2001, and capital flows returned to Latin America in the mid-2000s. If Argentina had built a sturdy currency board and had implemented supporting policies—as it was urged to do by the World Bank, the IMF, and a number of independent observers—it would have been able to withstand the temporary shocks of the late 1990s and early 2000s. And if instead of a rigid exchange rate Argentina had had a monetary system with built-in exchange-rate flexibility, it would have been able to endure these rough months without suffering a deep crisis.

The problem was not the shocks themselves; the problem was that Argentina was ill-prepared to sustain them. The country was unprepared because it had implemented the reforms halfway and had failed to put in place the policies required to support the currency board. As a consequence, these shocks had a very negative effect on the economy: unemployment skyrocketed, national income contracted, interest rates rapidly increased, and credibility declined. In 2000 the rate of unemployment climbed to 15 percent from 7 percent in 1992.

As time passed and the recession deepened, there was a growing sense that the government would renege on its promise to keep the exchange rate at one peso to the dollar and abandon the Convertibility Law by devaluing the peso. As a result of rumors and the perception that something of the sort would happen, the public withdrew its deposits from the banking sector—particularly deposits denominated in pesos. Fewer deposits meant fewer loans, and fewer loans meant further contractions in economic activity, output, and employment.

Faced with a dwindling credibility, the de la Rúa government sought assistance from the multilateral institutions, and in December 2000 it obtained a large loan from the IMF. Both government and IMF officials expected that

Argentina could buy some time and implement the policies required to shore up confidence and reassure investors that the Convertibility Law would not be abandoned. In August 2001 the IMF increased the size of the loan by $8 billion, but by then it was too late; the increase only prolonged the agony, making the costs of the collapse even higher.

Another Foretold Disaster

In late January 2001, a group of investors met in an exclusive Colorado skiing resort for a three-day conference on emerging markets. The keynote speaker was Domingo Cavallo, Argentina's former economic minister and the architect of the Convertibility Law. There was great expectation when Cavallo took the podium, as most of the men and women attending the conference had invested large amounts of their clients' money in Argentine securities.

Cavallo, a self-confident man who at the time was in his mid-fifties, acknowledged that his country was facing serious economic and political problems. However, he said, these difficulties were not related to the fundamentals of his Convertibility Plan. The currency board and the fixed exchange rate, he argued vehemently, should be maintained; they had served Argentina well. What the country needed, he explained, was to introduce some adjustments to the monetary and exchange-rate policies that had been pursued for more than a decade. He then proceeded to list the modifications that, in his opinion, were required: instead of being pegged to the U.S. dollar, the peso should be pegged to a group of currencies; a "competitiveness" plan consisting of higher import tariffs and export subsidies should be put in place; and the requirement that all pesos in circulation be backed by foreign currency holdings at the central bank should be eased. The questions that followed Cavallo's speech clearly reflected the participants' skepticism about the former minister's proposals. Implementation of these policies, one banker after the other said, would undermine whatever was left of the government's credibility and would result in confusion in the marketplace. Some even intimated that if such a plan were put in place they would liquidate all their Argentine investments.[21]

Seven weeks after this conference, President Fernando de la Rúa surprised the world by firing his recently appointed minister of the economy, Ricardo López Murphy, and replacing him with Domingo Cavallo. During the next few months the new minister proceeded to implement a program that closely followed his Colorado proposals. As a number of the investment bankers at the conference had anticipated, these policies had a negative effect on confidence and on Argentina's credibility. In retrospect it is clear that the year 2001 was fraught with mistakes.

Political dynamics during the first ten months of 2001 were dominated by the government coalition's concern about the congressional elections in October of that year. Campaigning required funding, and thus before October of 2001 provincial governors were unwilling to agree on any reforms that implied a reduction of federal transfers to the provinces. No one seemed to care that the large IMF loan was made on the condition that such reforms were indeed implemented; very few politicians even mentioned the fact that if no progress was achieved on the reforms front, the IMF could suspend further disbursements from the loan.

On April 16, 2001, Argentina's congress passed a bill that changed the exchange-rate peg from the U.S. dollar to a combination of the U.S. dollar and the euro. The intent was to effectively let the peso weaken against the dollar. However, this was widely perceived as a first step toward abandoning the convertibility regime, which had been credible precisely because it was based on a simple, transparent, and supposedly inviolable rule. As more and more people believed that the one-peso-to-one-dollar policy would be abandoned, the government was forced to pay increasingly high interest rates to attract investors. Investing in Argentina was rapidly becoming a gamble, and interest rates paid by Argentina in international financial markets skyrocketed, putting further pressure on its fiscal accounts.

In late April the government allowed commercial banks to use Argentine government securities (up to US$2 billion) as part of their liquidity reserves. This meant that a fraction of banks' deposits were now backed by securities issued by a government whose credibility was in doubt, rather than by bonds issued by the United States and other advanced nations with fully convertible currencies. This measure was perceived as a further indication that the de la Rúa administration was not committed to maintaining the currency peg. The change was resisted by central bank governor Pedro Pou, who argued that weakening the foreign currency backing of commercial banks would be destabilizing. On April 25, 2001, Pou was fired, further eroding the credibility of the government.

Between April and June of 2001, the de la Rúa administration tried to alleviate Argentina's short-term debt burden by exchanging bonds that were about to mature for longer-term bonds that would mature in 2006, 2008,

2018, and 2031. Some of the new bonds did not require payments for a few years, but they had very high interest rates; the 2018 bond, for example, paid an annual interest of 15.2 percent. The staff of the IMF Research Department concluded that any short-term savings obtained from the bond swap would be more than offset by extremely high longer-term interest rates.[22] The rationale for this exchange—which was known as the "mega swap"—was that it would ease Argentina's liquidity problems. However, it did not address any of Argentina's long-term economic weaknesses; the Coparticipation Law continued to be as disruptive as before, labor and *obras sociales* regulations were still a drag on competitiveness, trade policy continued to be restrictive, there were still fiscal expenses that were kept off the books, and thus the swap was perceived by the market as a ploy to buy time.

On June 15 the government announced the adoption of a plan aimed at improving competitiveness. This program consisted of subsidizing exports of nonenergy goods and imposing duties on imports. Many saw this policy as an attempt to increase exports without addressing the deeper problems that were keeping down competitiveness and productivity. As with other measures taken during this period, the public was skeptical; many analysts interpreted the "competitiveness plan" as an effort to "devalue without devaluing." The public's skeptical reaction to all these measures was aptly summarized in a *Financial Times* article that asked: "If Argentina's real problem is fiscal, as almost everyone agrees, is Mr. Cavallo just distracting people's attention with financial sleight of hand?"[23]

A month later Cavallo announced a "zero deficit" policy consisting of short-term measures such as a reduction in government employees' salaries and pensions. The Argentine press as well as the public expressed deep doubts and skepticism, as the package did not address the long-term factors behind the crisis and thus was not credible.

Immediately after the congressional elections, on October 15, 2001, the national government sought to reach an agreement with the provincial governors in order to send a signal that a permanent and credible solution to the fiscal problem would be achieved. Cavallo proposed a program that would reform the Coparticipation Law, reduce the size of the public sector, and restructure provincial debts. But once again partisan politics prevailed, and the governors refused to consider reforming the Coparticipation Law or enacting other long-term reforms. As the negotiations dragged on, deposits began to leave the banking sector at an increasingly fast rate, and Argentina lost additional cred- ibility. Two of the provinces that refused to sign an agreement with the federal government were San Luis, whose governor, Adolfo Rodríguez Saá, became president in December 2001 after the resignation of Fernando de la Rúa, and Santa Cruz, whose governor, Néstor Kirchner, was elected president in 2003.

In November 2001, Standard and Poor's lowered Argentina's long-term sovereign rating to "selective default." At this point, both the Argentine pub- lic and international actors lost nearly all confidence in the government of Argentina's willingness to support the currency board.

On December 1, 2001, Cavallo imposed wide-ranging controls on banking and foreign exchange transactions that effectively froze bank deposits. This policy made the commitment to convertibility meaningless. Freezing depos- its was a desperate measure that violated the government's social contract with the Argentine public and solidified expectations of devaluation and debt default. On December 9, the IMF suspended its assistance to Argentina, im- plicitly acknowledging that there was no way of avoiding a major crisis. On December 20, after two weeks of protests and rioting by a disappointed and furious public, Fernando de la Rúa resigned as president of Argentina. Eleven days later Argentina defaulted on its external debt, and a week after that the peso was devalued by 40 percent.

Devaluation, Default, and Pesification

On January, 6, 2002, the so-called Emergency Law was passed by Argentina's congress, and on January 8 the new government officially ended convertibility and devalued the peso. A new fixed exchange rate of 1.4 pesos to the dollar ap- plied for imports and exports; all other transactions were subject to a floating, market-determined rate. In addition, the government converted all dollar- denominated debts that did not exceed $100,000—regardless of whether they were government or private debts—into pesos at the old rate of one peso to one dollar.[24] On February 3, 2002, the government decided to go further and fully pesified all debts at the old exchange rate of one peso to one dollar and pesified dollar deposits at a rate of 1.4 pesos to the dollar. On February 11, 2002, the peso began to float in earnest and lost additional value. By the end of February, the exchange rate stood at 2.1 pesos to the dollar, and by mid-April it was almost 4 pesos per dollar.

By transforming dollar-denominated contracts to peso denominations at different rates—one dollar to one peso for debts and one dollar for 1.4 pesos for deposits—the Duhalde administration consciously benefited some groups and imposed severe costs on others. Corporations and individuals who had borrowed in dollars benefited from pesification, as did those who had dollar deposits outside the country. Those who had dollar-denominated deposits in the Argentine banking sector suffered losses, as did public utilities whose tariffs were transformed from U.S. dollars to pesos at the old unitary exchange rate. The political nature of the devaluation-cum-pesification policy was acknowledged in early 2002 by Duhalde's spokesman Eduardo Amadeo, who said: "At one point we wanted to float the peso but when we saw the social situation we knew this would be politically unsustainable."[25]

The political motives behind the asymmetric pesification were apparent. One of the basic political goals of the Duhalde government was to obtain the support of the middle class, which had become disenchanted with all political parties.[26] The Duhalde government blamed foreign banks, foreign public utilities, and foreign companies in general for the crisis.[27] The pesification of debts also benefited mortgage debtors—many of whom were members of the middle class—as well as large corporate debtors who had borrowed in dollars from Argentine banks. At the same time, the pesification of deposits at a higher exchange rate (1.4 pesos per dollar) provided partial compensation to dollar depositors.

Exporters were also bound to benefit from the devaluation of the currency, as they would get a greater number of pesos for every dollar's worth of goods they exported. The new Argentine government, however, decided to tax most exports and to use the proceeds to pay for transfers to a number of interest groups that had lobbied for a change in government and to end the reform effort.

Since 2002 successive Argentine governments have argued that the IMF was partially responsible for the crisis. According to former minister of economics Roberto Lavagna, the IMF contributed to the notion that during most of the 1990s the Argentine economy was a "stellar performer" but failed to point out with enough force that slippages in fiscal policies were extremely dangerous.[28] In particular, Lavagna argued that the IMF should have warned Argentina that the social security reform, which created individual savings accounts, would result in an increase in the fiscal deficit. Lavagna's remarks,

however, were disingenuous. The fact that a partial privatization of social security creates a fiscal imbalance was well known in the economic literature and
was certainly known to the Argentine policy makers during the late 1990s.[29]
Lavagna also criticized the IMF for not having assessed the appropriateness of
the fixed exchange-rate currency board regime for Argentina, for encouraging
complacency, and for not having a contingency plan that contemplated an
orderly departure from the fixed exchange rate during early 2001. So much
for taking responsibility.

There is little doubt that the IMF made serious mistakes in its dealings with
Argentina, including its failure to be forceful enough on the need for truly
supporting the currency board through appropriate policies and its granting
of loans in late 2000 and in August 2001 that allowed the de la Rúa administration to muddle through. These mistakes have been acknowledged by the IMF's
own independent evaluation report and by Michael Mussa, the former IMF
chief economist. However, a careful analysis of the historical record indicates
that the lion's share of responsibility for the crisis rests with Argentina's economic authorities, as was recognized by President Duhalde.[30] Simply put, the
adoption of the fixed exchange-rate regime and the currency board was a decision made by Argentina and not by the IMF—in fact, many World Bank and
IMF officials were skeptical about this policy. Moreover, in spite of repeated
suggestions and requests by the multilateral institutions and independent observers, the Argentine authorities failed to put in place the type of fiscal, labor,
and trade policies required to support and strengthen the currency board.

Blaming the IMF for the country's economic trouble is not new in
Argentina. In a remarkably candid 1966 interview, former strongman José
Domingo Perón, arguably one of the leading populists in the region's his-
tory, blamed the IMF for Argentina's economic crises after 1955. According to
Perón, during the 1960s the IMF "robbed" Argentina of half of the financial
loans it granted the country. With a great sense of self-importance he said:
"Since I left [the government] Argentina has been governed by the Interna-
tional Monetary Fund."[31]

In the months leading to the crisis, a number of economists argued that
the most direct and least costly way of avoiding it was for Argentina to give
up its own currency and adopt the U.S. dollar as legal tender. The debate over
the merits and drawbacks of this policy—usually called "dollarization"—went
beyond Argentina and was particularly heated in countries such as Ecuador,

El Salvador, the Dominican Republic, and even Mexico. In the end, despite the support of influential personalities such as Stanford University professor John Taylor, who was then Undersecretary for International Affairs at the U.S. Treasury, Argentina decided not to dollarize its economy; during the 1990s only Ecuador and El Salvador gave up their local currencies and adopted the U.S. dollar as legal tender.[32]

Social Costs, Recovery, and Populism

The social costs of the Argentine saga were substantial: in 2002 the proportion of households in greater Buenos Aires living below the poverty line was 42 percent, three times higher than in 1992; the rate of unemployment skyrocketed to almost 20 percent in 2002. Real wages declined substantially, and other social indicators, including public health indexes, worsened considerably.

Not surprisingly, Argentina's voters were deeply disappointed and very angry. They felt that once again they had been the victims of a major social experiment that had gone tragically wrong, and almost everyone thought of the experiment as nothing more than neoliberal reforms of the Washington Consensus. The public did not have the time or patience to undertake a nuanced analysis and postmortem or to deconstruct the causes of the crisis by making a distinction between the Convertibility Law and the fixed currency value on one hand and the reforms aimed at improving productivity, efficiency, and growth on the other.

The fact that the ultimate cause of the crisis was a weak currency board that was not supported by appropriate fiscal and labor policies was of little solace to Argentine voters. All they knew was that they had been promised stability, growth, and prosperity, but instead they had lost their jobs and life savings and their incomes had declined significantly. Under these circumstances it is far easier—and certainly very human—to find a handful of guilty parties on whom to blame the debacle. In this case the culprits were seen as former president Carlos Menem, Domingo Cavallo, the Washington Consensus, foreign banks and multinationals, and, of course, the IMF.

The sense of frustration and revulsion was such that generally negative sentiments toward all politicians spontaneously emerged, without regard to their political affiliation, ideology, or stance on globalization. In the streets of Buenos Aires and other cities large crowds demonstrated, demanding that their savings be returned in U.S. dollars and chanting again and again, "*Que se vayan todos!*"—Throw them all out!

In early 2002 political conditions were fertile for the emergence of a populist leader with massive backing from the population. But as is often the case in Argentina, things were more convoluted than even seasoned analysts expected. On January 2, 2002, Eduardo Duhalde, an old Peronist hand and former governor of the province of Buenos Aires, was appointed president by congress. Although he was an experienced politician and had often used populist rhetoric—the BBC described him as "a populist . . . known for blunt language and outspoken remarks"—he was more of a political operator than a natural charismatic leader. In the eyes of many he was seen as a loser, since he had lost the election in 1999 to Fernando de la Rúa.[33] During his sixteen months in office Duhalde made an effort to avoid the return of rapid inflation and implemented a number of measures aimed at undoing the Convertibility Law. As noted earlier, most of these policies affected foreign investors and redistributed income toward those firms and individuals who had become indebted in U.S. dollars.

In May 2003, Peronist Néstor Kirchner, the former governor of the southern province of Santa Cruz, was elected president of Argentina. He obtained 22 percent of the popular vote, the lowest percentage ever obtained by an Argentine president, and was declared the winner once his rival, former president Carlos Menem, withdrew from the runoff election. Kirchner's years in office were characterized by political discourse centered on anti-globalization and the ills of inequality. Like his predecessor, he blamed foreigners, in particular the IMF, for the country's state of affairs. When Kirchner took office international financial conditions had begun to turn in Argentina's favor. Global interest rates declined to an all-time low; prices of Argentina's exports—oil, minerals, and agricultural commodities—increased substantially; and the world economy continued to expand.

Throughout the Kirchner administration the antiglobalization and antiforeign rhetoric continued. The nation's external debt was restructured, and foreign investors were forced to take only 30 cents on the dollar. The combination of unparalleled positive international conditions and a debt that had declined significantly after the default and restructuring helped the country recover rapidly. Between 2003 and 2008 income per capita grew an average of 7.6 percent per year. Slowly, Argentina began to return to normal. For most of the people the years of the Convertibility Law were a bad nightmare triggered by the adoption of the wrong policies. As time passed Kirchner' popularity increased, thanks to a combination of growing incomes, his strong populist rhetoric, and a personal style that emphasized nationalistic themes. In December 2007, when his term was over and he was replaced by his wife Cristina Fernandez de Kirchner, Néstor Kirchner's approval rating was the highest of any retiring president in the history of Argentina.[34]

But behind this sense of progress and success, serious tensions had been simmering. Given the breach in contracts and hostile attitude toward the business sector, foreign direct investment declined markedly during the first decade of the twenty-first century. This represented a serious problem, since Argentina continued to need large volumes of funds in order to increase investment and productivity and achieve a sustainable rate of growth over the longer run. In 2003, for example, Minister Roberto Lavagna stated that "foreign investment . . . is essential for re-launching economic growth."[35] However, according to A. T. Kearney's prestigious *Foreign Direct Investment (FDI) Confidence Index*, starting in 2002 large international companies had limited interest in Argentina as an investment destination.[36] This contrasts sharply with the situation before the government of Argentina froze deposits, defaulted on its debt, and pesified contracts. In 1998 Argentina ranked eighth in the "investment intentions" of large international companies. In spite of its economic recession, Argentina still ranked fourteenth in 1999 and nineteenth in 2000 and was still ranked among the top twenty-five global investment destinations for large international companies in 2001. The reason for these high rankings was the perception that the country respected contracts and the rule of law. These rankings contrast sharply with those from the most recent A. T. Kearney survey: neither in 2006 nor in 2007 or 2008 was Argentina ranked among the top twenty-five investment destinations for the largest one thousand international corporations.[37] As stated in the 2005 A. T. Kearney index, "lingering political and economic uncertainty and numerous pending international investment disputes are all hindering Argentina's ability to regain the level of investment interest experienced in the late 1990s."[38]

The decline in infrastructure investment in Argentina has already had serious economic consequences. Since 2004 the country has faced natural gas shortages, which have resulted in electricity blackouts and threatened industrial production.[39] Another consequence of the post-2002 decline in investment in infrastructure is that Argentina has reneged on its contracts to export natural gas to Chile, generating diplomatic tensions.[40]

The administrations of the two presidents Kirchner have relied on the old Argentine tradition of taxing the export sector—including the vast agricultural sector—to subsidize urban dwellers, including, in particular, government bureaucrats, teachers, and health workers. Historically, this policy had reached its zenith during populist strongman Juan Domingo Perón's administration in the 1950s. Most experts agree that antiexport policies have historically been behind Argentina's dismal long-term economic performance.[41] As noted in chapters 2 and 3, an antiexport bias generates inefficiencies, low investment in key sectors, and public-sector accounts that are vulnerable to the vagaries of the international economy. This model—which is rationalized on the basis of distributional concerns—transfers incomes to privileged groups that for years have benefited from the state without substantially contributing to economic growth. The most important among these groups is, arguably, teachers' unions, which have systematically blocked any attempt at improving the quality of Argentina's educational system.

Since 2002 Argentina has taxed the majority of exports; the rates of taxation have varied by sector and product, however. For example, in April 2002 exports of some items were subject to taxes at a 5 percent rate (dairy products, processed vegetables and footwear among others); other exports were taxed at a 10 percent rate (fresh fruits, honey, tobacco, cotton fiber, and others); others were subject to a 14.5 percent tax rate (corn products); still other exports were levied a 17.5 percent tax (seeds and oil seeds); and some exports (crude oil) were subject to a 20 percent tax rate. In a paper on the Argentine devaluation of 2002, World Bank senior economist Daniel Lederman and Argentine professor Pablo Sanguinetti said: "There is no convincing economic argument in favor of having a differentiated export tax structure that favors manufactures over other exports."[42] As a result of increased political tension, higher export taxes, and strong antibusiness discourse, a number of investors have decided to move their operations to neighboring Uruguay or to Brazil, which in the mid-2000s surpassed Argentina as the world's largest beef exporter.[43]

Although export taxes are not illegal under the World Trade Organization, it is generally acknowledged that they constitute an inefficient and distortionary way of raising government revenue. Historically export taxes have been avoided by countries seeking to develop a healthy international trade sector and achieve rapid and sustained economic growth. The fact that export taxes generate significant distortions, reduce exports, and harm economic performance has led a number of countries, including Japan and the nations of the European Union, to suggest that their imposition should be prevented by international treaties.[44]

Increasing reliance on export taxes to finance an expanding public sector generated severe political tensions between the government of President Cristina Fernandez de Kirchner and agricultural producers. These problems became quite serious in March 2008, when the most important agricultural lobby groups called a strike to protest the decline in rural incomes.

The conflict with farmers is not the only problem faced by the administration of the second president Kirchner. In 2007 inflationary pressures began to increase significantly, threatening macroeconomic stability and triggering demands for very large wage increases. The government response appeared to be taken from a manual on populism: instead of acknowledging the problem and implementing corrective measures, the administration claimed that the higher inflation figures were the result of a flawed consumer price index. A number of members of the technical staff of the national statistical office were fired and replaced by political appointees willing to manipulate the data. With such a response the administration seemed oblivious to the fact that the country's dwindling reputation had been damaged further and possibly irreparably.

Part III
The Populist Reaction

Chapter 8
Populism, Neopopulism, and Inequality in the New Century

After the crises and disappointments of 1990s and early 2000s, Latin America became fertile ground for populist politicians. The Washington Consensus and the international institutions—particularly the IMF—were blamed for the increase in unemployment, the decline in wages, higher poverty incidence, and currency collapses.[1] Across the region, populist politicians criticized globalization, markets, competition, and capitalism and argued that in order to improve social conditions and reduce poverty the role of the state in economic affairs had to increase significantly. In a number of countries foreign companies were nationalized by newly elected governments, trade barriers were hiked, businesses were harassed, official statistics were doctored in order to show low inflation rates, business regulations were stiffened, and exports were taxed.

Populism is not a new phenomenon in Latin America. Historical examples of populist regimes include the presidencies of Getulio Vargas and João Goulart in Brazil, Juan Domingo Perón in Argentina, Salvador Allende in Chile, Luis Echeverría and José López Portillo in Mexico, Daniel Ortega and the Sandinistas in Nicaragua during the 1980s, and Juan Velasco Alvarado and Alan García in Peru. In all these episodes policies based on unsustainable fiscal expansion, monetary largesse, protectionism, and government intervention were put in place as a way of redistributing income and wealth. And in all of them the experiment ended in runaway inflation, higher unemployment, lower wages, and massive currency crises. For example, according to UN data, during the first Alan García administration in Peru (1985–90), inflation-adjusted wages declined by more than 60 percent. And during Sandinista rule, wages in Nicaragua collapsed by an astonishing 80 percent. Current episodes of neopopulism in countries as diverse as Argentina, Bolivia, Ecuador, Nicaragua, Paraguay, and Venezuela differ from historical manifestations in several respects, including the ways through which the populist leaders got to power—the current crop has won democratically held elections.

Before I proceed, three points of clarification are in order. First, there is nothing wrong with focusing on social conditions when designing economic policies. On the contrary, given the region's dismal social history, the reduction of inequality and poverty are legitimate—one could even say, required—goals of any comprehensive blueprint or program for economic development. The problem is not the emphasis on social objectives and goals. The problem is relying on policies that are unsustainable in the long run and that after a short period of euphoria generate stagnation, inflation, unemployment, and lower wages—policies that instead of improving the lives of the poor, make them more painful and frustrating. Second, populism is not the monopoly of the left; indeed, it is perfectly possible to have populism of the right. As it turns out, however, the majority of populist experiences in the region have been led by politicians with leftist and nationalistic leanings. And third, not every left-of-center government pursues populist policies. Indeed, side by side with the Hugo Chávez and Evo Morales, there is now a new generation of modern leftist politicians in Latin America whose goal is not to roll back the reforms of the 1990s but to make adjustments and corrections to these policies. More specifically, their goals are to increase social expenditures in an efficient way, implement modern regulatory systems that promote competition and avoid excesses like the ones that caused the global crash of 2008, use public investment as a catalyst to attract private investment, and introduce exchange-rate regimes that avoid the artificial strengthening of local currencies. These leaders—whom Mexican political scientist Jorge Castañeda has called Latin America's "modern left"—recognize the need to take advantage of global markets, and they fully understand the benefits of low inflation; they also acknowledge that innovation is behind growth and prosperity and that the market more often than not provides the right signals to guide investment decisions and encourage productivity gains.[2] Even in the aftermath of the global crash of 2008, these modern left-leaning politicians—including Brazil's Lula, Michelle Bachelet of Chile, and Tabaré Vázquez of Uruguay—were unwilling to implement protectionist policies or to roll back the reforms of the 1990s and 2000s.[3]

Populism and Neopopulism

Populism is a pejorative term. For a long time it has been tossed around by politicians to discredit their rivals. The expression has such a negative connotation that no politician I know of has ever called himself or herself a populist. So what is populism exactly? What are the elements of a populist regime? What are its ideological underpinnings and its main policies? When defining *populism*, political theorists and historians usually refer to political movements led by individuals with strong and charismatic personalities whose attractiveness to the masses stems from a fiery rhetoric that centers on the causes and solutions to inequality. Their discourse pitches the interests of "the people" against those of the oligarchy, corporations, financial capital, the business sector, and foreign companies. In his popular book on the history of Latin America, Edwin Williamson defines *populism* as "the phenomenon where a politician tries to win power by courting mass popularity with sweeping promises of benefits and concessions to . . . the lower classes. . . . [P]opulist leaders lack a coherent program for social change or economic reform."[4]

Political scientist Paul Drake has argued that populists use "political mobilization, recurrent rhetoric, and symbols designed to inspire the people" and draw on heterogeneous coalitions that include the working class as well as significant sectors of the middle class. He notes that populist programs "normally respond to the problems of underdevelopment by expanding state activism to incorporate the workers in a process of accelerated industrialization through ameliorative redistributive measures." In a classic book, Michael L. Conniff, another political scientist, has argued that "populist programs frequently overlapped with those of socialism."[5]

Populist leaders usually don't operate within the realm of traditional political parties but instead appeal directly to the masses to obtain support for specific policies. Other aspects of traditional populism emphasized by political scientists are an alliance between the lower and middle classes—who are, after all, the core of "the people"—a tendency toward prourban discourse and policies, and ambivalence toward, if not open disdain for, representative democracy. In fact, most historical episodes of populism in Latin America have shown a streak of authoritarianism.[6]

Most economists have followed the analysis proposed by MIT's Rudi Dornbusch and I in 1989 and have defined populism as a set of economic policies aimed at redistributing income by running high and unsustainable fiscal deficits and expansive monetary policies and by mandating wage increases for public-sector workers that are not justified based on increases in productivity. Dornbusch and I went on to argue that, invariably, macroeconomic populist episodes begin with great euphoria and end with rapid inflation—and in some cases hyperinflation—higher unemployment, and lower wages. Time after time these policies ultimately fail, hurting those groups (the poor and the middle class) that they are supposed to favor.[7]

The fiscal dimension of traditional populism is marvelously captured by the following statement in a 1952 letter from Argentina's Juan Domingo Perón to retired Chilean general Carlos Ibañez del Campo, who had recently been elected to the presidency:

> My dear friend: Give the people, especially to the workers, all that is possible. When it seems to you that already you are giving them too much, give them more. You will see the results. Everybody will try to frighten you with the specter of an economic collapse. But all of this is a lie. There is nothing more elastic than the economy which everyone fears so much because no one understands it.[8]

A clear statement of populist economic strategies and their disregard for basic budgetary and economic principles is provided by economist Daniel Carbonetto, who in the mid-1980s advised Peruvian president Alan García. Contrary to massive historical evidence in country after country and through the centuries, he asserts that fiscal largesse and very large public-sector deficits would *reduce* rather than increase inflation. He writes:

> If it were necessary to summarize in two words the economic strategy adopted by the government starting in August 1985 they are *control* [meaning control of prices and costs] . . . and *spend*, transferring resources to the poorest so that they increase consumption and create a demand for increased output. . . . It is necessary to spend, even at the cost of a fiscal deficit, because, if this deficit transfers public resources to increased consumption of the poorest they demand more goods and it will bring about a reduction in unit costs, thus the deficit is not inflationary.[9]

As Rudi Dornbusch and I pointed out in our 1991 book, historically there has been a common thread in populist episodes. At the outset of the experience the populist policy makers—and the population at large—are deeply dissatisfied with the economy's performance; there is a strong feeling that things can be better. In most cases, the country has experienced very moderate growth, stagnation, or outright depression as a result of previous attempts at reducing inflation or recovering from a severe currency crisis. This previous stabilization experience has often, though not always, been implemented under an IMF program and has resulted in reduced growth and lower standards of living. In addition, a high degree of inequality provides the justification for a radically different economic program. The preceding stabilization would generally have improved the budget and the trade balance sufficiently to provide some degree of freedom for financing a short-term highly expansionary program. But of course the fact that funds are available, making fiscal largesse feasible in the short term, does not mean that this is a wise way to proceed. Once in power, populists explicitly reject what they call the "conservative paradigm" and ignore the existence of any type of constraints on public-sector expenditure and monetary expansion. The risks of deficit finance emphasized in traditional thinking are portrayed as exaggerated or simply unfounded—recall the quote from Perón's letter to Ibañez del Campo. According to populist policy makers, fiscal and monetary expansions are not inflationary because there is spare capacity, and it is always possible to squeeze profit margins by means of price controls.

The Populist Cycle: From Euphoria to Regret

Most traditional populist experiences in Latin America have been characterized by a predictable four-stage cycle. In the first phase, populist policymakers are fully vindicated in their diagnosis and prescription: growth, real wages, and employment are high, and their policies appear to be highly successful. Generalized price controls assure that inflation is not a problem, and shortages are alleviated by imports. The depletion of inventories and the availability of imports—usually financed by using international reserves or suspending external debt payments—accommodate expansion of demand with little impact on inflation.

During the second phase the economy runs into bottlenecks, partly as a consequence of expansionary demand and partly because of a growing lack of foreign exchange. At this point currency devaluation, exchange control, protectionism, and allowing prices to reflect the true scarcity of goods become necessary, and an increasing black market for foreign exchange develops. Inflation increases significantly, but wages stay up thanks to automatic adjustment mechanisms or government-mandated increases. The budget deficit worsens tremendously as a result of pervasive subsidies on basic goods—including food, public services, and transportation—and foreign exchange.

The third stage, the prelude to collapse, is characterized by pervasive shortages, an extreme acceleration of inflation, and capital flight. To protect themselves from inflation, consumers shy away from domestic currency, and foreign currency becomes the preferred medium of exchange. The budget deficit deteriorates drastically because of significant declines in tax collection and increasing subsidy costs. The government attempts to curb inflation and stabilize the economy by cutting subsidies and by devaluing the currency. Inflation-adjusted wages fall precipitously, and policies become unstable.

Finally, the fourth stage is the cleanup following the disaster. Usually an orthodox stabilization takes over under a new government. More often than not, an IMF program will be enacted, and when all is said and done, the incomes— particularly those of the poorer segments of society—will have declined to a level significantly lower than when the whole episode began. The decline will be very persistent, because the politics of the experience and the growing economic disequilibria will have depressed investment and promoted capital flight. The extremity of inflation-adjusted wage declines is due to a simple fact: capital is mobile across borders, which can leave a country in disarray, but labor is not; capital can flee from poor policies, but labor is trapped. The final dismantling of populist policies is often accompanied by major political change, including violent overthrow of the government. The middle class tends to approve of these developments because of the inflationary and economic dislocations that have been brought about by the populist regime.[10]

The Policies of Neopopulism

Current populism, or neopopulism, is also based on a discourse that castigates the private sector, foreign companies, and the multilateral institutions for the country's ill, including its acute level of inequality. Like traditional populists, neopopulist leaders also have strong and charismatic personalities, tend to operate outside the channels established by traditional political parties, and appeal directly to the masses to obtain support for their initiatives. There are, however, some important differences between neopopulism and traditional or historical populism. First, the populist heads of government of the twenty-first century—the presidents Kirchner in Argentina, Hugo Chávez in Venezuela, Evo Morales in Bolivia, Rafael Correa of Ecuador, Daniel Ortega of Nicaragua, and Fernando Lugo of Paraguay—don't emphasize outright expansionist fiscal and monetary policies, nor have they engineered—at least as of the time of this writing—massive and unjustified increases in public-sector wages. In a way, these neopopulists seem to understand the need for maintaining overall fiscal prudence and reasonably low inflation (although, when it comes to inflation, what is "reasonably low" may be subject to debate: while most leftist politicians in Latin America are willing to tolerate inflation in the 8 to 15 percent range, most market-oriented politicians aim at a rate of inflation below 5 percent per year).

Having said this, it is still too early to know if these populist politicians will be willing or able to maintain fiscal caution during a major downturn such as those generated by the global crash of 2008. In fact, at the time of this writing, in mid-2009, there is already some indication that Argentina and Venezuela have slipped into the old practices of traditional populism. Whether these countries will go through the populist cycle discussed above, a cycle that invariably ends with frustration, is still to be seen.[11]

A second important difference between traditional populism and neopopulism has to do with the way in which power is gained. Many historical populists got to power, or maintained it, through undemocratic means. That was the case, for example, with Getulio Vargas in Brazil, Juan Domingo Perón in Argentina, Carlos Ibañez del Campo in Chile during the late 1920s, Juan Velasco Alvarado in Peru, and Daniel Ortega in Nicaragua. In contrast, and as political scientist Ignacio Walker and others have emphasized, all neopopulist leaders in Latin America have gained power through the democratic process.

A third difference between neopopulists and historical populists is their attitude toward globalization. To be sure, traditional populist leaders from Getulio Vargas to José Domingo Perón and from Salvador Allende to Alan García were staunchly nationalistic; they often criticized foreign investors and in many cases nationalized multinational firms. What is different about neopopulists, however, is that the criticism goes beyond specific foreign companies or banks. Neopopulists decry globalization as a system based on the massive international exchange of goods, financial capital, ideas, and people. Neopopulists often cling to national identity and denounce the loss of the nation's cultural heritage; they condemn McDonalds not because hamburgers are unhealthy and contribute to obesity but because the restaurants represent a foreign taste; they disparage Hollywood as shallow and frivolous; they revile modernity and are nostalgic for the "good old days," even if they don't specify when those good times took place or how good they really were or which groups enjoyed them. Their antiglobalization rhetoric became stronger after the financial crash of 2008 and the meltdown of the mortgage-backed securities market in the United States and other advanced nations.

Instead of relying heavily on fiscal deficits to redistribute income, up till now neopopulists have emphasized the use of increasingly intrusive government controls and restrictions as a way of attempting to redirect income to particular groups. For example, exchange controls have been imposed in Venezuela as a mechanism to keep inflation (as officially quantified by the government) in check and reduce the cost of food; foreign companies have been nationalized in Argentina, Bolivia, and Venezuela in an effort to capture profits and raise workers' salaries; contracts with foreign investors have been violated in Argentina as a way of keeping down electricity and gas tariffs and thus to obtain the support of the lower and middle classes; a black market for foreign exchange has sprung up in Venezuela; prices have been kept at artificial levels in Argentina, Bolivia, Ecuador, and Venezuela; import tariffs have been raised in Ecuador and Bolivia to protect local industries; export taxes have been hiked time and again in Argentina in an effort to collect revenues and finance social programs; archaic monetary systems that border on barter have been promoted in Venezuela; and the private sector has been harassed in various ways in every country that has given in to the neopopulist temptation.[12]

Inequality and Neopopulism in Latin America

Contrary to what neopopulists have argued, inequality in Latin America is not the result of the Washington Consensus or of globalization, market forces, or the incomplete reforms of the 1990s and 2000s. Inequality is a centuries-old problem that can be traced back to colonial times and to the types of goods produced during that era. As noted in chapter 2, there were already clear differences in the production techniques used in South and

North America in the eighteenth century. These differences affected the distribution of wealth as well as the types of institutions that evolved in North and South America. In Spanish America, for example, both sugar and mining were fundamentally important, and both required massive numbers of unskilled workers—indentured and slave labor—and substantial volumes of capital. This resulted in the concentration of property in the hands of a few families who ended up controlling the large mining concerns and the latifundia. In contrast, in the North American colonies—particularly in New England—the dominant crops required much higher land-to-labor ratios. In the northern colonies land ownership was generalized and widespread, helping create a more egalitarian society and more inclusive institutions of the type described by Alexis de Tocqueville in *Democracy in America*.[13] To be sure, in the southern North American colonies—the Carolinas and Georgia—crops and production techniques resembled those of Spanish colonies, as did the distribution of wealth and the institutions that were developed in the eighteenth and nineteenth centuries. It took the trauma of the Civil War in the 1860s to begin to change this and for the southern states to begin converging, in terms of income per capita and social conditions, with the rest of the United States.

The distribution of wealth in the South American colonies was greatly affected by the way in which the Spanish Crown assigned land to new settlers. Private property was granted to certain individuals in payment for their services, on the condition that the lands not stand idle. New owners had to put their lands to work and had to live on their property in order to take effective possession. This system received the name of *morada y labor* or *casa y labranza*, which may be translated as "homestead and work."[14] It was not clear, however, how the Crown monitored the land's cultivation or landowners' residence on a particular property. With time the concept of working the land became very flexible; in most cases it was enough to keep a small vegetable garden or to have a few animals grazing here and there. In the eighteenth century absentee ownership of vast expanses of land—the latifundia—had already become common throughout Latin America. According to political scientist Tatu Vanhanen, by the mid-nineteenth century in most Latin American countries farms owned and operated by families comprised less than 5 percent of arable land; family farms made up only 5 percent of total arable land in Argentina, 3 percent in Brazil, 3 percent in Colombia, and only 2 percent in Mexico. In contrast, 60 percent of families in the United States and 64 percent of those in Canada owned land.[15]

The system of land tenure based on extensive latifundia was complemented by the encomiendas, an institution created to help convert Indians to the Catholic faith. Large numbers of Indians were assigned to a specific settler, who could have them work his lands or mines as long as he fed them, provided them with shelter, and evangelized them. Although the Crown had established that no encomienda could have more than three thousand Indians, this limit was rarely observed, and in many cases a single landowner had control over more than thirty thousand Indians. This was the case, for example, of Rodrigo de Contreras in the mid-sixteenth century, in what is known today as Nicaragua.[16] The unequal distribution of land was also perpetuated by legislation that forbade landowners from dividing their holdings and precluded younger siblings from inheriting the land. In Bolivia and Peru, the *mita* system of forced labor, instituted by the Incas throughout their empire, was adopted by the Spanish colonizers as an inexpensive way of exploiting the silver mines. Although the Crown required that Indians subject to *mita* work be paid, the amounts received were paltry, and life conditions were miserable. This system was only abolished in the mid-1820s when Bolivia and Peru became independent.

Through time, institutions and economic policies helped maintain the historical structure of power and distribution of wealth and income. Stanley L. Engerman and Kenneth L. Sokoloff have argued that this is clearly illustrated by the different ways in which education evolved in South and North America. While schooling expanded rapidly in the North, it lagged desperately behind in the South. In the early twentieth century, for example, the literacy rate in the United States was approximately 90 percent; in contrast, it was only 52 percent in Argentina, 17 percent in Bolivia, 43 percent in Chile, 32 percent in Colombia, 41 percent in Cuba, 22 percent in Mexico, and 54 percent in Uruguay.[17]

One of the most important goals of the Alliance for Progress in the 1960s was to reduce income disparity and poverty through a number of policy initiatives aimed at expanding education, improving health care, and distributing land to peasants through market-based agrarian reforms. Over the next three decades, however, in spite of massive agrarian reforms in a number of countries, no major dents were made in inequality. In fact, as noted in chapter 2, between the 1960s and the early 1990s income distribution, as measured by the Gini coefficient—which ranges from 0 for perfect equality to 1 for absolute inequality—became more unequal in every country in Latin America with the exception of Mexico. Even Argentina and Uruguay, the only two nations that in the early 1950s had Gini coefficients similar to those of Western democracies, saw their distribution of income become significantly more disparate. And in spite of some progress, in Mexico the Gini coefficient in 1992 was still a very high 0.53.[18] In most countries the highest level of income inequality ever recorded occurred in the 1980s or very early 1990s, just prior to the Washington Consensus reforms. Inequality is definitely not a result of neoliberalism.[19]

It is also true that poverty and inequality did not decline during the Washington Consensus years, but given the entrenched interests opposed to reform and the limited extent to which better policies were implemented, that is not much of a surprise. According to a World Bank study published in 2006, for the region as a whole the percentage of the population living below the poverty line of two dollars per day remained virtually constant between the early 1990s and early 2000s.[20] The incidence of poverty declined in Bolivia, Brazil, Chile, Costa Rica, El Salvador, Nicaragua, and Panama; poverty as a percentage of the population increased in Argentina, Colombia, Uruguay, and Venezuela and remained nearly stable in Mexico. During the same period, the World Bank has estimated that the extent of income disparity also remained practically unchanged in Latin America. Not surprisingly, the data show differences between countries: there was a sizeable increase in inequality in Colombia, Argentina, Costa Rica, and Venezuela; in Uruguay, Bolivia, Ecuador, Honduras, Panama, Peru, and Paraguay income disparity increased slightly; and it declined in Brazil, Chile, El Salvador, Mexico, and Nicaragua.[21]

Openness, Globalization, Inequality, and Social Conditions

A popular belief among antiglobalization activists is that the opening of international trade throughout Latin America in the 1990s increased poverty and inequality.[22] This idea has been echoed in the media and has become a fundamental component of neopopulist rhetoric. However, it is more a myth than a fact. Indeed, economic research has failed to find hard and robust evidence relating trade openness to the systematic worsening of living standards for the poor as a group. This, of course, does not mean that all the poor gain from globalization or that trade liberalization in every country has been associated with improved social conditions. Existing evidence indicates that, in general, some among the poor win with trade liberalization and some lose; the evidence also indicates that under certain conditions the vast majority of people may benefit from increased trade openness.

A detailed review of the evidence on the relationship between globalization and social conditions is well beyond the scope of this book.[23] My interpretation of the data, stemming from my own research on the subject, as well as from reading scores of technical academic papers, articles, and books, may be summarized by the following eight points.

First, a greater degree of trade openness has a positive effect on economic growth. Some authors have argued that this effect is strong and lasts for a substantial period of time, while others have noted that this acceleration in growth is a temporary phenomenon.[24] Be that as it may, the important finding is that, at least for some years, countries with a greater degree of trade openness will tend to grow at a faster rate than they would if they had retreated from global markets. In that regard, most scholars who have looked at Chile over the last thirty years have argued that the opening of the economy in the mid-1970s is one of the most important factors behind the country's stellar performance, rapid economic growth, reduced poverty incidence, and improved social conditions.

Second, individuals who work in the export sector tend to experience increases in wages and income after trade liberalization reform. On the other hand, those employed in industries formerly protected by import barriers tend to experience income reductions once trade is liberalized. Thus, facilitating the reallocation of workers from formerly protected importing industries to exporting industries is important for countries to reap the full benefits of increased globalization. Easier reallocation of workers requires, in turn, flexible labor markets, where there are no major restrictions to hiring or dismissing workers. This, however, is an area where the vast majority of the Latin American countries have made very little progress.[25] According to the Doing Business data set, the Latin American countries are ranked 122nd on average in the category of ease of employing workers. In contrast, on average the Asian Tigers are ranked 78th, and the advanced commodity exporter countries referred to in chapter 4 are ranked 13th on average.

Third, income inequality and poverty tend to decline in regions, states, and provinces that receive significant volumes of foreign direct investment. In turn, higher investment by foreign firms is generally a consequence of greater trade openness. This result comes out very clearly in research on social conditions in Mexico's thirty-one states. Economists Fernando Borraz and José Ernesto López-Cordova found that poverty and inequality declined significantly in those states that have received a larger volume of foreign direct investment.[26]

Fourth, trade reform and export expansion have given low-income women greater opportunities to find formal, stable, and relatively well-remunerated jobs. This is a particularly important finding for Latin America, since in many countries—including Chile—the percentage of women who participate actively in the formal labor market is significantly lower than in countries in other parts of the world that have a comparable level of economic development.[27]

Fifth, by forcing companies to become more efficient, trade liberalization induces firms to adopt sophisticated production techniques. As a consequence, wages of skilled workers who can operate complex machinery tend to increase relative to those of unskilled workers. This in turn tends to increase inequality.[28] This suggests that trade liberalization reforms need to be accompanied by improvements in the educational system, particularly in training programs for displaced workers. However, this is more easily said than done. As discussed below, the quality of education in Latin America is extremely low and has not improved in the last few decades.

Sixth, the effects of trade reform on poverty depend on accompanying policies; countries that have a safety net or put in place an effective transfer system that assists those displaced by heightened foreign competition have been able to avoid some of the negative effects of openness on some segments of the poor. This is the case, for example, of Mexico's Procampo and Progresa, two programs aimed at assisting poor families, mostly in the rural sector. Other programs that provide targeted assistance to the poor include Bolsa Família in Brazil, Familias en Acción in Colombia, and Red de Protección Social in Nicaragua. Countries that lack safety nets or whose social programs are too small, inefficient, or corrupt—and there are many of these in Latin America—are likely to see an increase in the incidence of poverty following trade reform.[29]

Seventh, cross-country comparative studies suggest that while trade openness reduces inequality in middle-income and richer countries, it increases inequality in very poor countries. Specifically, there is evidence suggesting that for countries with an income per capita in the upper half of world income distribution, a greater degree of trade openness will tend to reduce inequality. The reason for this is that countries that are higher up on the development ladder have the ability and institutional capacity to put in place programs that mitigate the negative effects of trade reform on certain groups and regions. They are able to put in place effective safety nets and workers' training programs or to implement legislation to increase the degree of workers' mobility across sectors.[30] Interestingly, most Latin American countries are above this critical income per capita threshold, which has been calculated at approximately six thousand dollars per year.

And eighth, macroeconomics crises such as the ones in Mexico and Argentina increase poverty significantly and tend to make income distribution more unequal.[31] This point deserves particular attention, as external crises have historically been at the center of deteriorating social conditions in Latin America. Currency crises generate enormous dislocations; companies go bankrupt, unemployment increases rapidly, wages decline, and many people lose their life savings.[32] Since most Latin American countries have a very precarious social safety net, after a crisis a large number of people plunge into destitution and desperation. This was precisely the case in the Mexican and Argentine crises discussed in this volume. After the Argentine peso collapse of 2001–2 the percentage of the population living in poverty increased by 15 percentage points—indeed, who can forget the image of scavengers looking for food in the streets of Buenos Aires in 2002? After the 1994–95 crisis, poverty in Mexico increased by almost 11 percentage points. Because of these dramatic and very visible episodes, the impression that the reforms have generated an increase in poverty has become widespread. In many ways, however, the evidence from countries that have avoided major crises, have opened their economies to international competition, and have modernized their policies and institutions is more relevant to this debate. In that regard, the case of Chile—the nation that has made the greatest progress on the reform and modernization front and the only country in the region that has reached the third phase of growth transitions discussed in chapter 1—is particularly revealing: between 1989 and 2003 the proportion of people living below the World Bank's poverty line in Chile declined from 24 percent to 5 percent of the population.

The fact that major crises generate dislocations, increased unemployment, lower wages, and generalized suffering doesn't imply that market orientation or openness is the ultimate cause of Latin America's persistent degree of poverty and inequality. Three points are particularly important in this respect. First, currency crises are not an exclusive feature of the post–Washington Consensus era. In fact, as I document in chapter 7, currency failures in Argentina began as early as the 1820s. Similar historical patterns have been observed in the rest of the region. Second, as noted earlier, in most countries income disparity reached a peak in the early 1990s, before the launching of the reforms. And third, as I show in this book, in the vast majority of Latin American countries—Chile being the sole exception at this time—the reforms have been incomplete and have only partially addressed the region's historical inefficiencies and institutional weaknesses. It is not possible, therefore, to blame something that has not really happened—the implementation of a modern and competitive capitalist and market-oriented system—for social problems that have affected the countries of the region for centuries.

Income Disparities and Education

If neither the reforms nor globalization are the culprits, what are the main causes of Latin America's entrenched poverty and persistent income inequality? More specifically, what are the policy areas that should be tackled by politicians—including those of a populist persuasion—interested in reducing inequality and poverty?

Historical economic research singles out three factors that have played a fundamental role in determining the region's poor social conditions: The oldest one is the unequal distribution of assets, particularly land, that has affected Latin America since colonial times. A second factor behind the region's historically skewed income distribution is the pattern of public-sector expenditure. In contrast to the advanced nations, in Latin America public-sector transfers and subsidies are not geared toward lower-income groups. Compare the United Kingdom with the average Latin American country: in the UK public-sector transfers and subsidies reduce the Gini coefficient by 0.18 points—from 0.53 before transfers to 0.35 after transfers—while in the typical Latin American country the Gini coefficient barely declines by 0.02 points after transfers are taken into account.[33]

But without any doubt the most important cause of Latin America's social ills—including poverty and income inequality—is the historical dreadful state of the region's educational system. By neglecting education the vast majority of the Latin American countries have failed to upgrade their labor force skills and have lagged behind other nations in the key areas of human capital formation and productivity growth. It is not an exaggeration to say that workers in many Latin American countries are among the least prepared to meet the high skill requirements of the twenty-first century.[34]

Children from Latin American nations score very poorly on international tests, indeed much more poorly than children from the Asian Tigers, the advanced commodity exporters, and the southern European nations. Paradoxically, during the last fifteen years there has been a significant increase in access to education throughout the region, and spending in education has grown from an average of 2.7 percent of the region's total income in 1990 to more than 4.1 percent in 2006. In some countries, such as Argentina, Chile, and Costa Rica, there is now almost universal coverage of secondary education. The problem, however, is that neither coverage nor spending are by themselves that important in determining the effectiveness of education as a tool for enhancing productivity, generating social mobility, and improving social conditions. As the World Bank has recently recognized, "access to education is not enough: the key is learning."[35]

In 1995, Colombia was the only Latin American country to participate in the Trends in International Mathematics and Science Study, or TIMSS, a highly respected international standardized test taken by eighth-graders in forty-one countries.[36] The results were telling: in both the mathematics and science parts of the test Colombia was ranked next to last, in fortieth place. In part as a consequence of this poor showing, the Colombian authorities decided to withdraw from the test in 1997.

In 1999 Chile replaced Colombia as the only Latin American participant in the TIMSS. To the surprise of some observers, and to the dismay of Chilean educational authorities, the results left much to be desired: in mathematics Chilean eighth-graders ranked thirty-fifth out of thirty-eight nations. Their average score was 392 points, significantly below the average of 487 points for all countries. Moreover, Chile's scores were below those of countries with lower income per capita, including Indonesia, the Philippines, Morocco, Thailand, Iran, Turkey, Tunisia, and Jordan. In the science part of the test, Chile's children also ranked thirty-fifth out of thirty-eight countries. These dismal results generated a major political storm. Government officials gave long speeches and assured voters that they were committed to improving education. Expenditure was increased, and a major program aimed at building new schools was unveiled.

In spite of all the talk, statements, and press releases, Chile's results didn't improve in the 2003 TIMSS test: Chile's eighth-graders ranked thirty-ninth out of forty-five countries in mathematics. In absolute terms, however, the score declined relative to 1999. In science, on the other hand, the results were slightly better, with Chile's children taking thirty-seventh place out of forty-five nations. However, the average score (413 points) was significantly lower than the average for all countries (474 points). The 2003 TIMSS scores provided important and disturbing insights into Chile's educational system. In mathematics, girls did much worse than boys; in fact, Chile's gender gap was the third highest in the sample, only behind Tunisia and Ghana. In science, boys outperformed girls by an even greater margin; the gender gap was the second largest after Ghana. The results also showed that Chilean children did particularly poorly in the "knowledge" category of the test, suggesting that Chilean teachers are particularly weak in transmitting knowledge to their students.

In 2006 a handful of Latin American countries participated in the Program for International Student Assessment, a standardized test administered by the OECD. The results confirmed that the Latin American educational system is in disarray. Every one of the six Latin American countries that participated in the science assessment ranked in the lower half of the sample. Out of 57 countries, Chile was ranked 40th, Uruguay 42nd, Mexico 48th, Argentina 50th, Brazil 51st, and Colombia 52nd. They were clearly outperformed by the advanced commodity exporters—Canada was 7th, New Zealand was 11th, and Australia was 13th—as well as by the southern European countries and most of the East Asian nations. Mexico's results were typical for the region: its fifteen-year-old students scored significantly below what was expected based on the country's income per capita and expenditure per student.

Unprepared teachers, poor curricula, excessive centralization, and lack of accountability are some of the problems at the center of the region's poor education results. The political forces that today oppose globalization, market orientation, and economic reform have traditionally also opposed major reforms aimed at improving the quality of education. Some populist regimes—including the governments of Evo Morales in Bolivia, Daniel Ortega in Nicaragua, and Hugo Chávez in Venezuela—have made efforts to improve the coverage of education and have implemented major literacy campaigns. The results of these programs have been modest, however, and do not include lasting improvements in the learning experience. (See chapter 9 for a discussion of Hugo Chávez's education policies.)

In most Latin American countries efforts to reform and modernize the educational system have been strongly opposed by teachers' unions and left-of-center political parties. The most dramatic case of frustration in education reform took place in Argentina in 2001, during the presidency of Fernando de la Rúa. The effort was led by respected minister of education Juan Llach and was aimed at improving educational quality and raising Argentina's ability to compete effectively in a technologically oriented global economy. Llach's reform program was both simple and ingenious. It relied on decentralization, debureaucratization, choice, merit-based compensation for teachers, accountability for school principals, and greater parent involvement. But it was strongly opposed by the powerful teachers' unions and by politicians from both President de la Rúa's own political party and the Peronist opposition party.[37]

The quality of Argentina's educational system has declined significantly through the years. International comparisons indicate that while the country spends more on secondary education than nations of comparable development, its performance—measured, for instance, by the percentage of students who graduate on time—is significantly below the international norm. Worse, the quality of education has gradually deteriorated. While in 1962 more than 35 percent of students who had started the secondary education program graduated on time, by 1997 that figure had declined to only 24 percent, and today it still hovers around that level. The quality of education also varies significantly across provinces. While rich provinces do relatively well, poor ones don't do much better than the more destitute countries of the world.[38]

Under Argentina's federal political system, education policy is the responsibility of the provinces. But instead of viewing this as an impediment to change, Llach saw it as a springboard for reform. He developed an incentive system for the provinces: those that were willing to go along with the basic tenets of reform would be eligible for special federal educational funds. He called this the "Federal Educational Pact" and asked the government to provide $450 million to fund it. According to the pact the provinces could have used these additional monies for any educational purpose, including increasing the salaries of highly rated teachers.

During his campaign for the presidency in 1999, de la Rúa talked repeatedly about the importance of education. However, when it was time to deliver, he balked under teachers' union pressure and left his education minister standing alone without political or financial support. As time went by, it became increasingly clear that the president was unwilling to use any political capital to bankroll Llach's program.

Paradoxically, Latin America's populist politicians—both historical figures as well as current neopopulists—have never faced the educational challenge head on and effectively. Of course they have talked about improving education, but they have been unwilling to confront teachers' unions or to introduce merit pay, accountability, decentralization, or competition. In avoiding conflict with powerful unions, time and again populists have chosen shortcuts over substantive measures to improve social conditions for the poor. The problem is that in the long run shortcuts never work.

Populism and Political Institutions

Latin American politicians are not the only ones who have used populist rhetoric to gather support or rally the masses. Rhetoric based on class and income disparities has been common in many countries, including in the United States and Europe. What has set Latin America apart, however, is that again and again, populist politicians have been able to implement these policies, to the great disadvantage of their people. How can we explain, then, why Latin America has been such a fertile ground for populist policies? The historical high degree of inequality and the succession of currency crises that time and again have devastated these nations' economies have contributed to this outcome. But these are not the only causes behind the recurrence of populism in the region. The nature of political institutions has also played an important role, as it has allowed strong-willed, charismatic leaders to pass legislation that negatively affects economic efficiency.

Pablo Spiller, a professor at the University of California, Berkeley, and Mariano Tommasi of the Universidad de San Andrés in Buenos Aires, Argentina, have argued that the quality of economic policies is directly related to the quality of political institutions.[39] Using a battery of quantitative indicators, they constructed an index of the overall quality of public policies during the 1990s and early 2000s in seventy-seven countries, including eighteen Latin

American nations.[40] From the region's perspective their results are disturbing: the three countries with the lowest-quality policies in their overall sample are Latin American—Paraguay, Guatemala, and Nicaragua. All but one of the countries in the bottom 10 percent of the distribution are from the region—in addition to the three mentioned above, these include Ecuador, Bolivia, Venezuela, and Argentina. Only three Latin American countries are in the top 50 percent of the public policies quality index—Costa Rica, Uruguay, and Chile—and only one, Chile, is in the top 25 percent.

This research also shows that countries with high-quality public policies tend to have political institutions that constrain the power of the executive and make it somewhat difficult to pass legislation that violates property rights, introduces major economic controls, or unilaterally reduces the degree of openness of the economy. Spiller and Tommasi have also shown that countries with successful public policies tend to have a legislative branch that focuses on long-term goals and implications, a judiciary that enforces laws and regulations, a stable and highly professional cabinet, and a civil service made up of adequately trained and skilled bureaucrats. In that regard, countries with high-quality public policies seldom grant extraordinary powers to the president that allow the executive to govern through decrees that are neither discussed nor approved by the legislature. Interestingly, in recent years both Venezuela's Hugo Chávez and the presidents Kirchner in Argentina have relied extensively on extraordinary powers to advance their populist agendas.

A simple yet powerful implication of this analysis is that in countries where there is a weak system of political checks and balances, a president with populist inclinations will be able to implement all sorts of policies without much debate and without going through a legislative process; he or she will be able to alter contracts unilaterally, violate property rights, change the rules, and expropriate private companies. This indeed has happened in Venezuela, where Hugo Chávez has used presidential decrees to nationalize oil companies partially owned by U.S. corporations (ExxonMobil, Chevron, and Conoco-Phillips), Total of France, British Petroleum, and Norway's Statoil ASA; he has also nationalized steel producer Ternium, telecommunications giant CANTV, and power companies partially owned by U.S. utilities AES Corporation and CMS Energy.[41] Evo Morales of Bolivia has also relied extensively on the use of presidential decrees to nationalize a number of companies.[42] In countries where executive power is constrained, and where the legislature is an equal branch of government, it is significantly more difficult for strong popular leaders to enact profound changes that will have positive effects in the short run but will lead to inflation, unemployment, and stagnation in the long run.

Mariano Tommasi's research on politics and public policies indicates that Chile has the strongest political institutions in Latin America. That is, Chile has institutions that impose strict checks and balances on the executive and encourage politicians, including members of the legislature, to focus on longer-term implications. He also finds that political institutions are particularly weak in Nicaragua, Argentina, Paraguay, and Venezuela. It is not surprising that populist policies have been implemented in some of the latter countries over the last few years.

Tommasi's research suggests that in order to make real, long-term progress in modernization and economic policies, it may be necessary to implement important political reforms that would strengthen democracy and put the legislative and judiciary powers on the same footing as the executive branch. However, this will not be easy to do, as entrenched interests will resist any changes that could reduce their influence and result in income and power being redistributed away from them. What is particularly disturbing about recent trends in many Latin American countries is that the popularity of drafting new constitutions of a peculiar sort is formalizing the interests of groups opposed to reforms and at the same time strengthening the executive by weakening the other branches. With their vast lists of constitutional obligations, responsibilities, and mandates, they are likely to clog the judiciary, reduce the protection of property rights, and give the executive branch—through the indefinite reelection of the president—greater discretion and power.

Neopopulism and Neoconstitutionalism

Neopopulists have not only come to power through elections, they have also used the legal system, by means including the writing of new constitutions, to further their cause. In the last decade new constitutions have been approved in Venezuela, Ecuador, and Bolivia, and a law allowing the legislature to take the first steps toward reforming the constitution has been approved in Nicaragua. All three of these new constitutions have been written with the purpose of refounding these nations, recognizing some inalienable rights of the indigenous populations, and granting vast and very detailed economic rights to the people, especially the poor, and to regional interests. These legal charters have been written with the assistance of teams of scholars from Spain's Fundación Centro de Estudios Políticos y Sociales (CEPS), a legal think tank directed by Roberto Viciano Pastor, a law professor at the University of Valencia.

From a doctrinal and constitutional theory perspective these new constitutions are very different from most constitutions around the world. In particular, they differ significantly from the concepts behind the U.S. Constitution, which throughout the years has been the model for most Latin American nations. Legal scholars Roberto Viciano Pastor and Rubén Martínez Dalmau have argued that the modern Latin American constitutions are unfinished documents, always subject to being amended by the people, which are the true depositary of sovereignty and power. First, according to their "new Latin American constitutionalism," political constitutions should be changing documents that adapt quickly and flexibly to new political conditions. They should be easy to amend and reform, and they are not expected to endure more than ten years without going through major changes.[43] The result is to increase uncertainty for all actors, especially businesses and investors. With ever-shifting rules of the game, which can be changed at the whim of political leaders, investors' expectations for stability are naturally reduced along with their willingness to engage in long-term planning and investment, which in turn will have adverse effects on economic growth.

Second, these new constitutions are supposed to help attain certain political goals. That is, all pretense of political impartiality and evenhandedness is forgotten. In the case of Venezuela, the goal of the 1999 constitution—and of its 2009 amendment that allows the unlimited reelection of the president and other officials—is to construct a political system based on the principles of "socialism of the twenty-first century."[44]

Third, according to Latin America's new constitutionalism, two additional powers of the state are added to the executive, legislative, and judiciary powers: citizens' power and electoral power.[45] Because of these two additional powers, the new constitutionalism accepts ands promotes extensive reliance on plebiscites and referenda to advance political and social agendas. That is, this new doctrine has elevated one of the fundamental characteristics of populism—the direct appeal to the masses by populist leaders to attain their goals—to the constitutional level.

In stark contrast with the U.S. Constitution and traditional constitutions in Latin America, the new constitutions of Venezuela, Ecuador, and Bolivia are not brief documents. On the contrary, they are long and massive legal charters that cover every aspect of life; regulate considerable facets of social, political, and economic activities; and establish vast economic rights for individuals, groups, and regions. The Venezuelan constitution has 350 permanent and 18 transitory articles. Ecuador's constitution of 2008 has 442 permanent articles, and the Bolivian constitution of 2008 has 411 permanent articles.[46] Argentina's constitution, in contrast, has only 129 permanent and 17 transitory articles; Chile's constitution has 119 permanent and 49 transitory articles; and the U.S. Constitution has only 7 articles.[47] Enshrining very detailed economic rights in the constitution, rather than establishing them at the level of laws and regulations, has a precedent in the 1991 Colombian constitution. However, the new constitutions of Venezuela, Ecuador, and Bolivia are much more detailed than any ever seen in Latin America—including in Colombia's—or in other parts of the world, for that matter.

In many ways, these new Latin American political charters fall within the category of what legal scholar Robin West and others have called aspirational constitutions, based upon the present society's goals and ambitions, as opposed to more traditional constitutions that "record historic victories."[48] According to West, "at the core [aspirational constitutions] would be the true ideals of liberty and equality toward which aspirational and political goals are, or should be, aimed." Colombian constitutional scholar Mauricio García-Villegas has argued that aspirational constitutions are very different from "protective" constitutions. The former are maximalist documents that aim to politicize the judicial system in order to achieve the people's political goals, while the latter—of which the U.S. Constitution is a premier example—seek to protect the status quo, including the rights of the people, from possible future abuses. From a doctrinal and philosophical perspective, García-Villegas associates aspirational constitutions with the ideas of Rousseau and protective constitutions with Montesquieu.[49]

The view that constitutions should be long documents that capture a nation's goals contrasts markedly with those of constitutional economists who argue that constitutions should be short documents that protect individual rights and help societies solve issues related to credibility by making sure that the government does not fall to the temptation of taking individuals' property and reneging on other promises. Along these lines, Cass Sunstein has argued that the constitution should protect a society against the weaknesses and temptations that spring from its own traditions and political customs.[50]

Ecuador's constitution of 2008 establishes, for example, that it is an obligation of the state to seek Latin America's political, economic, and financial integration (article 423). It is also a constitutional obligation of the state to seek "food sovereignty" (article 410) and fund scientific research (article 388). The Ecuadorian constitution forbids the privatization of social security (article 367) and requires that the state guarantee all senior citizens free access to health services and medicine, regardless of their income or wealth (article 37). The constitution also establishes, following its aspirational mode, that Ecuadorian citizens have a responsibility not to lie or be lazy (article 83).

Not a word is said, however, about how the very long list of constitutional mandates and obligations will be financed. Given Ecuador's limited capability to collect taxes and its traditionally deficient tax administration system, it is likely that many of these obligations will be unfunded and that the state will fail to provide many constitutionally mandated services to the population. This situation is likely to result in a long list of unmet aspirations and could lead to a serious constitutional crisis. What makes the case of Ecuador particularly interesting is that because it uses the U.S. dollar as its currency, it cannot resort to inflationary financing to deal with the state's constitutional obligations. This suggests that the country's current dollarized monetary regime could be abandoned in the future. This could be done by passing a simple law, as the use of U.S. dollars as legal tender is not enshrined in the constitution.[51]

Viciano Pastor and Martínez Dalmau's comments on the doctrinal bases of the Venezuelan constitution of 1999 bear repeating at some length:

> This is a new constitutional approach that emphasizes an integral concept of sovereignty, a new role for the State in society, and the usefulness of democratic and participative constitutional processes in order to promote an advanced democracy. It is an approach that has changed the classical model of the Constitution in order to reinforce its mechanisms of internal strength, the validity of the people's sovereignty and a new relationship between the State and society. . . . [This is] a Constitution that establishes forms of democratic control over all public powers, mechanisms of participative democracy, public property of national resources, new forms of distributing wealth and the broadest catalog of rights recognized anywhere in the world. From this point of view, the Bolivarian Constitution is not only a product of the new Latin American constitutionalism, but it is also one more link in the chain of constitutional processes that move away from

the tradition of Latin American constitutionalism to enter into more genuine and original formulas, that are adapted to the true needs of the Latin American people.[52]

With respect to the relation between the Venezuelan constitution of 1999 and Hugo Chávez's political quest to create an economic and political system in accordance with the principles of the socialism of the twenty-first century, Viciano Pastor and Martínez Dalmau say:

> the Bolivarian Constitution is . . . by necessity, an unfinished constitution. It could not have been in any other way, since the *destruction of the previous system*, and the *construction of a new system* are two projects that move parallel to each other, but are not simultaneous in time. . . . Thus, the goal of the Constitution [of 1999] was not to establish a final model, but to provide the time required to think about the new model, without facing the threat of a return to the old system.[53]

In February 2009 the Venezuelan constitution was amended through a referendum, opening the way for Hugo Chávez—and other Venezuelan elected officials—to be reelected an unlimited number of times. Many analysts expect that this unrestricted reelection provision will make it into the constitutions of Bolivia and Ecuador and possibly into other constitutions in the region. Supporters of these provisions have argued that all they do is to incorporate the wish of the people—the ultimate sovereign—into the fundamental legal charter of the country. In addition, they have argued that parliamentary systems such as those in most European countries allow for unlimited reelection of a given party or coalition and that as long as that party maintains its leader, he or she could head the executive for an unlimited period of time.[54] These arguments, however, miss two important points. First, in parliamentary systems it is possible to censure the prime minister, an option not available in the Venezuelan constitution, where ministers can be censured but not the chief executive. And second, in most Latin American countries government intervention in the political process tends to be rampant, and allowing unlimited reelection is likely to increase government intrusion and interference. Under the cover of returning power to the people, populist leaders with authoritarian leanings have created conditions to perpetuate their rule, benefit their cronies, and provide themselves with a semblance of legitimacy both as true conduits of the people's will and as adherents to constitutionalism. The results have been dire. There is already evidence suggesting that in the period leading to the February 2009 referendum in Venezuela the government used public funds to bolster support for the option of unlimited reelections. According to journalist José de Córdoba,

> The electoral process was marked by the massive spending of state resources on the Chávez campaign, where, among other things, the state-dominated media endlessly broadcast Mr. Chávez's message. . . . As has become usual in Venezuelan campaigns, there were implied threats that thousands of state workers would lose their jobs if they voted against the measure. . . . Police also broke up protest marches by university students calling on Venezuela to oppose the measure.[55]

Chapter 9
Chávez's Challenge and Lula's Response

On February 4, 1992, a little-known army lieutenant colonel named Hugo Chávez led a coup d'état attempt in Venezuela. After intensive fighting that left several people dead and scores wounded, the forces loyal to President Carlos Andrés Pérez were able to repel the insurgents. After surrendering, Chávez—a stocky man of dark complexion who looked very different from Venezuela's elite—talked briefly on national television and said that his Bolivarian movement had failed "for the time being."[1] Six years later, after serving four years of his prison term, Hugo Chávez was elected president of Venezuela with Bolivarism as his rallying call. A vocal critic of globalization, capitalism, and free markets, Chávez has nationalized foreign companies, appointed his supporters to the supreme court, interfered with other countries' affairs, supported guerrilla movements that have made kidnapping the center of their operations, implemented vast social programs aimed at improving the health of the poor and ending illiteracy, and managed to change the constitution in a way that would ensure his permanent reelection. During the last few years no one in Latin America has been immune to Hugo Chávez: while many revere him, others despise him. Contrary to what people think, Chávez is not the product of economic reforms or globalization; he is the product of the government-led import substitution policies that had prevailed in Venezuela since the late 1950s and of the policies of the out-of-touch political elite who had governed the country since 1958.

Much has been made—and rightly so—of the fact that Brazil's president Luiz Inácio Lula da Silva rejected the populist temptation. This, however, is not enough if Brazil is to take off and fulfill its economic potential. For this to happen Brazil needs to put in place a massive modernization program that creates efficient institutions and encourages innovation, competition, and productivity growth. From 2003 to 2008 Brazil's gross domestic product grew on average at 3.9 percent per annum, a figure that, although not particularly low, is not exceptional, especially considering the very positive external environment. In fact, during this period Brazil posted the lowest rate of economic growth of the four BRIC countries (Brazil, Russia, India, and China). Moreover, Brazil continues to be highly vulnerable to external shocks. This was made clear by the rapid slowdown in exports, investment, and growth following the global crash of 2008. The differences between Hugo Chávez and Lula provide rich material for a study in contrasts.

Hugo Chávez and the Path to Bolivarian Populism

Thousands of pages have been written about Hugo Chávez. Most analysts agree that he epitomizes neopopulism, and many have argued that his policies represent a challenge for market orientation and modernity, not only in Venezuela but also in the rest of Latin America. Almost every ingredient of neopopulist leadership is present in Chávez: he is a charismatic, strong leader who uses egalitarian rhetoric and attacks on the wealthy to mobilize the masses, and he has contempt for the institutions of representative democracy and resorts to referenda—although he doesn't always win them—and direct pressure from the masses to attain his goals. Chávez's disdain for democratic institutions is captured in the following assessment by his supporter and former Venezuelan vice president José Vicente Rangel: "Chávez is above institutions, because he personifies the people."[2]

The distortionary economic policies that generate optimism in the short run are also present. Chávez has controlled prices, nationalized all sorts of firms, ladened the central bank with political appointees, and considered creating a monetary system partially based on communal currencies.[3] He has implemented transfer programs aimed at helping the poor, promoted literacy campaigns, and provided assistance to indigenous people and the unemployed. However, as Venezuelan economist and former Chávez supporter Francisco Rodríguez has argued, there are serious questions about whether these measures have resulted in a real and durable improvement in the living conditions of the least fortunate. What is unquestionable, however, is that under Chávez Venezuela has had an increasingly rapid inflation, food shortages, and an economy that has grown thanks to record high oil prices.[4]

Hugo Chávez is not only the perfect textbook example of a neopopulist leader. He is also a very lucky politician. When he took over as president the price of oil was $15 per barrel; in July 2008, oil hovered around $135 per barrel; and in September 2009 it was $70 per barrel, more than four times what it had been when he took office. Chávez has used this windfall to finance social programs that, as I will argue below, have had dubious effects on the well-being of the poor and to further his political causes throughout the region. He has provided massive aid to Bolivia and Nicaragua and financial assistance to Argentina. Whether he helped finance the Revolutionary Armed Forces of Colombia (FARC) guerrillas in Colombia is still unclear; what is certain, however, is that he has provided political support to the Colombian insurgents and has urged the Western democracies to take them off the terrorist list.[5] On June 8, 2008, in what the media called a "surprising turnaround," President Chávez called on the FARC leadership to put down their arms and release the hostages that they have held for years.[6]

In spite of the vast literature on Hugo Chávez and the populism of his Bolivarian regime, there is a misunderstanding about the historical causes behind his ascendance to power. In order to comprehend this phenomenon fully it is important to recognize that Chávez's election in 1998 was not an immediate reaction to the reforms of the Washington Consensus. Venezuela had stopped implementing any meaningful modernization reform in 1993, five years before Chávez was elected. Indeed, Chávez was preceded as president by Rafael Caldera, who ran on a populist platform and whose administration undid most of the rather timid reforms implemented by the administration of Carlos Andrés Pérez.

Venezuela's populist experience did not begin with Chávez or Caldera; it began in the mid-1980s during the administration of Jaime Lusinchi, when the country's fiscal deficit, foreign debt, and inflation increased dramatically. After a brief interregnum from 1989 to 1993, when Pérez attempted to restore economic order, reduce inflation, and introduce some mild modernization reforms, populist policies returned with Caldera. When Chávez took power in 1998, Venezuela was arguably the country that had implemented the fewest reforms in Latin America. As Moisés Naím, the editor of *Foreign Policy* magazine has put it, "the Venezuelan experiment with neoliberal reforms was modest, short-lived, clumsily executed, and often reversed."[7]

Strictly speaking, then, Chávez's rise to power was not the result of the Washington Consensus; it was the result of decades of corruption, economic stagnation, and complacency on the part of the Venezuelan elite. In that regard, more than being a product of neoliberalism, Chávez's ascendancy is the result of the failed policies followed by Venezuela since the late 1950s.

Thanks to its immense oil resources, Venezuela had the highest income per capita in Latin America in 1950. In 1958, after years of dictatorship, the Venezuelan political elite reached an agreement—the Punto Fijo Pact—for maintaining democratic rule and succession of power. During the next three decades, as most of the region experienced coup d'état after coup d'état, Venezuela had a succession of democratically elected governments. In the early 1970s things got even better, when a dramatic increase in the international price of oil allowed the government to embark on vast social programs that resulted in important improvements in social conditions and a decline in inequality. Venezuelans lived in a kind of paradise, or so it seemed to thousands of middle-class Latin American professionals who left their countries of birth to try their luck in Caracas, Maracaibo, Valencia, and other Venezuelan cities.[8]

Abundance, however, can be a double-edged sword and can incubate the seeds of social discontent. In Venezuela this process had three elements: the elites' complacency toward the political system, corruption on a grand scale, and government-led protectionist and interventionist policies that in spite of the country's vast wealth and riches resulted in economic retrogression after 1980. Between 1980 and 1995 Venezuela's income per capita *declined* by 18 percent; during the same period income per person increased by 45 percent in Chile, 27 percent in Colombia, and 17 percent in Uruguay.[9] Venezuela's record during this period is particularly poor when one considers that the country "was barely touched by the 'Tequila Effect' that rippled through all of Latin America's economies as a result of Mexico's [1982] financial crisis."[10]

As the years passed without the military getting involved in politics, the Venezuelan elites became persuaded that their country was "exceptional." They were convinced that theirs was a country with superior political institutions, a satisfied electorate, and inclusive social policies. But while the elites were in a permanent self-congratulatory mode, the people became increasingly disillusioned. Few participated in the political process, and there was a general resentment toward the two traditional political parties, which had stifled political competition. In the late 1970s and early 1980s, as the price of oil increased again, there was mounting sentiment that the elites were becoming more and more corrupt. Political analyst Andrew Templeton has used polling data to document the evolution of public sentiment in Venezuela during the 1980s and 1990s. He shows that in early 1983 more than 60 percent of the population was already unhappy with the country's economic conditions.[11]

During the oil boom years the government embarked on a series of investment projects aimed at rapid industrialization. As it turned out, most of these projects were highly inefficient and did not contribute to growth. As a result of this strategy, in 1978 the public-sector deficit reached 14 percent of gross domestic product. By 1983 the foreign debt had grown significantly, and the trade deficit had widened to unsustainable levels. In February of that year, after significant losses of central bank international reserves, a major devaluation of the Bolivar was implemented. The public was shocked by the turn of events and sensed that corruption on a massive scale had taken place. According to a 1984 poll, 69 percent of the population believed that the country's growing external debt was due either to government mismanagement or, plainly, to corruption.[12]

Between 1984 and 1988, in spite of falling oil prices, the government of Jaime Lusinchi continued to run expansionary fiscal and monetary policies. In December of 1986 the Bolivar was devalued again, losing almost half of its value. In 1987 inflation increased to 42 percent, a figure not seen in Venezuela in generations.[13] Instead of stepping on the brakes and trying to restore balance to the economy, the government continued to increase public expenditures and to print money liberally. According to Harvard economist and former Venezuelan minister of planning Ricardo Hausmann, "To contain the accelerating inflation caused in part by its disregard for monetary discipline, the government fell into the well-known populist trap of price controls and froze prices for agriculture and the public sector . . . accentuating the public sector deficit, which reached 9.9 percent of GDP [gross domestic product] in 1988."[14]

In 1989, when Carlos Andrés Pérez was inaugurated as president, Venezuela was on the brink of collapse. The external debt was immense, the fiscal deficit was out of control, there were food shortages, and credit had all but disappeared. The new government decided to tackle these problems with the assistance of the IMF and a massive "shock program." At the center of the plan was a major devaluation that reduced the value of the Bolivar by two-thirds.[15] Supporting polices included a major fiscal adjustment, a substantial increase in gasoline and public transport prices, a reduction of import tariffs, and a large increase in interest rates to reflect the true cost of credit. The program was announced in general terms by the president himself in mid-February

1989. In the days that followed, members of his cabinet provided details of the agreement reached with the IMF.

On February 26 the minister of transportation informed the nation that the price of public transportation would be raised by 30 percent for the next ninety days; additional price increases, he added, would be announced after that period. The public reacted badly; in their view Pérez had been elected to save the country and return Venezuela to the good old days of his first presidency, from 1974 through 1979, and not to make the lives of the people more difficult. On the morning of February 27 demonstrations began in the poor suburbs of Caracas; as the day progressed, the demonstrations spread, and by the afternoon there were massive riots in the capital as well as in other important cities. Supermarkets were looted and businesses destroyed; buses were set on fire, and private citizens were attacked.[16]

The rioting and looting continued for five days. The authorities handled the situation with remarkable incompetence. It took hours to send policemen to those neighborhoods where violence was particularly intense, and when the police and the military arrived, they acted without any restraint. At the end of the fifth day of violence more than three hundred people had been killed.[17] The "Caracazo," as the uprising came to be known, was a turning point in Venezuela's modern history. The Pérez administration never recovered, and the next three years were characterized by attempts to explain what had happened. Surprisingly, President Pérez never acknowledged that the demonstrations and riots were a reaction to his economic policies. He spent the rest of his administration trying to survive politically and putting in place what Moisés Naím has called "modest reforms."[18]

In retrospect, one of the most important consequences of the Caracazo was that Hugo Chávez attempted a coup d'état in February 1992. Although he did not succeed, he became a household name, and large segments of the population, including those who were convinced that corruption was at the center of the country's misfortunes, considered him a hero.

In 1993 President Pérez was accused of corruption and removed from power by the Venezuelan congress. In February 1994 Rafael Caldera, who had been president between 1969 and 1974, was elected to a new term in office on an antireform and antiglobalization platform. The early years of his administration were characterized by rapid inflation, price controls, a plunging value of the Bolivar, foreign exchange controls, a massive banking crisis, and economic stagnation. In 1994 he freed Hugo Chávez from prison, and in 1996 he signed an agreement with the IMF; in exchange for $1.6 billion in financial assistance, he put in place an adjustment program aimed at reducing inflation and reigniting growth.

The Bolivarian Revolution and Its Disappointment

Many analysts and international observers greeted Hugo Chávez's election to the presidency in 1998 with great enthusiasm. The former paratrooper was a fresh face and had promised to eradicate corruption and tackle the country's pressing economic problems, including poverty and social inequality. The fact that merely six years earlier he had attempted a coup, showing little respect for democratic institutions, was brushed aside as a minor youthful peccadillo.

During the early months of his presidency, Hugo Chávez took major steps toward revolutionizing Venezuela's political and economic systems. Politically, his main objective was to put an end to the influence of the traditional parties that had signed the Punto Fijo Pact in 1958 and to move the country toward a more egalitarian society. A constitutional assembly was elected in July 1999—Chávez's supporters got 95 percent of seats—and a new constitution was adopted in December of that year.

The new constitution changed the official name of the country to the "Bolivarian Republic of Venezuela," replaced the bicameral congress with a unicameral national assembly, greatly increased the power of the executive branch, and assured free quality health care to all citizens. It also introduced major changes to the judiciary, giving the executive great influence in the appointment of judges.

From early on, Chávez's economic policy had three goals: to nationalize key strategic companies, to accelerate the rate of economic growth, and to revolutionize the provision of social services.

In 1999 he abolished the Ministry of the Family and centralized social assistance through the Fondo Único Social, a new institution run by the military that disbursed billions of dollars in oil monies. In 2002, after a failed coup attempt that removed Chávez from power briefly—he was detained for two days—he launched a series of new social programs called "missions," or, in Spanish, *misiones*. The first was the Misión Barrio Adentro, whose objective was to provide medical services to the poor in their own neighborhoods.

Most doctors were Cuban and came to the country as part of a mutual assistance program signed between Venezuela and the Caribbean island. The Misión Barrio Adentro was massive and controversial; more than thirteen thousand Cuban health professionals participated, and more than eight million people received preventive medical care. The government has claimed that the program has been a great success, claiming that a number of clinics and hospitals have been built and poor people's health has improved substantially; the opposition, on the other hand, has argued that the program has been pure propaganda and a failure and that public health indicators have worsened, including infant mortality rates and incidence of infectious diseases.[19]

Literacy campaigns were implemented through the Misión Robinson, and a program aimed at improving primary education coverage and quality was organized around the Misión Robison II. The Misión Ribas dealt with high school students and dropouts, and the Misión Sucre focused on higher education. These missions spent billions of dollars that came directly from the state oil giant PDVSA and were channeled outside normal budgetary conducts.[20] The Misión Mercal was aimed at providing affordable food to the poor by creating a number of markets in shantytowns and poor neighborhoods. As I elaborate in the pages that follow, a number of observers and analysts have criticized these programs for being ineffective—illiteracy, for example, barely declined during the Chávez presidency—and fraught with corruption.[21]

Political scientist Michael Penfold-Becerra analyzed whether there was a connection between the expenditure patterns of the Bolivarian missions and political support for Chávez and his regime. He found that while the health-oriented Misión Barrio Adentro was not guided by political considerations, the other programs had a political "carrot and stick" element. That is, expenditures were used to reward Chávez's supporters and punish his opponents. Penfold-Becerra argues that the massive expenditures channeled through these programs helped Chávez defeat a recall referendum that would have ousted him in 2004. The use of social programs for political purposes—what political theorists call "clientelism"—has traditionally been considered a favorite tool of populist politicians.[22]

Chávez's rhetoric and economic policy became more radicalized in 2002 after a failed coup d'état against the Bolivarian president was linked to the U.S. government. The White House denied any involvement, but its endorsement of the interim government led by businessman Pedro Carmona damaged its relations with Chávez beyond repair.[23] One of the consequences of Chávez's radicalization was the dismissal of seventeen thousand employees from the state-owned oil giant PDVSA. This gave the president direct control over oil revenues. However, the removal of engineers and other technical staff resulted in a major decline in Venezuela's oil production. According to independent estimates, Venezuela's daily output at the time of this writing is approximately 2.5 million barrels, significantly below its OPEC quota of 3.3 million barrels a day.[24]

A three-month national strike called by the opposition and the business sector between December 2002 and February 2003 also hardened Chávez's policies. After 2002 public expenditures increased drastically, and money creation by the central bank became more liberal. As a result, inflation shot up—in 2008 official inflation exceeded 30 percent—prices were controlled, and there were shortages of many basic products.

Professor Chang-Tai Hsieh of the University of California, Berkeley, and his colleagues Edward Miguel, Daniel Ortega, and Francisco Rodríguez used a data set with information on the political preferences and opinions of more than 10 million Venezuelan voters to investigate whether their political views influenced their economic well-being.[25] They found that voters who supported the Chávez recall in 2004 experienced a statistically significant decline in personal income (4 percent) after the referendum. They also found that Chávez supporters were more likely to get public-sector jobs following the referendum, while opponents would more likely move to the private sector. According to Hsieh and his colleagues, "Pro-opposition firms (those whose owners signed the petitions calling for Chávez to be ousted) have shrinking profits, less access to foreign exchange (50% less), and pay significantly higher taxes (27% higher) than other firms post-2003. Local media reports indicate that selective tax audits of opposition firms is a leading explanation for the tax result."[26] Professor Hsieh and his associates also investigated whether political tension affected the country's overall performance and economic growth. Their analysis suggests that political volatility and infighting in Venezuela has resulted in a decline in the country's gross domestic product of approximately 6 percent. This is a large number, indeed much larger than what other authors, including Harvard's Alberto Alesina, have found for other nations experiencing political turmoil.[27]

Chávez and Social Conditions

After twelve years of Chávez's presidency there is a sense among international observers that, although the former paratrooper is a colorful and sometimes abrupt man, he has delivered on his promises to improve Venezuela's economic performance and to help the poor and the destitute attain a better standard of living. In fact, however, this does not seem to be the case: growth has been mediocre at best, and his social programs have been ineffective. A revealing statistic is that during Chávez's tenure the proportion of the budget devoted to social programs—health, education, and housing—has not increased: it is still about 25 percent of total expenditures.[28]

When Chávez's tenure as president is considered as a whole, the average rate of growth is far from impressive: between 1999 and 2007 Venezuela's gross domestic product grew on average at 3.5 percent per annum; this is almost identical to Latin America as a whole; however, it is lower than the rate of growth attained by Chile (3.8 percent), Costa Rica (4.6 percent), and Peru (5.0 percent) among others. What makes Venezuela's performance particularly meager is that during this period its export prices experienced a remarkable increase. Between 1999 and 2008 Venezuela's terms of trade—defined as the ratio of export to import prices—improved by more than 100 percent. To put this in perspective, consider that during the same period Latin America as a whole experienced a terms-of-trade improvement of merely 18 percent. Although the price of oil started increasing during Chávez's first year in office, a significant expansion of the economy was not seen until 2004.

In a series of articles I used large data sets and advanced statistical techniques to analyze the dynamics of economic growth in the emerging economies. This work focuses on the way in which severe shocks affect the deviation of economic growth from its long-term trend. My research indicates that a 10 percent improvement in terms of trade translates to approximately 1 percent acceleration in the rate of economic growth above its long-term trend.[29] This means that all of Venezuela's growth during the Chávez administration may be attributed to higher oil prices. Indeed, the data suggest that if it weren't for the oil boom, Venezuela would have experienced a negative rate of growth in income per capita during the years of the Bolivarian revolution.

Some have argued that there is a trade-off between encouraging economic growth and pursuing greater equality. According to this view, countries that want to improve social conditions for the poor and reduce inequality will grow more slowly than countries whose economic policies focus exclusively on growth and ignore social goals. It is possible, then, that Venezuela's mediocre record of growth could be justified by great improvements in the well-being of the poor. Unfortunately, there is little evidence that conditions for the poor have improved greatly. In an article published in *Foreign Affairs*, economist Francisco Rodríguez has argued that Chávez's social policies record is mediocre—indeed, that it is arguably worse than the country's economic growth record. Rodríguez's article is noteworthy because he has not been particularly enthusiastic about the Washington Consensus; quite the contrary, for years he was an articulate critic of globalization.[30] Using official statistics Rodríguez concluded: "Most health and human development indicators have shown no significant improvement beyond that which is normal in the midst of an oil boom. Indeed, some have deteriorated worryingly, and official estimates indicate that income inequality has increased. The 'Chávez is good for the poor' hypothesis is inconsistent with the facts."[31]

Rodríguez acknowledges—as other Chávez critics do—that the incidence of poverty has declined from almost 50 percent of the population in 2003 to 29 percent in 2007. However, he argues that this decline in poverty is lower than one should expect given the spectacular increase in the international price of oil. When one looks at detailed data, Rodríguez says, the results are deeply disappointing. Specifically, according to official statistics, during the Chávez administration the percentage of underweight babies has increased, as has the percentage of households without potable water and the number of families who live in houses with earthen floors. Although infant mortality has declined, it has done so at a slower pace than in other Latin American countries such as Argentina, Chile, and Mexico. And in spite of Chávez's claims, it is not true that illiteracy has disappeared in Venezuela. A study by Professor Rodríguez and his colleague Daniel Ortega using official data indicates that the number of illiterate Venezuelans only declined from 1.1 million in 2003 to just over 1 million in 2006.[32]

Rodríguez's criticisms of Venezuela's social policies sent shockwaves among progressive politicians and defenders of Chávez and his Bolivarian revolution. Responses were rapidly drafted and published, and a vociferous debate took place on the Internet.[33] An important issue in this debate is which type of government expenditures constitutes true social expenditures. Are pensions—

most of which accrue to the middle class—true social spending? Professor Rodríguez believes that they are not; pensions are not earned by those who toiled for years in the informal sector, and those are, precisely, the disadvantaged and the poor. He also argues that oil giant PDVSA's transfers to the Ministry of Defense and Ministry of Finance for debt reduction should not be counted as social spending. The debate has also addressed other work by Rodríguez. Economists David Rosnick and Mark Weisbrot, for example, have argued that the analysis by Rodríguez and Ortega of the ineffectiveness of the large literacy program (Misión Robinsón) under president Chávez lacks statistical validity and reaches the wrong conclusions.[34]

At the center of these discussions are three of the most important issues that have often come into play in controversies in the social sciences. The first one has to do with data availability and data quality. How good are the data, and can they be trusted? How do we know that they have not been manipulated or doctored by the authorities? (This issue became very pertinent in Latin America in 2008, after the Argentine and Venezuelan governments manipulated the data on inflation.) The second issue has to do with the role of independent scholars or experts who evaluate evidence related to controversial issues. The question here is, who evaluates the data and who interprets the effects that some controversial policies have on economic well being? And the third and most difficult issue has to do with what social scientists call "the counterfactual"—that is, evaluating the outcome of certain policies or government interventions not with respect to the particular country's past but relative to what would have happened in the absence of those policies or if those policies had been undertaken by a different government (which is even more difficult to determine). In the case of Venezuela the relevant way of evaluating the evolution of social conditions during the Chávez presidency is not relative to Venezuela's history but relative to what would have happened if a different type of government with a different perspective on policy had been in office.

Most experts seem to agree that the quality of Venezuela's data on poverty, income distribution, and other social indicators are acceptable, especially when compared to that of other countries of a similar level of economic development. Analysis of the poverty data shows that in recent years the incidence of poverty in Venezuela has declined significantly, from almost 50 percent of the population in 2002 to 29 percent in 2007. An interesting question is how this accomplishment compares with those of other countries. According to

UN data only Bolivia, Brazil, Honduras, and Paraguay managed to reduce poverty incidence as fast as or faster than Venezuela during this period.[35] If one considers a broader set of social policy objectives, such as the Millennium Goals—which include poverty reduction, employment provision, and hunger alleviation—Venezuela's achievements do not look very different from those of the rest of the region during the same period.[36]

Interestingly, the data suggest that the reduction of Venezuela's poverty incidence has been largely the result of the bonanza induced by the oil boom and not of the redistributive policies undertaken by the Chávez government after 2002. According to calculations made by the UN Economic Commission on Latin America, redistribution policies were more effective in Bolivia, Brazil, Chile, Costa Rica, El Salvador, Panama, and Paraguay than in Venezuela; in all of those countries redistribution policies account for more than half of the reduction in poverty in the 2002–7 period.[37]

UN data suggest that between 2002 and 2006 income inequality declined in Venezuela by more than any other country in the region. This reduction in income disparity had two fundamental sources: higher wages for blue-collar workers and, more important, an increase in the number of people employed. At first glance, it would appear that these data are quite clear and unequivocal and that they do show that, at least on the inequality front, there has been significant progress during the Chávez years. But these results are also controversial, as alternative data on income disparities give a different picture. Francisco Rodríguez's reply to the critics of his *Foreign Affairs* article is indicative: "The World Bank, using the same base data as the [Venezuelan government's] National Institute, found that the share of income received by the poorest quintile declined from 4.1 percent to 3.7 percent between 1998 and 2005—a period for which the National Institute reported that it increased from 4.1 percent to 4.6 percent."[38]

Controversies over evaluation of the results of economic policies are not new. In 1963 Albert O. Hirschman argued that one of the most important roles of foreign advisors in the formulation of policy is to act as umpires. They can provide an uninterested outsider's view on the different options being considered in the country in question and can help politicians decide which of them is correct and which is suspect.[39] Foreign experts play a similar role in evaluating the effect of policies undertaken in the past: they are able to evaluate the historical record without the biases and passion that usually come with evaluations undertaken by interested parties. Interestingly, however, at the time of this writing multilateral institutions such as the World Bank, the IMF, and the Inter-American Development Bank have undertaken no broad evaluations of Chávez's social programs. A detailed search of these institutions' publications results in hundreds of titles on Venezuela. But not one of them provides an in-depth, technical, data-rich, comprehensive evaluation of social programs in Venezuela during the Chávez presidency. It is not clear whether this is a coincidence or the result of pressure by the Chávez administration on the multilaterals, but what is obvious is that work on the subject by these organizations would help move the debate forward.[40]

What about the "counterfactual"? How would things have looked if a different set of policies had been in place? Although a detailed counterfactual analysis is still to be done, existing research casts doubts on the premise that the Bolivarian regime has been successful and positive for the lower-income people of Venezuela. First, there is evidence that most of the acceleration in economic growth in Venezuela after 2002 was the result of the acute increase in oil prices. Second, as the UN has indicated, the reduction in poverty incidence during this period was mostly the result of growth induced by higher oil prices; it was not the result of redistributive policies. Third, public-sector expenditures on core social areas have not increased. Fourth, there are contradictory data on the evolution of income distribution, and the evidence suggests that whatever improvement did take place was mostly the result of higher employment generated by the oil boom and not the result of the Bolivarian policies. And fifth, there are some doubts about the effectiveness of both the health and educational misiones, especially if their effects are compared with the trends observed in other countries during the same period. When considering these factors it is difficult to avoid the conclusion that the most important element behind the improvement in social indicators and the surge in growth is the oil boom of the last few years.

What makes Venezuela's story particularly troubling is that when the price of oil declines significantly—and by early 2009 it already dropped by two-thirds relative to the peak achieved in July 2008, with the result that the government has had to scramble to adjust its budget—economic activity is very likely to crumble, greatly affecting the poor and those who are unable to migrate to Miami or to protect their savings from inflation by moving their money to the Cayman Islands or other tax havens. Worse yet, this disturbing scenario may even present itself if oil prices remain high; indeed, the deterioration of Venezuela's productive capacity is every day more apparent. We should not be completely surprised, however. After all, this has been the story of repeated populist regimes throughout history. What is different under the Bolivarian regime is that luck has been on the side of Chávez. But luck and good fortune—and as poet Joseph Brodsky has said, even sorrow—have a limit.

The Surprising Absence of Populism in Brazil

In 2002, after three attempts, Luiz Inácio Lula da Silva became president of Brazil. A former union leader who had lost a finger in an industrial accident, Lula was the quintessential leftist politician. The period leading to his election was fraught with uncertainty and instability, as analysts from around the world predicted that a new era of runaway inflation, government intervention, and nationalization of industry would take over Brazil. In late 2002, as the second round of the elections approached, Brazil's currency lost 30 percent of its value, and the country's cost of borrowing in international financial markets increased to historical records. Investors and analysts feared that if Lula were elected there would be a repeat of the Argentinean crisis of a few months earlier. Interestingly, there was no concern in the media, or among U.S. officials for that matter, that Lula would become another Hugo Chávez, suggesting that at the time, the Venezuelan president had not yet achieved the reputation of an enfant terrible and a fierce critic of markets and globalization.

The perception that Lula's government would rely on short-term populist policies was not completely farfetched. His political party, the Partido dos Trabalhadores (PT), had long had a platform based on land redistribution, strong government regulation, expansive fiscal policies, and the nationalization of privately owned companies.[41] Brazil also had a long tradition of leaders who, on the basis of progressive, nationalistic, and redistributive rhetoric, had implemented populist policies that, after a brief period of rapid growth, had resulted in inflation, stagnation, and a succession of crises. President Lula, however, surprised pundits and experts of all stripes by strictly avoiding the populist temptation. During his tenure Brazil has shown strict respect for property rights and as a result has attracted large volumes of direct foreign investment. In 2008, for example, net direct foreign investment in Brazil was

US$38 billion, representing more that one-third of the amount of foreign investment received by Latin America as a whole.

In the 1930s Getulio Vargas, who was president for nineteen years between 1930 and 1954 (he was out of office briefly from 1946 to 1949), used a combination of regionalist, nationalist, and egalitarian arguments to launch an economic program aimed at accelerating growth on the basis of fiscal imbalances and higher inflation. In the early 1930s Brazil was hit particularly hard by the Great Depression, as the international price of coffee collapsed. In 1933 Vargas responded by creating the Brazilian Coffee Institute, a government body that purchased large amounts of coffee from private producers in order to sustain the domestic price. These purchases were mostly financed through monetary expansion that fueled inflation. Of course, this measure did not by itself represent a move to populism; it did, however, set the tone for the type of economic policy that would prevail during the next five decades. Throughout this period the government became increasingly involved in production decisions at every level, and the inflationary financing of public-sector activity became the norm rather than the exception.[42]

Vargas argued that in order to develop and become a world economic power, Brazil needed a strong state that was actively involved in every sphere of economic life—the so-called Estado Nôvo, or New State. This view was incorporated into the constitution of 1937, which allowed for the nationalization of basic industries, natural resources, and the banking system. For Vargas and his successors, issues related to regional inequalities—both economic and political—were of paramount importance. In particular, there was a strong rejection of the implicit power-sharing agreement forged by the leaders of the states of São Paulo and Minas Gerais that had been in place since the inception of the republic in 1889. During the Vargas administrations the industrial sector was developed behind the protective walls of high import tariffs and strict import controls. In little less than a decade Brazil's export-led growth was replaced by a development program based on import substitution and protected industrialization. According to historian Edwin Williamson, "the rapid industrialization favored by nationalists required high levels of investment, which the state could finance only with foreign capital—of which the nationalists intensively disapproved—or by printing money, which caused even higher inflation."[43]

Vargas's successors to the presidency pushed on with the plan to achieve rapid industrialization and status as a developed country. Juscelino Kubitschek, elected president in 1956, promised "fifty years of development in five."[44] In the attempt to attain this goal shortcuts were taken, additional protectionist measures were implemented on top of the already existing high import barriers, exports were further discouraged, government regulations were stiffened, and inflationary pressures were increased. Although the country posted impressive rates of growth, poverty continued to be rampant, especially in the northeast, and the degree of income inequality continued to be among the highest in the world.

In 1964 the armed forces staged a coup and deposed President João Goulart, whose politics had veered too much to the left, and who had forged a tight diplomatic relationship with the Soviet Union. In spite of its clear anticommunist stance—characterized by systematic violation of human rights and persecution and torture of dissidents—the military continued to pursue a government-led, inflation-financed import substitution economic policy. Regulations were tightened further and competition was suppressed. Monopolies, both governmental and private, had a free hand, and the economic plan overruled the market in most investment decisions. Throughout the military dictatorship under five different strongmen, economic policies that accelerated growth in the short run were implemented—leading to what was known as the "Brazilian Miracle"—without concern for long-run sustainability or inflationary impact.

As time passed, the industrial sector, which was supposed to have matured and become competitive internationally, continued to require protective tariffs to survive. Without domestic or international competition, most companies failed to innovate or become more productive.[45] Worse yet, inflation moved to higher and higher plateaus. For some time it was thought that indexation—a mechanism used to periodically adjust prices and wages according to past inflation—would help Brazil live with rapidly rising prices. This was, however, an illusion. As inflation increased, all indexation did was validate price pressures, moving the country to higher and higher inflationary levels. First it was 40 percent per year, then it was 100 percent, then 200 and 400 percent per annum, until in 1990 inflation was almost 3,000 percent per year; the country was rapidly moving toward hyperinflation and self-destruction. In 1985, with the economy devastated by the debt crisis, Brazil returned to democracy. During the late 1980s and early 1990s there was a clear sense of frustration and circularity as the nation moved from higher inflation to crises to failed stabilization programs to even higher inflation.

In the 1989 presidential elections, Fernando Collor de Mello, a former state governor, defeated an up-and-coming young trade union leader nicknamed Lula and was elected president. Collor de Mello was the closest thing to a right-wing populist that Brazil had ever had. He despised political parties, and in his speeches he attacked bureaucrats, politicians, and both private and public-sector monopolies, all of whom in his view were responsible for the country's ills, including its high degree of poverty and income disparities. One day before the election the *New York Times* wrote: "Mr. Collor's deep appeal to the poor is attributed to his vigorous campaign against corruption. Last year, he captured the nation's fancy by uprooting 'marajahs,' or overpaid, corrupt government officials, from state bureaucracies."[46]

Collor de Mello's economic program had three fundamental elements: a "shock policy" to bring down inflation, the privatization of a number of state-owned enterprises, and the modernization of the state. In 1989 inflation was 1,400 percent, and in 1990, when Collor took over the presidency, it accelerated to the remarkable level of 2,900 percent per year. His anti-inflation plan was based on a rapid and draconian reduction in bank liquidity through forced conversion of short-term deposits into longer-term ones and a freeze on prices and wages. The plan had a rapid effect, and by 1991 inflation had declined to 430 percent. The government, however, was unable to control the fiscal deficit, and in 1992 inflation once again increased, reaching 950 percent for the year. In 1993 things were even worse, as the annual rate of price increases climbed to 2,000 percent.[47] But Collor de Mello's privatization program was successful and had a lasting impact: for the first time since the creation of the Estado Nôvo by President Vargas in the 1930s, the notion that state-owned enterprises were required for development was challenged. A number of large public companies were put on the block, opening the window to the emergence of a handful of very successful Brazilian multinationals in the twenty-first century, including jet manufacturer Embraer and mining giant CVRD, now known as Vale.

In May 1991 Collor was accused by his own brother of corruption. The core of the accusation involved illegal deals made by one of his aides and former campaign manager, Paulo César Farias. It was alleged that Farias bilked businessmen and collected enormous bribes, which he shared with President Collor.[48] In September 1992 Collor was impeached and found guilty of corruption by the Brazilian congress, and Vice President Itamar Franco took over for the rest of the presidential term. In 1994 a new plan aimed at reducing inflation—the Real Plan—was put in place by Finance Minister Fernando Henrique Cardoso, a progressive intellectual who in the 1960s had written extensively on the relationship between poor and rich countries.[49] The plan had four components: the introduction of a new currency, the real; the elimination of indexation, which had contributed to the creation of an inflationary vicious circle; the reduction of the fiscal deficit through the imposition of a tax on financial transactions; and the pegging of the currency to the U.S. dollar. Like other anti-inflation programs the Real Plan was successful initially: in 1994 inflation was down to 64 percent, a modest level for Brazil at that time.

In 1994, largely thanks to the success of the Real Plan, Cardoso was elected president. During his eight years in office Cardoso did not draw from his academic writings, nor did he close up the economy in order to minimize the relationship between Brazil and the rich nations; instead, he relied on his experience as finance minister and implemented policies aimed at moving Brazil toward economic stability and growth.[50]

As early as 1996 MIT economist Rudi Dornbusch expressed his doubts about the Real Plan. His main concern was that, as had been the case in so many countries throughout Latin America—Argentina, Chile in the early 1980s, Colombia, and Mexico among others—the currency would become artificially strong and would eventually collapse. He wrote, "Brazil has a tradition of disregarding foreign experiences and more so foreign advice. . . . The strategy [of pegging the value of the currency] is being followed once again."[51]

Dornbusch was right. As in other Latin American nations this policy resulted in currency overvaluation, encouraged speculation, reduced exports' competitiveness, and generated a bloated trade deficit. In January 1999, Brazil faced a serious crisis that resulted in the loss of 20 percent of its currency's value. In the aftermath of this crisis, with a remarkable sense of pragmatism President Cardoso appointed former hedge fund manager Arminio Fraga to preside over the central bank and asked him to lead the country into stability and recovery. Fraga, who had been trained at Princeton and had worked with financier George Soros, allowed the currency to float freely and to respond to market forces. He also implemented a modern monetary program based on targeting a declining rate of inflation. With the assistance of the IMF a realistic fiscal plan aimed at keeping the nation's public-sector debt below a certain threshold was put in place. During 2001 and 2002, the last two years of the Cardoso administration, inflation averaged 10 percent per year; growth, on the other hand, averaged a modest but still positive 2 percent per annum. Fernando Henrique Cardoso, the former professor, the intellectual who had popularized dependency theory in Western universities, the man who had been critical of capitalism and multinational corporations in the 1960s and 1970s, pulled it off. He avoided a new meltdown of the Brazilian economy, stabilized the currency, and prepared the basis for what could be an economic take off.

In the 2002 presidential elections the establishment candidate was José Serra, a studious economist who had worked closely with President Cardoso in many capacities and had spent most of the 1960s in exile in Chile. Serra was seen by international analysts as the candidate of continuity and as an assurance that the Cardoso reforms would move forward. Lula, on the other hand, was seen as somewhat of a radical, whose policies would endanger the economic progress made during the Cardoso administration. After a hard-fought runoff election, in October 2002 Lula was elected president of Brazil with almost 60 percent of the votes.

Stability and Social Programs in Lula's Brazil

From early on, to the surprise of doomsayers Lula proved to be a pragmatic president who understood clearly the challenges faced by Brazil in the early twenty-first century. There is little doubt that the control of inflation has been one of Lula's greatest achievements. He understood early on that inflation is a tax that affects the poor in a disproportional way. It is a tax that falls mostly on those who cannot move their savings abroad. Worse yet, in an inflationary environment it is very difficult for consumer credit to develop, and the poor are forced to live in a strictly cash economy. Without credit small businesses cannot develop and prosper, and employment suffers accordingly. And in the absence of credit the middle classes and the poor have limited access to housing—mortgages are among the first victims of inflation—and durable goods such as refrigerators and cars are beyond their reach.

Under most circumstances, reducing inflation is a difficult and protracted process that requires maintaining high interest rates for a prolonged period of time and running an austere fiscal policy. Successful anti-inflationary programs involve patience and resolve. It is precisely for this reason that populist leaders, with their characteristic short-termism and propensity for taking shortcuts, have never been able to control inflation; on the contrary, accelerating inflation has been one of the hallmarks of populism.

In spite of criticism from his own supporters who wanted to favor income distribution over price stability and growth, Lula persevered, and eventually price increases began to abate. The control of inflation was supported by an austere fiscal policy that generated sizable surpluses in the primary fiscal accounts.[52] In addition, after 2003 Brazil reduced its foreign debt significantly, and the government was able to borrow at longer maturities and lower costs. During this period the authorities accumulated a very large volume of international reserves in the central bank as a precaution for an uncertain future.

With inflation under control and reduced overall economic instability, consumer credit soared, and for the first time in a generation the lower middle class and the poor had widespread access to white goods, vacations and automobiles and, perhaps more important, could obtain mortgages and become homeowners.[53] Not surprisingly, these developments were extremely well received by the public and resulted in a very high approval rate for Lula, who in 2006 was easily reelected to a second term in office.

The central theme of Lula's social policy has been the eradication of hunger. In order to accomplish this his government implemented a number of programs known as *bolsas*, which provide cash transfers to poor families. The precursor was a very successful program developed in the state of Brasilia during the late 1990s called the Bolsa Escola. The system was built on very simple premises: Families with an income level below the national poverty line were eligible to participate. In order to receive the transfer all children in the family had to be enrolled in school and could not miss more than two days of classes per month. Very quickly after being implemented this conditional cash transfer program became a model emulated around the world; at the Dakar meeting on Education for All in 2000, UN Secretary General Kofi Annan referred to it with great enthusiasm and urged other countries to follow Brazil's example. During the Cardoso administration the program was extended to the federal level, and the resources devoted to it were greatly increased.

In 2001 the Cardoso government launched a highly innovative program aimed at providing food to poor children and pregnant and breastfeeding mothers, the Bolsa Alimentação. Preliminary evaluations of these two programs by independent research institutions suggest that they have been successful: the intended target groups have been reached, the condition of their lives has improved, school attendance has increased, and food intake by poor children has gone up substantially. Further analysis, however, is needed in order to gain additional insights on the programs' strengths and limitations and their applicability in other parts of the world.[54]

In 2003 the Lula administration combined a series of programs including Bolsa Escola and Bolsa Alimentação to form the Bolsa Família, its most important antipoverty program, and the largest conditional cash program in the world. Some of the Bolsa Família's most innovative aspects are that the transfers are usually given to mothers (or adult females in the family) and that the cash is provided through electronic debit cards. According to the World Bank, in 2007 the program reached 11 million people. In a recent study the World Bank stated:

> The virtue of the *Bolsa Família* is that it reaches a significant portion of Brazilian society that has never benefited from social programs. It is among the world's best targeted programs, because it reaches those who really need it. Ninety-four percent of the funds reach the poorest 40 percent of the population. Studies prove that most of the money is used to buy food, school supplies, and clothes for the children. . . . (...) Although inequality is still very high, the *Bolsa Família* seems to be helping Brazil progress.[55]

The program is still being formally evaluated, and it is too early to know precisely and in detail its overall impact and cost-effectiveness. What is clear, however, is that Bolsa Família is very popular with the people. Indeed, many analysts credit it for Lula's very high approval rating and his easy reelection to the presidency in 2006. And partially as a result of Bolsa Família's popularity and perceived effectiveness a large number of countries in the region have begun to increasingly rely on conditional cash transfer programs to address poverty and destitution. Some of the better-known ones are Mexico's Progresa, Colombia's Familias en Acción, Honduras's Programa de Asignación Familiar, and Nicaragua's Red de Protección Social.

Lula's Pragmatism and Chávez's Ideology

What explains Lula's pragmatism and rejection of the populist temptation? Why, on the other hand, did Hugo Chávez embrace populist policies with such enthusiasm and gusto? What, in short, is behind the differences between Brazil and Venezuela? There are, I think, three interrelated factors behind the divergent paths followed by these two nations during the first decade of the twenty-first century: ideology, their recent history, and institutional differences.

I will first deal with ideology. Lula spent a lifetime in trade union circles and at a young age became familiar with the nuances of left-wing and particularly Marxist doctrines. His view of the world was guided by a coherent and sophisticated perspective. More important, Lula recognized very early that the fall of the Berlin Wall had changed the world, forcing left-wing parties—including his own Workers' Party—to alter their political visions, goals, and strategies. Chávez, in contrast, spent most of his life in the barracks. In 1998 he was a newcomer to politics, a self-taught politician who borrowed from different and often contradictory doctrines to form his own ideology. He combined the thinking of nationalistic historical figures such as Simón Bolívar with that of biblical ones—for him Jesus Christ was the first Socialist—as well as the ideas of modern intellectuals such as Noam Chomsky. The result was a messy blend of nationalism and anticapitalism that tended to ignore the teachings of history and the fact that many, perhaps most, of his policy proposals had been tried in the past—in Cuba, in Nicaragua, in the former Soviet Union, in Allende's Chile, and in other places—and had largely failed.

Lula developed a pragmatist and eclectic point of view that adapted quickly to new circumstances; throughout his presidency his goal has been to transform Brazil into a modern social democracy, not very different from those of western Europe. Moreover, during the late 1990s Lula became aware of the failures of rigid attempts at imposing socialism. He recognized that economic incentives matter, that inflation is always a deterrent to growth and prosperity, and that investment—including foreign investment—is crucial for generating productivity improvements and accelerating growth. He also understood that in order to be effective, social programs have to eschew excessive bureaucracy and waste and must be focused on those it expects to reach; these are precisely the main characteristics of his successful Bolsa Família. Chávez, on the other hand, has a nostalgic view of the world, a view in which Fidel Castro's Cuba serves as a role model. It is true that he also avoided using old and corrupt bureaucracies to deliver social services—indeed, he created the misiones—but he replaced them with new ones that operate on the basis of political favoritism. In spite of all his talk of socialism of the twenty-first century, Chávez's brand of socialism is stale and tired; if anything, it resembles the socialism of the mid-1960s.

Recent history also plays a role in explaining the differences between Venezuela and Brazil. The 1990s were a horrible decade in Venezuela. Growth was dismal, and the demonstrations, riots, looting, and killings of the 1989 Caracazo had a tremendous impact on people's minds. There was a generalized sense among voters that corruption was rampant and that the elite—including powerful businesses—had ransacked the country. In short, in 1998 Venezuela was ripe for major change, and Chávez offered appealing rhetoric that castigated the political class, the private sector, and foreigners. For Brazil, in contrast, the late 1990s and early 2000s were years of important achievements—not years of great successes, it is true, but years of solid accomplishments nonetheless. The most important of these was the reduction of inflation and the incipient movement toward openness and modernization initiated during Fernando Collor de Mello's presidency and intensified by his successors Itamar Franco and especially Fernando Henrique Cardoso. While in 1998 (when Chávez was elected) the mood in Venezuela was one of deep frustration, in 2002 (when Lula came to power) the atmosphere in Brazil was one of hope and expectation.

But neither ideology nor recent historical developments are the main causes behind the different paths followed by Brazil and Venezuela. The most important factor is the deep institutional differences between the two countries. While Brazilian institutions effectively constrain the executive from implementing irresponsible policies, Venezuelan institutions lack the required checks and balances to restrict such policies. In Venezuela, the lack of legal constraints on the executive became particularly clear after the new constitution of 1999 was approved. In analyzing the institutional differences between the two countries, it is useful to make a distinction between institutions that affect the policy-making process on one hand and political institutions on the other. Both Venezuela's policy-making institutions and its political institutions are much weaker than Brazil's.

From an institutional perspective, the policy-making process in Venezuela is one of the most inefficient in the world. In an effort to evaluate the quality of public policy institutions in a number of countries, Argentine economist Mariano Tommasi analyzed six characteristics of the policy-making process in seventy-seven nations. His analysis ranks Venezuela's institutions the seventh weakest. The same index indicates that Brazil's policy-making institutions are stronger—not stellar, but significantly stronger than Venezuela's. Brazil's institutions are ranked the thirty-third weakest among the same seventy-seven countries. According to this study, public policies in Brazil are more stable, coherent and better enforced than in Venezuela. They are also more likely to promote the general welfare, and to allocate scarce resources to those uses that have a higher payoff for the population at large. Furthermore, Brazil is more likely to change course if certain policies have obviously failed.[56] Data collected by the Fraser Institute confirm these findings and suggest that in Venezuela the degree of independence of the judiciary, the extent of law and order, and the degree of protection of property rights are lower than in Brazil.[57] Furthermore, Transparency International reports that in 1998 the degree of perceived corruption in Venezuela was substantially higher than in Brazil; in that year's ranking Venezuela was in seventy-seventh out of eighty-five nations (the lower the ranking the more corrupt the country), while Brazil was ranked forty-sixth; again, Brazil was not a very highly ranked country, but was ranked much higher than Venezuela.

As noted in chapter 8, in countries where there are no checks and balances or congressional oversight, public policies are weak. Moreover, if the judiciary is not independent, a strong leader is able to pursue extreme policies, even policies that border on illegality and are clearly detrimental to the general welfare of the population. This has been to a large extent the recent story of Venezuela, where Hugo Chávez has governed by decree during long stretches of his tenure. Mariano Tommasi has analyzed the characteristics of political institutions in seventeen Latin American countries.[58] He focused on the scope of political parties' vision, political parties' ability to forge national and long-term programs and platforms, the capacity of the legislative branch to pass legislation efficiently, the strength of the civil service, and the ability of the judiciary to enforce laws. In every one of these categories Brazilian institutions are stronger than those in Venezuela. All of this suggests that even in the absence of the ideological and historical factors discussed above, from a purely institutional point of view it would be more difficult for a populist leader in Brazil to implement the type of policies that Chávez has put in place in Venezuela.

Brazil's Challenges in the Post-Lula Era

In 2003 Goldman Sachs published its celebrated study "Dreaming with BRICs: The Path to 2050," in which, on the basis of a framework similar to the one used in this book, it forecast economic growth of the four largest and most promising emerging markets: Brazil, Russia, India, and China.[59] The results of this study were startling, suggesting that by 2040 Brazil, Russia, India, and China would collectively surpass the G-6 in gross domestic product. The authors forecast that of those four countries, Brazil would be the one with the slowest rate of growth over a thirty-year period, but it was still expected to have a healthy rate of economic expansion, almost 4 percent per year on average over the long run. The report, however, recognized that Brazil faced important challenges if it were to achieve high and sustainable growth; the study mentioned particularly the need for Brazil to increase its openness to international competition and to undertake further modernization and deregulation.

In the years following the BRICs report, analysts' enthusiasm for Brazil grew considerably. In early 2008 Standard and Poor's gave the country's national debt the coveted "investment grade" rating, and a number of people ventured that, finally, the South American giant was about to take off. Soon, they said, it would stop being the subject of the old joke "Brazil is, and always will be, the land of the future." At the center of these positive sentiments is the notion that, after a long history of false starts and a tendency to take shortcuts, Brazil is ready to do the hard work required for moving forward and achieving true international prominence as an economic power.

In spite of recent achievements—growth was 5.4 percent in 2007 and 5.5 percent in 2008 and averaged slightly better than 4 percent for 2005–8—a number of important questions remain. If Brazil is truly to become a world economic force and do as well as the Goldman Sachs study has forecast, it will have to face a number of challenges successfully. In particular, productivity growth will have to increase significantly and continue to grow at a rapid pace for a prolonged period of time; the rate of investment in capital, equipment, machinery, and infrastructure will have to increase from its current 22 percent of gross domestic product to around 30 percent, a figure closer to the historical average of the Asian Tigers; and the skills of its labor force will have to improve substantially.

Brazil appears to be entering phase one of the growth transition process outlined in chapter 1. The realization that it is possible to have a left-of-center government that does not take shortcuts and does not fall to populist temptations, coupled with an improvement in the country's export prices, has generated an acceleration in productivity growth. The challenge now is to move from this first stage to phases two and three of the growth process. What will make this transition particularly difficult is that it will have to happen at a time when there is great uncertainty in the world economy and it is not clear how long the repercussions of the global crash of 2008 will last.

A decisive move to the higher stages of the growth transition process will require that institutions be strengthened and policies streamlined in order to encourage competition and innovation. An analysis of the indicators computed and collected by a number of institutions and think tanks, including the Fraser Institute, the World Bank, and others, suggests that the task ahead is formidable and should not be underestimated. Consider the following results from the World Bank's 2009 Doing Business index: Brazil is ranked 125th out of 181 countries in ease of doing business; Chile in contrast is ranked 40th, and the Asian Tigers are ranked 36th on average. In dealing with licenses Brazil is ranked 108th, in ease of employing workers it is ranked 121st, and in ease of registering a property it is 111th. In fact, Brazil is ranked below the 100th position in seven of the eleven categories in the data set and is in the bottom half in all but two of them. For the average businessperson Brazil is a highly inefficient country: it takes 152 days to obtain the licenses and permits required to start a business, compared with 27 days in Chile and 35 days on average in the Asian Tigers. In Brazil it takes 616 days to enforce a rental contract; it takes 480 days in Chile and an average of 389 days in the Asian Tigers.

The list of inefficiencies goes on and on, covering almost every category analyzed, prospected, and investigated by experts in productivity, innovation, and entrepreneurship such as the World Economic Forum. In the 2008–9 Global Competitiveness Index Brazil is ranked 64th out of 134 countries; Chile is 28th, Thailand is 34th, Malaysia is 21st, and the Republic of Korea is 13th. In the same study China is ranked 30th, India 50th, and Russia 51st.[60]

In the key category of protecting investors the World Bank ranks Brazil 70th; this is not as high as Chile (38th) or the Asian Tigers (30th), but it is significantly better than Latin America's average ranking as a group (96th) and that of the emerging Asian nations (90th). Brazil also does relatively well in the voice and accountability category in the World Bank study on governance and institutions.[61] This is partially good news, suggesting that there are some foundations on which to begin an effort to strengthen institutions.

Other institutional indicators are weak, however, and show that the road to modernity will be long and difficult. In terms of rule of law, the World

Bank gives Brazil a relatively low grade ($-.44$ on a scale from -2.5 to 2.5), indeed significantly lower than Chile's (1.17) and the averages for the emerging Asia nations (-0.17), the Asian Tigers (0.64), the southern European nations (0.91), and the advanced commodity exporters (1.85). Brazil also receives poor grades—again lower than Chile, the Asian Tigers, southern Europe, and the advanced commodity exporters—for control of corruption, government effectiveness, and quality of regulations.

Data collected by the Fraser Institute on the quality of institutions confirm the results discussed above and illustrate the need to undertake a major institutional overhaul. On a scale of 1 to 10, in 2006 Brazil got a score of 3.6 in judiciary independence; compare this to Chile's 5.4 and the Asian Tigers' 6.4. Brazil's score for the legal enforcement of contracts is 4.8; Chile's score is 5.8, and the Asian Tigers' average is 7.0. For protection of intellectual property Brazil gets a score of 5.2, while Chile gets 7.0 and the Asian Tigers get 7.4.

In terms of trade openness, Brazil is also behind some of the comparison groups. In Brazil it costs on average US$1,240 to export a container (that is, to put it on board a ship). The corresponding figures is US$745 in Chile and US$626 on average in the Asian Tigers. According to the prestigious AT Kearney/*Foreign Policy* magazine Globalization Index, Brazil is ranked sixty-seventh out of seventy-two countries. The importance of this index is that it goes beyond measurement of trade openness and economic variables to measure countries' exposure to global forces, their degree of global connectivity, and the ease and efficiency with which they move in the current world economy. Among other variables, this index considers data on Internet users, Internet hosts, secure servers, and extent of technological networks.

Brazil has an enormous attractiveness that is unmatched in Latin America; it is a very large country: Gross domestic product was US$1.5 trillion in 2008, and its population had reached almost 190 million people. Figures related to the Brazilian economy are almost always large, including the numbers of computers, cars, refrigerators, life insurance policies, and cell phones sold per person or per year. These numbers are always much greater for Brazil than for other Latin American nations or most countries in other regions. Size definitely matters. But it is not all that matters. Being a large country is certainly not enough to truly take off and prosper. What is ultimately needed is an innovative economy in which productivity improvements are the norm rather than the exception, the quality of the educational system is high, and investors and entrepreneurs are willing to devote time and effort to achieve lasting results.

The data discussed above indicate that in spite of recent investors' enthusiasm, Brazil is still very far from being a country with efficient, pro-innovation policies and strong institutions. It is important to emphasize that the vast majority of indicators analyzed show a major gap between Brazil's current conditions and those of countries and regions that have been successful. When referring to what Brazil needs to do next, I am not talking about tinkering at the margins; the challenge is not improving this or that indicator or changing one or two laws or regulations. Brazil needs major changes to free the productive forces of its population. Only major reforms will allow the country to move to the higher phases of the growth transition process. Politically, these will be difficult to achieve but not impossible. Lula's accomplishments show that Brazilian politicians are able to deliver and to take a long-term view, and a handful of very efficient Brazilian global companies have demonstrated that, given the opportunity and the right incentives, Brazil's businesses can indeed be innovative and productive. Whether Brazil will make it this time around is still an open question. Indeed, it will take years before a final verdict is possible. Two things are clear, however: the challenges ahead are formidable, and Brazil has never been as well positioned to truly break away from its long history of frustrations than at this time.

Part IV

Challenges for the Future

Chapter 10
A Three-Speed Latin America for the Twenty-first Century

The global financial crash of 2008 contributed significantly to the appeal of populist politicians and populist ideas. In many ways this is understandable, as the collapse of the advanced countries' financial markets was correctly seen as the result of the excesses of an unregulated capitalist system in which greed became the norm and cutting corners the preferred way of getting rich rapidly. There is little doubt that the lack of regulation and a dogmatic belief in the unfaltering efficiency of markets was behind the succession of events that led to the meltdown of the international financial system.[1] Indeed, it is difficult to disagree with Paul Krugman's assessment that "American bankers, empowered by a quarter-century of deregulatory zeal, led the world in finding sophisticated ways of enriching themselves by hiding risk."[2] But these excesses in financial markets in the advanced nations—the creation of extremely complex and risky securities, the increase in leverage to unthinkable levels, and the lax lending standards, among others—have nothing to do with the core of a modern competition-based capitalist system that encourages innovation, efficiency, and creativity. Indeed, the idea of ditching all regulations and allowing a free-for-all in financial markets was never part of what Joseph Schumpeter had in mind when he wrote almost a century ago about competition, innovation, and "creative destruction."

In 2006 a myth of sorts began to emerge among Latin American analysts, observers, and politicians. The region, it was said, was finally taking off and moving toward prosperity and reduced poverty. A very significant increase in export prices—mostly prices of commodities such as oil, iron ore, copper, natural gas, and soybeans—and the plentiful availability of international financing were behind this optimistic prophecy. The price of oil, which in the early 2000s had been $30 a barrel, had climbed to almost $150 a barrel in mid-2008; the price of copper had gone from 85 cents per pound in 2003 to

$4 per pound in 2008; soybeans prices had jumped from $500 per metric ton in 2002 to over $1,600 dollars in early 2008; and the price of natural gas per thousand cubic feet went from $2 in 2000 to more than $13 in 2008. These improved export conditions were attributed to the unquenchable demand for raw material by the new economic wonders China and India.

In São Paulo, Buenos Aires, Mexico City, and Bogotá, analysts and gurus assured their Latin American audiences that the world had changed for good. The era of commodity producers had not only arrived but would continue into the future indefinitely. Analysts of various stripes talked with vehemence and conviction about Latin America's "decoupling" from the rest of the world. According to this view the Latin American nations had become immune to the international business cycle. It didn't matter what happened in the United States, the European Union, or Japan, Latin America would continue to enjoy the fruits of high commodity prices and to move toward prosperity. After all, they said, glancing at their fancy Power Point presentations, a virtuous cycle of "emerging markets to emerging markets" had developed: China and India bought commodities from Latin America, and Latin America bought manufactured goods and software from the Asian giants. Who needed the industrial world and globalization? Those who questioned this rosy scenario and insisted on the old-fashioned notion of "no pain, no gain" while pointing out that Latin America continued to be mired in bureaucracy and red tape were brushed aside and labeled as, well, old-fashioned. According to this optimistic vision, there was no need, then, to improve efficiency, become more competitive, improve the skills of the labor force, or reform the educational system so Latin American children would be as well prepared as those in Asia or the emerging nations of central and eastern Europe; there was no need to suffer the difficulties of strengthening institutions, reducing corruption, improving the impartiality and efficiency of courts, or deepening democracy. Finally, it was said, God had decided to favor Latin America.

The fact that Argentina and Venezuela, two countries at the forefront of the populist resurgence, were doing so well and growing so fast during the mid-2000s made many believe that the policies of Hugo Chávez and Néstor Kirchner were, after all, the key to future prosperity. Between 2004 and 2008 Argentina's gross domestic product grew at an average rate of 8.5 percent, while in Venezuela gross domestic product expanded at an average rate of 10.4 percent per annum.[3] On the basis of the Argentine experience some even argued that defaulting on foreign debt—as Argentina did in 2001—and imposing severe losses on international investors had no negative effects whatsoever. The idea that the global market punished those countries that did not stand by their obligations seemed to many to be old-fashioned and stale.

But the global financial crash of 2008 showed that the notion of a Latin American decoupling from the global economy was nothing more than an illusion. It was wishful thinking at its worst. The decline of commodity prices, the disappearing demand for the region's exports, and the drying up of financing showed that the gurus of optimism had not understood the lessons of history. Rather, these events showed that the majority of the Latin American nations remained as vulnerable to the vagaries of the international economy as they had always been. Reality came back forcefully and reminded perceptive analysts that the only way for a country to reduce poverty permanently and move toward prosperity is by educating the population, encouraging innovation, and having efficient mechanisms for resolving conflicts and strong institutions that protect property rights and deepen democracy. But not everyone is perceptive or wants to recognize the difficult lessons of history. Latin America is still replete with politicians, analysts, and academics who cling to the notion that it will be possible to take shortcuts.

It is not a coincidence that Argentina is one of the countries that, at the time of this writing, faces the bleakest prospects. Argentina has enormous financing requirements in the years to come—it needs to refinance an ever-growing public sector debt—and since the crisis of 2001–2 it has failed to promote meaningful policies aimed at modernizing its economy, encouraging innovation, improving the quality of its educational system, strengthening its institutions, or advancing efficiency. On the contrary, a succession of populist governments headed by Néstor Kirchner and his wife Cristina Fernandez de Kirchner took additional shortcuts, demonized foreign investors, and relied on extraordinarily positive export prices of oil, soybeans, and other commodities to finance an ever-growing and inefficient state. With virtually no new investments in machinery, equipment, and infrastructure and no improvements in its people's skills, Argentina's long-term prospects look bleak. The fact that in mid-2009 the Kirchners lost some support in midterm congressional elections is of little solace. The forces that gained power represent other factions of the Peronist Party that continue to be skeptical toward, if not strongly opposed to, major reforms.

But of course Argentina is not the only country facing a difficult future. Ecuador is particularly vulnerable to a prolonged period of global stagnation, as is Venezuela. If the price of oil does not recover, both of these nations will face major reductions in income and large fiscal imbalances. In Venezuela this would translate into rapid inflation, price controls, scarcity, black markets, and lower wages. In Ecuador the path to inflation is somewhat impeded by the fact that the country uses the U.S. dollar as its currency, and thus the government cannot use the central bank as a way of financing the deficit. There will be a serious temptation for the government of Rafael Correa to remove this constraint and reintroduce a domestic currency. If this occurs, the road to full-blown inflation and a populist crisis will be wide open.

It will take many years to recover from the global financial crisis of 2008. But eventually the world economy will rebound. In Latin America the country that will emerge fastest and with the least damage will be Chile; Peru is also likely to do relatively well. This is not a coincidence but a direct result of Chile's having transformed its economy into a relatively flexible one by streamlining business processes, emphasizing the role of exports and innovation, maintaining a healthy banking system that has avoided excesses and extravagances, and saving a large proportion of the monies from the copper boom of the mid-2000s as an emergency reserve. Polls conducted in March 2009, in the midst of the global recession and crisis, show that the Chilean public's support for the economic model based on markets, trade openness, innovation, and efficiently provided social services has gained in popularity. Whereas 55 percent of respondents stated in 2007 that the prevailing model was the best for the country, in March 2009 the approval rate for Chile's market-oriented and proglobalization economic policies had climbed to 63 percent of respondents.[4]

The Institutions of the State and the Narcotics Trade

Throughout this book I have emphasized the key role of institutions. Progress and prosperity require the rule of law, protection of property rights, low levels of corruption, an independent judiciary, and a strong democracy. I have documented the fact that in the vast majority of the Latin American countries very little if any progress has been made on the institutional front. But what is more troubling is that a number of nations face the risk of major institutional failure. This danger comes directly from production and distribution of illicit drugs.

In order to understand the nature of the narcotics challenge, it is useful to go back to the mid-1990s, when the United States changed its policy toward the supply of drugs coming from Latin America. In November 1993, President Bill Clinton signed the Presidential Decision Directive for Counternarcotics, "which instructed Federal agencies to shift the emphasis in U.S. international antidrug programs from the transit zones such as Mexico, Central America and the Caribbean to the source countries such as Colombia, Peru and Bolivia."[5] Since that time, most of the U.S. effort has focused on reducing Colombia's role as a producer and distribution center. This effort has been financed through Plan Colombia, an assistance program that provides funds to train Colombia's police and military in anti-insurgency and antidrug tactics. Most analysts acknowledge that, with an annual budget of approximately $650 million, the plan has been successful in reducing the power and reach of Colombian drug lords. That is the good news. The bad news, however, is that a decade after the launching of this plan, narcotics production and trafficking in Latin America has not declined. In fact, it has increased. What the efforts to eradicate drugs from Colombia have accomplished is to move the industry closer to the United States, where the bulk of the demand for illicit drugs is located. Mexico—and in particular the states of Chihuahua and Sinaloa—has become the illicit drug capital of the world.

The proliferation of drug operations in Mexico has resulted in massive violence and, in some states, thousands of deaths. It is estimated that in 2008 alone, more that six thousand people died as a result of drug violence in the state of Chihuahua. Most of the violence was concentrated in Ciudad Juárez, a sprawling border city just south of El Paso, Texas. In late 2008, Ciudad Juárez's chief of police declared an all-out war on traffickers. Far from being intimidated, the cartels accepted the challenge and went on a violent rampage. Kidnappings and assassinations increased, and there was no visible decline in drug-related activities. Then the drug mafia demanded the ouster of the Ciudad Juárez police chief. Since the mayor refused to fire him, the cartel threatened to kill one policeman every forty-eight hours. After a number of murders of law enforcement officers the authorities got the message, and on February 20, 2009, the chief of police tendered his resignation. The mayor reluctantly accepted it.[6]

In February 2009 the U.S. Justice Department made the shocking announcement that the Sinaloa drug cartel had expanded its direct operations into the United States. The cartel had hundreds of operatives in almost every

U.S. metropolitan area, peddling drugs, collecting money from street-level distributors, keeping the books, kidnapping members of competing gangs, and assassinating turncoats and informers. During a twenty-one-month period law enforcement authorities in different parts of the United States arrested 730 individuals connected to the Sinaloa cartel.[7]

Mexico's attorney general Eduardo Medina Mora estimates that in 2008 his country's drug cartels received more than $10 billion from U.S. consumers. According to his figures, approximately half of the cartels' revenues come from marijuana, while the other half derive from harder drugs including cocaine, heroin, and amphetamines.[8]

The situation has become so dire throughout Mexico that in late February 2009 Admiral Dennis C. Blair, the U.S. director of national intelligence, testified before Congress that "the corruptive influence and increasing violence of the cartels had undermined the Mexican government's ability to govern parts of its country."[9] According to U.S. attorney general Eric Holder, the Sinaloa mafia has transported tons of marijuana, methamphetamine, and cocaine into the United States and has laundered tens of millions of dollars of ill-gotten monies. And according to the Phoenix police, the Sinaloa cartel was responsible for almost four hundred kidnappings for ransom in that Arizona city during 2008. Most of them were drug-related, and several involved U.S. citizens.[10]

In February 2009 a group of Latin American intellectuals and opinion leaders chaired by three former presidents—Fernando Henrique Cardoso from Brazil, César Gaviria from Colombia, and Ernesto Zedillo from Mexico—and composed of a number of luminaries including historian Enrique Krauze, magazine editor Moisés Naím, and novelists Mario Vargas Llosa and Sergio Ramírez released a document in which they argued that the U.S. war on drugs had failed and demanded a change in paradigm.[11] Interestingly, the commission had representatives—all of them prominent in their own right—from Argentina, Bolivia, Brazil, Colombia, Costa Rica, Mexico, Nicaragua, Peru, and Venezuela but not from Chile. Was this a coincidence? Was no Chilean intellectual—and there are many well-known ones—included because drugs are not a serious problem in that Andean country? Or was it because, due to its progress in economic and institutional modernization, Chile is gradually no longer being seen as a true Latin America country? Be that as it may, the absence of a voice from Chile in this document is an interesting reflection of the country's status as the region's solitary economic star.[12]

This group, which calls itself the Latin American Commission on Drugs and Democracy, makes a number of important points, including the obvious one that dealing with the demand for illicit drugs is a key element in any solution to Latin America's economic problems. This point is obvious to everyone who has looked into the illicit drug problem except the successive U.S. administrations that have continued the war on drugs launched by President Richard Nixon in 1971. It is worth quoting from the Commission's report:

> A long-run solution to the illicit drug problem will require reducing the demand in the main consumer countries. The point is not to search for guilty parties . . . but to point out that the United States and the European Union are co-responsible for the problems faced by the [Latin American] region, since their markets are the largest consumers of drugs produced in Latin America. It is desirable, therefore, that they implement policies that diminish consumption levels and reduce significantly the size of this criminal business.[13]

The commission goes on to make four main recommendations. First, addiction should be treated as a public health problem. Addicted consumers should not be put in prison; instead they should be treated as patients in the national health system. Second, personal consumption of marijuana should be decriminalized. It makes no sense to clog up courts, prisons, and jails with individuals that are recreational users of marijuana. Third, there should be a determined and focused effort to combat organized crime. The negative impact of mafias and cartels on society should not be underestimated. And fourth, a serious effort should be made to offer peasants who currently grow illicit drugs financing and technical assistance for growing alternative crops.

These recommendations are shared by numerous scholars, journalists, and opinion leaders.[14] Politically, however, it will be difficult to convince U.S. politicians to move in this direction. European political leaders are likely to be more sympathetic to the commission's suggestions, but whether a major shift in paradigm takes place is still an open question.

What makes things particularly pressing is that there is a complex, two-way interaction between drug production and trafficking on one hand and economic performance and social progress on the other. In countries where the economy falters, employment is stagnant, and wages decline, there is an increase in informality and lawlessness. A culture of corruption and bribes evolves, and the rule of law declines precipitously. These countries are prone to experience an increase in drug-related activities. Under these circumstances it is highly unlikely that there will be massive innovation or that investment in machinery and equipment will take off. Indeed, as the discussion on El Salvador in chapter 5 shows, foreign investment will not flow into a country that lacks safety and security. And in countries where crime takes over, it is almost impossible to have a well-functioning educational system, let alone one that improves skills in order to allow workers to successfully face the challenges of the global economy. And thus a vicious circle evolves, in which a culture of crime and corruption impedes economic progress, and economic failure feeds into crime and lawlessness. There is little doubt that as Latin America enters the second decade of the twenty-first century a major effort should be made to avoid this cycle of desperation.

Three Latin American Clusters for the Twenty-first Century

At the time of this writing, economic discussions around the world are centered on the great global crash of 2008. Analysts, politicians, and the public at large look at the meltdown of the global financial system with disbelief. This concern is understandable. In little more than six months almost $10 trillion of wealth were wiped out in the global economy, unemployment increased drastically, and prospects for income collapsed. There is a threat of protectionism, and nations that until recently thought they had an assured path to prosperity—including many of the countries of eastern Europe—are facing the ugly prospect of insolvency and debt default.

Eventually, however, the world economy will rebound. It may take years, but it will happen. Almost certainly, the global economy that will emerge will be different from the freewheeling one of the 1990s and first decade of the twenty-first century. The financial sector will be smaller, and regulations will be stiffer, broader, and more general. Financial innovation will proceed with caution, and there will be more and better supervision. One hopes that there will also be less arrogance and that investment bankers will understand that markets are not always fully efficient and the tools of "financial engineering" are not the most adequate to understand the public's psychology, fears, obsessions, moods, fads, and panics. We will also see more protectionism around the world. However, it is unlikely that the hike in import tariffs, licenses, and quotas will be as severe as during the Great Depression. Every economic historian agrees that the protectionist Smoot-Hawley Tariff Act of 1930 contributed significantly to the downward economic spiral that the world experienced during that period. It seems that most policy makers have learned some lessons from history.

All of this may be true, but what will not change is the irremediable fact that in the long run the things that matter for economic growth, prosperity, and higher incomes are the rate at which the economy becomes more efficient, the pace at which productive capacity expands through investment in machinery and infrastructure, and the upgrades that are brought about in labor force skills through training and education. In all three of these areas—efficiency, investment, and improvement of workers' skills—most of the Latin American nations have done poorly for long periods of time, and unfortunately, they are likely to do as poorly in the future as they have done in the past. Sadly, the political reality of Latin America is that most countries show no political willingness to embark on the reforms required to spur productivity improvements or higher investments. Furthermore, every effort to introduce educational reform has run into the unyielding opposition of teachers' unions and other interest groups. In most countries this is likely to continue in the future.

In the years to come it is highly likely that we will see three groups of countries in Latin America. The first will comprise those nations that will cling to populist policies. In these countries there will be very little innovation or improvements in efficiency. The quality of education will continue to be dismal and institutions weak. In the name of the poor and the dispossessed, policies that violate property rights and eliminate incentives for entrepreneurs and innovators will be put in place. Growth is likely to be very low, informality in the labor market will increase, there will be rapid inflation, black markets are likely to emerge, and social conditions will worsen. The usual suspects—capitalism, multinational corporations, the IMF, the United States, and the European Union—will be blamed by the populist leaders for the dreary economic conditions. It is also likely that insecurity will be higher and that the level of corruption will rise; in many of these countries it is likely that the institutions of the state will lose ground in their struggle with organized crime and drug mafias.

Eventually, and as has always been the case with populism, the economic situation will become so dire that voters will become tired of the old populist rhetoric. At that time new governments will be elected. The timing of these political changes will depend on three factors: future commodity prices, the extent of domestic inflation, and the degree to which those in power manipulate the electoral system in order to stay afloat. If commodity prices rebound significantly, these countries will be able to finance their largesse and survive for some additional time without implementing efficiency- and productivity-enhancing policies. Some may even experience a short-lived bonanza. In these countries the end of populism may be delayed for some years, but it will eventually happen. That is what history teaches us, and there are no reasons to believe that this time around things will be different; not even high export prices can offset the damage done to the economic fabric of a nation by a heavy government hand and inflation. When all is said and done, we will find that those most hurt by these populist experiments were the poor. They are affected the most by inflation, by violence and insecurity, by the collapse of the institutions of the state, and by the low quality of the educational system. And as always, there will be some that will learn how to play the system and become enormously rich in the process. There will be individuals and companies that will take advantage of the inefficiency and corruption of populism and will be able to reap enormous profits as the national economies collapse before their eyes.

Of course, it is difficult to know precisely which countries will fall in this populist category, but some cases are easier to predict than others. Venezuela, Ecuador, Bolivia, and Nicaragua are likely to stay in this first group. Given the current political mood and forces, it is even possible that other countries will join them in the populist camp. After all, the rhetoric is attractive, and it is true that the incomplete reforms of the 1990s and 2000s produced little in terms of palpable results. Also, the devastation generated by the global crash of 2008 has resulted in a greater rejection of capitalism and in a search for alternatives. An important question is whether Mexico will fall into the populist trap. That will depend on how well the U.S. economy does in the next few years—a vigorous U.S. recovery will be a boon for Mexico, since most of its exports (more than 86 percent) go to its neighbor to the north—and on whether the administration of President Felipe Calderón is able to get the upper hand in its fight against organized crime and the drug cartels. But be that as it may, in the years to come Mexico is likely to be in a fragile situation, with the populist danger waiting on the sidelines. Only if the next necessary steps toward institutional strengthening and enhanced competition policies are taken will this populist threat recede.

A second group of countries will be formed by those that will neither fall for the populist temptation nor move forward in the implementation of the procompetition policies and institutional reforms needed to spur productivity growth. Like the Prince of Denmark, these countries will doubt, hesitate, and be undecided; they will not move forcefully in one direction or the other. Their leaders will have the wisdom to understand that government controls and intrusion, rapid inflation, autarkic policies, and authoritarianism will not lead their nations toward rapid growth, reduced poverty, and prosperity. At the same time, they will not have the courage—or the political ability—to implement the policies required for taking off and moving to the higher stages of economic growth transition. Their economies will not collapse, but their performance will not be spectacular. They will struggle and move forward rather slowly. Their performance will conform to the Latin American historical norm, and their income gap with the emerging nations of Asia and eastern Europe will widen. The reduction of poverty will be slow, inequality will continue to be significant, and people's aspirations will be frustrated. In some of these countries the disillusionment may even lead to political apathy and the withdrawal of people from voting and other activities that are central to modern representative democracies.

In late 2009, as the global financial crisis began to ebb, international investors became increasingly enthusiastic about Brazil's economic prospects. There was talk of a miracle in the making and of a major take-off. Some observers argued that Brazil was about to join China and India as a super global performer. Success and rapid growth were predicted. This, it was said, would be accompanied by improved social conditions and reduced inequality. The fact that the World Cup and the Olympics are to be held in Brazil in 2014 and 2016 has added to the sense of enthusiasm and anticipation. A key question, however, is whether these exuberant prospects are rooted in reality and fundamentals or whether, on the contrary, they are a mirage and a reflection of generalized wishful thinking. The answer is that while Brazil has much going for it—a sizable population, a growing middle class, newly discovered oil deposits, and ample natural resources—it continues to be (as documented above) a country mired in inefficiencies, red tape, weak institutions, and noncompetitive markets. A serious analysis of the country's *longer-term* prospects would suggest that unless these major impediments to growth are tackled, Brazil is bound to disappoint. At the time of this writing, the most likely scenario is that Brazil will become the most important country in the middle group of so-so performers. It is unlikely that after Lula's rejection of populism the country will fall into its trap. It is even possible that, after having suffered the blow of the crash of 2008, Brazilian politicians will finally realize that low inflation and high commodity prices don't automatically result in rapid and long-lasting economic growth. If Lula is followed by a true reformer and modernizer—be it the candidate from the Workers Party or from the opposition Partido da Social Democracia Brasileira—and if the legislature recognizes the importance of efficiency improvements, entrepreneurship, and creative destruction, we may see the awakening of what until now has been the eternal "country of the future." If this does indeed happen, then Brazil will rightfully gain a spot as a Latin American star. If, on the other hand, the status quo prevails and politicians are content with having reduced inflation and don't move decisively on the efficiency and institutional fronts, the country will not become the world power that so many Brazilians dream it might become.

Argentina raises several important questions. Will the populist forces of presidents Néstor Kirchner and Cristina Fernández de Kirchner muster enough support to stay in power? Or will the populist crisis that is already affecting the River Plate region be deep enough to change the winds of political support and bring new leadership? Whatever happens, it is unlikely that Argentina will move at full speed and with great enthusiasm toward innovative capitalism. The memories and wounds from the 2001–2 crisis are still too fresh in people's minds, and they continue to blame neoliberalism for their nation's misfortunes.

Most of the countries of Central America are also likely to belong to this second group and will struggle to achieve higher economic growth and improved social conditions. In particular, it is unlikely that they will be able to generate the political support to implement real educational reform.

And then there will be a very small group of countries that will embrace the innovative, productivity-based path to development and prosperity. These will be the countries that will understand that Schumpeter's process of creative destruction is required in order to move forward, experience substantial income growth, improve social conditions, and reduce poverty and inequality. These countries will continue to improve their social services and will put together sufficient safety nets to deal effectively with the "destruction" entailed in Schumpeter's view of innovative development. They will strengthen their institutions and will remember Joseph Conrad's phrase in *Heart of Darkness*: "What saves us is efficiency—the devotion to efficiency." Increasingly, these countries will separate themselves from the rest of the region and will see a convergence of their income and standards of living with those of the advanced nations of North America, Europe, and Asia.

Chile will continue to be the leader of this group. The key question, however, is who will join it in its effort to achieve developed-country status in a decade or so. How many other countries will see that hard work pays and that shortcuts and populism invariably backfire? It is possible that Peru, Colombia, and Costa Rica will join this modernizing effort in earnest. And, as noted above, even Brazil and Mexico could do so. I must say, however, that I am not particularly hopeful about the prospects for new Chiles. Modernizing the economy, strengthening institutions, improving the efficiency of social services, and taking on interest groups and monopolies are politically costly. Launching these types of reforms usually follows a major crisis that breaks the old social and political equilibrium. I don't see many Latin American countries being willing or able to incur the political costs required to move decisively toward an economic system based on innovation and competition. There are also additional problems—real and perceived—that may deter politicians from going all out in the modernization effort. For Chile one of the most significant costs of success has been its isolation. Increasingly, analysts believe that Chile does not truly belong to the ranks of the Latin American nations. This has been costly from a diplomatic perspective, as in many neighboring countries there is a sense that Chile has become arrogant and detached.

A Final Word

As the first decade of the twenty-first century comes to an end, Latin America is at a crucial juncture. In the next two or three years there will be presidential elections in every one of the larger countries, and in many of them there will be attempts to change the constitution as a means of keeping the current president in office.

As one looks into the future, the key question is whether the region will continue to move in the direction set by Hugo Chávez and his Bolivarian movement or will follow Chile's lead and opt for markets and openness. To put it another way, the fundamental question is whether more countries will opt for shortcuts, government controls, and inflation or will understand that prosperity requires adopting Schumpeter's concept of innovative capitalism, with all that it implies: the need to increase productivity, improve the quality of education, control inflation, foster competition, open the economy, and avoid monopolies. As I argue in chapter 1, this question is important not only for Latin America but also for the advanced nations, particularly the United States and the members of the European Union. A populist Latin America will be xenophobic and will tend to nationalize investments from the industrialized nations. A populist Latin America will sooner or later follow the fate of all historical populist experiments and will fail. With failure will come more poverty, inequality, and destitution, more violence and illicit activities, and more illegal migration to the advanced nations. Failure will perpetuate Latin America's long history of sorrow and frustration. If, on the other hand, there is the vision and political courage to move forward in the effort to finish the fractured modernization agenda of the 1990s, it is possible that the region will become a land of success, opportunity, and prosperity. If this happens, if politicians and voters recognize the need to modernize policies and institutions, if they are able to defeat the inertia and blocking tactics of entrenched interest groups—including local monopolists and teachers' unions—then Latin America will take off; at that time a true giant will awaken and begin moving forward. We will then see sustained and rapid economic growth, better jobs, higher incomes, better wages supported by a world-class educational system, lower inflation, reduced poverty, and better income distribution. At that time a true and sustained process that will close the standard-of-living gap with North America and other advanced nations will begin.

Notes

1. The Workers' Party has always had numerous factions with different ideologies, including a very significant Marxist contingent. For an engaging political biography of Lula, see Bourne (2008). Lula was not the first socialist elected to the presidency of a Latin American country—that was Salvador Allende of Chile, in 1970—but he was the first socialist union leader to reach the highest office.
2. The trade representative is a member of the cabinet, but the position does not have the status or carry the symbolism expected by the Brazilian public and media for this occasion.
3. *Forgotten Continent* is the apt title of Michael Reid's excellent 2007 book on Latin America's political and economic development since 1820.
4. On the main characteristics of the trend referred to as "twenty-first century socialism" by leftist intellectuals and academics, see http://www.monografias.com/trabajos43/el-socialismo/el-socialismo.shtml.
5. See *International Herald Tribune* (2008).
6. See Vinogradoff (2009).
7. See Castañeda (2006).
8. On the surge of illegal activities around the world, including in Latin America, see Moisés Naím's excellent book (2006).
9. For an early and influential study on the contrast between Latin America's and North America's economic development, see Stein and Stein (1970). On the Washington Consensus reforms, see John Williamson (1990). On recent challenges faced by the region, see Oppenheimer (2007).
10. These observations are based on the UN Comisión Económica para América Latina's (CEPAL's) "Average Real Remuneration." See CEPAL (2009).
11. For an analysis of the early reforms see Edwards (1995). For a technical analysis of Latin America's growth see Loayza, Fajnzylber, and Calderón (2005). The present book considers all countries in the region that were colonized by the Spanish or the Portuguese as Latin American. That is, I exclude Haiti from the analysis; also the Caribbean nations are not included in averages or other measures.
12. Of course, not every populist leader has acted outside the realm of traditional political parties. Both presidents Echeverría and López Portillo belonged to Mexico's powerful Partido Revolucionario Institucional (PRI), and Alan García was and is a member of Alianza Popular Revolucionaria Americana (APRA). On historical populist experiences, see chapter 9 of this book.
13. Dornbusch and Edwards (1991).

14. The fundamental role of institutions in the economic growth process has been emphasized by Nobel laureate Douglass North; see North (1990) and North (1993). For a political perspective on the quest to strengthen the institutions of the state in Latin America, see Geddes (1994).
15. See Easterly (2001) and Acemoglu, Johnson, and Robinson (2005).
16. Weil (2005), 182.
17. See Acemoglu, Johnson, and Robinson (2005) and Barro and Sala-i-Martin (1995).
18. The importance of well-established property rights has been emphasized by Peruvian economist Hernando de Soto, who has calculated that "dead capital," or assets that cannot be collateralized due to a lack of property rights, is as high as US$9.5 trillion (U.S.) worldwide. See Soto (2000).
19. The role of institutions was emphasized by classical economists, including Adam Smith in his 1776 *The Wealth of Nations*.
20. See Schumpeter (1939). For an early exposition of the insights of the new theories of growth see Barro and Sala-i-Martin (1995). Also see Easterly (2001).
21. The discussion that follows draws partially on Baumol, Litan, and Schramm (2007); Acemoglu, Johnson, and Robinson (2005); and Edwards (2008a).
22. See the discussion in chapter 8 and the references cited therein.
23. See Easterly (2001) and Easterly (2006).
24. For a breakdown of the sources of growth in the Latin American countries see, for example, Loayza, Fajnzylber, and Calderón (2005).
25. Ricardo Hausmann, Lant Pritchett, and Dani Rodrik (2005) have analyzed the determinants of more than eighty episodes of "growth acceleration." Their analysis is broadly consistent with the three-phase model discussed in this chapter.
26. See Easterly (2001).

CHAPTER TWO

1. Hanhimaki (2004), 92.
2. See the essays in Edwards, Esquivel, and Márquez (2007), especially Prados de la Escosura (2007). See also World Bank (2003) and Cardoso and Helwege (1991).
3. See Maddison (2007). See also Fukuyama (2008) and the essays collected there.
4. Bates (1978), 83.
5. See Coatsworth (2004), Przeworski (2008), and Bulmer-Thomas (1994).
6. See Prados de la Escosura (2007).
7. See Prados de la Escosura (2007) and Maddison (2007).
8. Astorga, Berges, and Fitzgerald (2005), 784; Thorp (1998), 159.
9. Prados de la Escosura (2007), 44–45.
10. The "advanced countries" were Australia, Denmark, France, the Netherlands, Sweden, the United Kingdom, and the United States. I focus on the comparison of gross domestic product per capita because it goes farthest into the past—all the way to 1820. However, other comparisons presented by Prados de la Escosura provide an almost identical picture of Latin America's relative economic performance over the very long run. See Prados de la Escosura (2007), 44–45 (emphasis added to quotation).
11. Fukuyama (2008), 284. Economists' interest in institutions was inspired by Nobel laureate Douglass North. See North (1990) and North (1993).

12. See Robinson (2008). Other authors who support this institutional-based explanation include economic historians Kenneth Sokoloff and Stanley Engerman, MIT economists Daron Acemoglu and Simon Johnson, and Harvard economist Dani Rodrik. I have made similar points in several of my works, including in the 2006 Figuerola Lecture that I delivered at the Universidad Carlos III in Madrid.

13. Quoted in Véliz (1994), 3.

14. See Weber (1958).

15. Hume (1875), 210. With time, Weber's analysis of the success of Protestant countries became one of the better-known culture-based explanations for differences in institutions and economic performance.

16. Bates (1878), 82–83.

17. See Elliott (1994).

18. See Fernandez-Armesto (2003) and Elliott (2006).

19. See Elliott (2006), 407.

20. See Syme (1958) and Lang (1975); see also Fernández-Armesto (2003).

21. Robinson (2008), 180.

22. See Véliz (1994).

23. As Berlin points out, the first author to make this comparison between the hedgehog and the fox was Greek poet Archilochus. See Berlin (1953), 1.

24. See Véliz (1980), 13. Véliz, like a number of authors before him (including Mexican poet Octavio Paz), identifies Spanish-American culture and institutions with the baroque. In his 1994 book Véliz expands this metaphor and associates the English fox with the gothic style.

25. Landes (2000), 2.

26. See García Hamilton (2002).

27. Tocqueville (1835), 46.

28. See Acemoglu, Johnson, and Robinson (2005), 429.

29. See Haber (2001), Maurer and Haber (2007) and Engerman and Sokoloff (2002).

30. See Engerman and Sokoloff (2002), 11.

31. Ibid., 14.

32. Ibid., 17.

33. See Vanhanen (1997), appendix 5. Robinson (2008) has pointed out that slaves and indigenous populations did not benefit directly from the landholding system in North America. The proportion of slaves in North America's southern colonies was small (approximately 20 percent of the population). It was much higher in Brazil and the Caribbean colonies.

34. See Wilde (1899).

35. See Marichal (1989).

36. Ibid. On Argentina's and Colombia's external debt in the nineteenth century, see Della Paollera and Taylor (2001) and Junguito (1995).

37. A currency board is defined as a monetary arrangement characterized by three main features: (a) a fixed exchange rate serves as a macroeconomic "anchor"; (b) the "monetary base" is fully backed by international reserves; (c) the central bank (or monetary authority) is not permitted to finance the government.

38. See Della Paollera and Taylor (2001) and Della Paollera and Taylor (2003).

39. See Dornbusch and de Pablo (1989).

40. See Marichal (1989).

41. Chile briefly suspended conversion to gold during its war with Spain in 1865–66. See Fetter (1931) and Molina (1898).

42. See Fetter (1931), chapter 7.

43. See Edwards and Edwards (1991).

44. Lewis (1961), xi.

45. These data are from appendix 5 of Vanhanen (1997).

46. On the Gini coefficient, see Atkinson (1970).

47. The Gini coefficient in the United Sates has increased from 0.39 in the late 1960s to 0.47 in the twenty-first century.

48. See Perry et al. (2007).

49. Ibid.

50. Ibid. See also World Bank (2008).

51. See Thorp (1998) and Astorga, Berges, and Fitzgerald (2005).

52. See Sarmiento (1845).

53. See Sarmiento (1849).

54. Ibid., 193.

55. See Rodó (1900).

56. "Ariel" is written as a letter addressed to "America's Youth." The title of the essay, as well as references to Prospero and the monster Caliban, comes from Shakespeare's *The Tempest.*

57. Rodó (1900), 99.

58. Some, however, believed that Rodó was an elitist and a racist. The image, values, and ideal of Ariel represented those of white Europeans and completely ignored those of South America's indigenous population. One of his most important critics was José Carlos Mariátegui, a Peruvian intellectual. On Mariátegui's views on the "Indian Problem," see Alonso (2009).

59. See Darío (2005).

60. There are several translations of this poem. This translation is my own.

61. See Krauze (2008).

62. See Neruda (1950). The translations that follow are my own.

63. See Krauze (2008).

64. Ibid.

65. See Neruda (1973).

CHAPTER THREE

1. See Cuadra (1974).

2. In 1961 Matthews published a book in which he recounts his famous Castro interviews and defends strongly, and with great naïveté, the Cuban Revolution. See Matthews (1961). Another important book supporting the Cuban Revolution was written by Columbia University sociologist C. Wright Mills (1961).

3. Matthews (1961), 131.

4. See Goodwin (1996) and Guevara (1997).

5. President Kennedy's March 16, 1961, can be found at http://www.fordham.edu/halsall/mod/1961kennedy-afp1.html.

6. The complete text of the Charter of Punta del Este may be found at http://avalon.law.yale.edu/20th_century/intam16.asp.

7. See Edwards (1995).

8. See Sheahan (1987), table 2.4. These data come originally from CEPAL.

9. Prebisch joined CEPAL in 1949, after he had formed his ideas on the need to industrialize. See Prebisch (1984). The most influential CEPAL publications at the time were *The Economic Development of Latin America and Its Principal Problems* (1950) and *Economic Survey of Latin America 1950: Recent Trends and Events in the Economy of Cuba* (1951).

10. Hirschman argued that inefficiency would be avoided if the productive process and the institutional setting "lacked latitude" for errors but conceded that how to ensure a "lack of latitude" was a difficult question. In time he came to argue that three mechanisms were usually at work: "voice," "loyalty," and "exit." He associated the latter with economic competition. See Hirschman (1984).

11. Diaz-Alejandro (1984), 113.

12. These data on the extent of protection are from Cuadra (1974) and Edwards (1975).

13. Incredibly, import tariffs, quotas, and licenses were not the whole story. In the mid-1960s the importation of a number of goods was also subject to a 10,000 percent prior deposit at the Central Bank of Chile.

14. See Edwards (1975).

15. See Balassa (1971) and Bulmer-Thomas (1994).

16. Krueger (1978) and Sheahan (1987) also provide data showing that other countries in the region had levels of protection similar to those in Chile.

17. See Edwards (1995).

18. See Thorp (1998), tables 6.3 and 6.4.

19. Most of the figures in this section have been calculated using data from the IMF's International Financial Statistics data set.

20. See Cooper (1971).

21. This calculation assumes that besides their proclivity to crises both countries are identical. For the formal analysis see Edwards (2007b).

22. López Portillo was born in 1920 and died in 2004. Many of his obituaries remembered both his promise to "administer abundance" and the corruption that plagued his administration. See, for example, *El Mundo* (2004).

23. The currencies of El Salvador, Guatemala, Honduras, and Nicaragua were for decades pegged to the U.S. dollar. Costa Rica was an exception in Central America and suffered from periodic currency crises.

24. The account of the first days of the crisis presented here draws on Kraft (1984) and Boughton (2001), as well as on my discussions with Mexican and other officials involved in the negotiations.

25. The income per capita data are from CEPAL's data bank. See CEPAL 2009. The data on inflation-adjusted wages are from Edwards (1995).

26. See Williamson (1990).

27. See Edwards (1995), chapter 3.
28. See Domínguez (1997).
29. See Williamson (1990). Williamson has a knack for labeling economic policies with apt and easy-to-remember terms. In the 1960s he referred to the exchange-rate system based on small and periodical government-controlled adjustments of the value of the currency as a "crawling peg" exchange-rate regime. That is precisely how such exchange-rate regimes have been known among economists ever since.
30. See Birdsal and de la Torre (2003) and Kuczynski and Williamson (2001).
31. See World Bank (2009b) and the IMF's International Financial Statistics data set.
32. The overall average rates of inflation were skewed by hyperinflation in some countries. During the same period, the median rate of inflation declined by half, from 26 percent to 13 percent.
33. For a report on improprieties during Chile's privatization process see, for example, the report prepared by the lower house of parliament in 2004. See Cámara de Diputados (2005). For a reaction to the report see Dittborn (2005), a commentary from the right-of-center think tank Libertad y Desarrollo.

CHAPTER FOUR

1. The title of this chapter comes from an article published by Columbia University professor Guillermo Calvo in the 1986. In the discussion that follows the Asian Tigers include Hong Kong, Indonesia, South Korea, Malaysia, Singapore, Taiwan, and Thailand. The southern European nations include Greece, Portugal, and Spain. The advanced commodity exporters group comprises Australia, Canada, and New Zealand. Occasionally I also refer to the emerging Asian countries; this group includes thirty-three developing Asian countries, excluding the seven in the Tigers group.
2. See Levine and Renelt (1992).
3. See Fukuyama (2008). See also Vargas Llosa (2005).
4. See Smith (1776), part 2, book 5.
5. North (1990), 3.
6. See North (1993).
7. Robinson (2008), 167.
8. See chapter 2.
9. See, for example, Domingo Cavallo's 1984 manifesto and Chile's Chicago Boys' 1973 economic blueprint in Centro de Estudios Públicos (1992).
10. See Economist (2008).
11. See Rodrik, Subramanina, and Trebbi (2002) and Edwards (2007a).
12. This index is one of the six categories included in the World Bank's Worldwide Governance Indicators project. See Kaufmann, Kraay, and Mastruzzi (2008).
13. See La Nación (2008).
14. The court-reform bill presented to Congress in February of 1937 allowed the president to add a new judge for every sitting justice who did not resign within six months of turning seventy years of age. Given the age composition of the Court at the time, this would have meant that six new justices would have been appointed.

15. These data are from the 2009 edition. See World Bank (2009a).

16. See Djankov et al. (2003).

17. See La Porta et al. (1998).

18. On institutional differences between North and South America during colonial times see, for example, Elliott (2006) and Véliz (1994).

19. For studies that show the negative effects of higher corruption on economic growth see, for example, Mauro (1995).

20. On ethnic conflicts see Alesina et al. (2003) and Easterly and Levine (2001).

21. See Polity Index Task Force (2009).

22. See Lora (2007), 6. The original data come from surveys done by Latinobarómetro.

23. See http://www.doingbusiness.org/ and http://www.freetheworld.com/.

24. There are two additional categories, which are related to institutional strength: the degree of protection of investors and enforcement of contracts.

25. On labor regulation see Botero et al. (2004).

26. The nonwage component of labor costs is higher in the southern European nations than in Latin America: 28 percent versus 16 percent.

27. See Soto (2000).

28. See *La Nación* (2007).

29. All the data here are from the 2009 edition of the Doing Business report, which contains information for the year 2008.

30. See KOF Swiss Economic Institute (2009).

31. See Erzan et al. (1989).

32. Parente and Prescott (2000), 143; see also Frankel and Romer (1999).

33. As is always the case with statistical analyses in economics, this statement is made "with other factors given." The evidence is summarized in Harrison (2007). See also Frankel and Romer (1999) and Wacziarg and Welch (2008). For a critical view see Rodrik and Rodríguez (2001).

34. Data on mean tariff rates for various years are from the Fraser Institute.

35. See, for example, Rodrik (2006).

36. These data are from the Fraser Institute. See Gwartney, Lawson, and Norton (2008).

37. Stiglitz (2002), Forbes (2007a), and Forbes (2007b).

38. See http://www.airliners.net/aircraft-data/stats.main?id=198.

39. See, for instance, "Update 1—Petrobras Makes New, 'Important' Light Oil Find," http://www.reuters.com/article/rbssEnergyNews/idUSN2936978620080529.

40. See http://www.marginalrevolution.com/marginalrevolution/2008/03/pollo-campero.html, and http://www.codelco.cl/prensa/presentaciones/pdf/america_economia_500.pdf. On the surge of Chile's wine industry see Bustos, Peña, and Willington (2008).

41. See http://www.bnamericas.com/story.jsp?idioma=I&sector=6&noticia=435988.

42. See Heckman and Pages (2004), 2.

43. See Hamermesh (2004), 557.

44. See A. T. Kearney (2005) and A. T. Kearney (2009). On the size of the unofficial labor market in a number of countries see Botero et al. (2004) and ECLAC (2006).

45. See Perry et al. (2007).

46. See Edwards (1989).

CHAPTER FIVE

1. See Friedman and Friedman (1998).
2. In his letter Pinochet, dated April 21, 1975, Friedman himself refers to his recommended anti-inflationary policy as "shock treatment." See Friedman (1998), 591.
3. See Arancibia and Balart (2007) and Fontaine Aldunate (1988).
4. For the Chilean experience during this period see Edwards and Edwards (1991) and the references cited therein.
5. See Klein (2007) and the references cited therein.
6. The election of Salvador Allende in 1970 had been preceded by political polarization and turmoil. For instance, Felipe Larraín and Patricio Meller (1991) report that the number of labor strikes went from 586 in 1966 to 1,127 in 1969.
7. Kissinger (1979), 654.
8. Rosenstein-Rodan (1974), 7. This paragraph draws on Dornbusch and Edwards (1991). For Rosenstein-Rodan's views on economic development see Rosenstein-Rodan (1984).
9. On the Chicago Boys see Valdés (1995); see also Edwards and Edwards (1991).
10. See de Castro's interview in the WGBH documentary *Commanding Heights* at http://www.pbs.org/wgbh/commandingheights/shared/video/qt/mini_p02_07_300.html.
11. See Valdés (1995).
12. Of course, as in any country, there were some restrictions based on phytosanitary and safety concerns. In addition there were price bands for a handful of agricultural products. See Edwards and Lederman (2002) for details.
13. See Fontaine Aldunate (1988).
14. For a comparative quantitative study of the growth process in Latin America, see the World Bank study by Loayza, Fajnzylber, and Calderon (2005).
15. For details, see Edwards and Edwards (1991).
16. See Edwards and Edwards (1991).
17. See Boeninger (1992).
18. See Agosin and Bravo-Ortega (2007).
19. See, for example, Rodrik (2004).
20. In 2008, concerns about the safety of Chilean farm-raised salmon resulted in a reduction of the demand in the United States. Local producers rapidly sought FDA support to clear any apprehension by foreign consumers. The Chilean government supported the industry's efforts by providing technical assistance.
21. Fundación Chile was created in 1976 by the Chilean government and ITT Corporation of the United States. In 2005, BHP Billiton, majority owner of Escondida Mining, became a partner in the organization.
22. Manuel R. Agosin and Claudio Bravo-Ortega (2007) provide a discussion of the role of Fundación Chile. See also Hausmann and Rodrik (2003). These authors, however, misinterpret the role of the Fundación, claiming that it provided significantly more direct support—of the industrial policy type—than it actually did. In particular, they ignore the important point that it is not a government institution and doesn't provide subsidies or preferences.
23. The only sector that has received tax advantages since the mid-1970s is forestry. This policy was based on the then revolutionary idea that there was an environmental

need to encourage a sustainable forestry sector. Also, in 1974 the military government of Augusto Pinochet passed a bill (the "Ley Austral") aimed at encouraging investment in the southernmost regions of Chile. This legislation benefited salmon producers as well as other industries that located plants in that part of the country. In 1997 the U.S. Department of Commerce determined that Chile's salmon industry was not subsidized either directly or indirectly, and as a result a temporary countervailing duty was eliminated.

24. See, for example, Edwards and Rigobon (2008).

25. Quoted in Uchitelle (1998). See also Edwards (2004) and the references cited there.

26. See Mundell (1995).

27. See Forbes (2007a) and Forbes (2007b).

28. According to the Fraser Institute's index—which ranges from 1 to 10—in 1995 the degree of protection of property rights in Chile was 6.8 and that of the Mediterranean nations was 7.4.

29. On El Salvador's reforms and growth potential see, for example, Hinds (2006) and Edwards (1999).

30. To be sure, even at 17 percent, the investment ratio for this period was significantly higher than that of the war era (1980–90), when fixed capital formation over gross domestic product averaged only 12.8 percent. But from a growth perspective—and in particular from a phase two perspective—a 17 percent investment rate is low, and unless total factor productivity growth maintains a spectacular pace, it is incompatible with maintaining sustained rapid growth.

31. See U.S. Department of State, Bureau of Democracy, Human Rights, and Labor (2007).

CHAPTER SIX

1. On the Mexican reforms from a policy maker's perspective see Aspe (1993). Pedro Aspe was the secretary of finance during the Salinas administration. For a historical view on Mexico's policies, see Schlettino (2007).

2. This chapter does not go beyond the eruption of the crisis. Readers interested in President Vicente Fox's administration should read the Pastor and Wise (2005) article on the lost "sexenio" and the references cited therein.

3. On the Mexican reforms before 1993 see, for example, Loser and Kalter (1992) and Lustig (1998).

4. Krugman (1995), 321.

5. See, for example, El País (1990).

6. See Edwards (1998) for a discussion along these lines.

7. Malpass and Chon (1994).

8. See Edwards (1998).

9. Aspe (1993), 23–24.

10. Some controls were maintained, however. In particular, it was not possible for nationals to short the peso.

11. Dornbusch (1993), 369.

12. World Bank (1992), 359.

13. See Banco de México (1993), Banco de México (1994), and Aspe (1993).

14. *Economist* (1992).
15. Milesi-Ferretti and Razin (1996).
16. See Edwards (1998) for details on this and other pronouncements from that time.
17. See Dornbusch and Werner (1994).
18. See D'Amato (1995).
19. After two weeks in the field, an IMF mission returned to Washington in early June without having obtained data from Banco de México authorities on the recent evolution of international reserves. Gil-Díaz (1997) argues that the level of international reserves was "timely revealed for the third occasion of the year on November 1st, 1994" (19).
20. See Edwards (1998).
21. D'Amato (1995), 381, 383–84.
22. See Wessel, Carroll, and Vogel (1995).
23. The memo's date has been cut off in the D'Amato papers. Its date can be approximately established by the following statement: "I estimate their reserves were $11.8 at cob Friday, December 16." D'Amato (1995), 428.
24. See, for example, Conger (1994).
25. D'Amato (1995), 428.
26. See *Economist* (2006).
27. Dornbusch (2000), 125.
28. Ahamed (2009).
29. Dornbusch (1997), 131.
30. Bruno (1995), 282.
31. See Dornbusch (2000), 54. The article was originally published in 1996.
32. Eichengreen et al. (1998), 18–19.
33. Dornbusch (2000), 53.

CHAPTER SEVEN

1. See Stiglitz's influential 2002 book. In his 2006 follow-up book Stiglitz devotes a long section to the Argentine crisis (220–25). See also Klein (2007).
2. On Colombia, see Edwards and Steiner (2008).
3. Duhalde (2002), emphasis added.
4. See Edwards (1995).
5. See Forbes (2005).
6. In 1992 the new peso replaced the Austral. The new peso's value was set at 10,000 Australes.
7. See Corden (2002).
8. See, for example, Dornbusch (2000). The data on inflation in this chapter are from the IMF.
9. These three pieces of legislation are sometimes referred to by their numbers: Convertibility Law, 23,928; Law of Reform of the State, 23,696; Economic Emergency Law of 1989, 23,697.
10. All these figures are rounded.
11. See Blustein (2005).
12. See Teijeiro (2001).

13. See the discussion on Sarmiento in chapter 2.

14. See Blustein (2005).

15. Some have argued that the social security deficit following the reforms was the responsibility of the IMF. It is hard to make this point, however. It was well known at the time—certainly well known by Argentine policy makers—that a partial privatization of social security would generate short-term fiscal needs.

16. Some of this increase is explained by higher international interest rates. The bulk of the larger deficit, however, was related to public-sector expansion.

17. See Meade (1951); see also Corden (1994).

18. See Heckman and Pages (2003).

19. See Forteza and Rama (2001).

20. Stiglitz (2006), 219.

21. As one of the speakers at that seminar, I was in the audience when this exchange between Cavallo and investment managers took place.

22. Blustein (2005).

23. *Financial Times* (2001).

24. See Hornbeck (2002).

25. Quoted in Lapper and Mulligan (2002).

26. See Catan (2002).

27. See *Economist* (2002).

28. Lavagna's remarks are provided at the end of the IMF's Independent Evaluation Office Report of 2004; see International Monetary Fund (2004), 115–19.

29. See Edwards (1998) and Feldstein (1998) and the literature cited there.

30. See Mussa (2002).

31. Quoted in Martínez (2004), 62. For a recent book on Argentina's stormy relationship with the IMF, see Tenembaum (2004).

32. Dornbusch (2000), 50.

33. For the January 2, 2002, BBC remark, see http://news.bbc.co.uk/2/hi/americas/1738176.stm.

34. See http://www.soitu.es/soitu/2007/12/02/info/1196618014_799981.html.

35. *La Nación* (2003).

36. See A. T. Kearney (2005), 16.

37. See A. T. Kearney (2008).

38. A. T. Kearney (2005), 16.

39. *La Nación* (2004).

40. *La Nación* (2005).

41. See, for example, Della Paollera and Taylor (2001), Della Paollera and Taylor (2003), and Coatsworth and Taylor (1998).

42. Lederman and Sanguinetti (2003), 131.

43. See Barrionuevo (2008).

44. See Yen (2006).

CHAPTER EIGHT

1. Marco A. Morales (2008) has shown that many people who defined themselves as centrists at this time voted for populist candidates. This suggests that many voters

wanted to repudiate the politicians who had embraced the Washington Consensus reforms.

2. See Castañeda (2006).
3. For a discussion of Latin America's recent turn to the left, see the essays in Castañeda and Morales (2008).
4. Williamson (1992), 347.
5. Drake (1982) 218; Conniff (1982), 82.
6. See Conniff (1982) and Walker (2008). See also Cardoso and Helwege (1992).
7. See Dornbusch and Edwards (1989).
8. Quoted in Hirschman (1979), 65. I first came across this quote when I read Ignacio Walker's (2008) paper on populism and democracy in Latin America.
9. Carbonetto (1987), 82.
10. Populist experiences go beyond rhetoric; they entail populist policies. In that sense, the characterization of Alberto Fujimori's administration in Peru as populist by Roberts (1995) is unconvincing. Equally unpersuasive is the discussion in Weyland (2003) of "neoliberal populism."
11. See the analysis in Inter-American Development Bank (2007).
12. See *La Tercera* (2008).
13. See Engerman and Sokoloff (2002).
14. See Hirschman (1963), 96.
15. Vanhanen (1997) defines "family farms" as farms that provide employment to no more than four people.
16. See García Hamilton (1998), 75.
17. Engerman and Sokoloff (2002).
18. See Thorp (1998).
19. For data on income distribution for several years, see World Bank (2006) and López and Perry (2008).
20. Perry et al. (2006).
21. Not every country has enough data to calculate the evolution of inequality during this time span. See López and Perry (2008). On social conditions in Mexico during this period see Levy (2008).
22. See Klein (2007).
23. See, for example, Harrison (2007). Other recent works on the subject are cited in the discussion that follows. The academic literature on the relationship between globalization and social conditions is vast and complex and at times seems contradictory. Some of the issues raised in this literature include the way in which poverty and inequality are measured, the way globalization is defined, and which other variables are included in the analysis. There has also been discussion of what type of analytical framework should be used to analyze the potential distributive effects of slashing import tariffs.
24. For an influential study on trade openness and growth, see Frankel and Romer (1999). To be sure, some economists are skeptical about the positive effect of trade openness on growth. See Rodrik and Rodríguez (2001).
25. See, for example, Goldberg and Pavcnik (2007) and the references cited therein.
26. See Borraz and López-Cordova (2007).

27. In the last few years there has also been an increase in the number of women working in the informal sector. See Harrison (2007) and Borraz and López-Cordova (2007).
28. See, for example, Goldberg and Pavcnik (2007).
29. See Ferranti et al. (2003) and Lustig (1995).
30. See Ferranti et al. (2003), Edwards (1995), Easterly (2007), and Milanovic and Squire (2006). See also Dollar and Kraay (2002) and Chen and Ravallion (2006).
31. See Edwards (1995).
32. For a historical analysis of currency crises in the emerging countries, see Edwards (1989). For a classic work on the subject see Cooper (1971).
33. See the detailed analysis in López and Perry (2008) and the sources cited therein.
34. See issues of the World Economic Competitiveness Report published annually by the World Economic Forum. The 2008 issue may be found at http://www.weforum.org/en/initiatives/gcp/Global%20Competitiveness%20Report/index.htm.
35. See http://go.worldbank.org/4PYTKZ3K20.
36. See Harmon et al. (1997).
37. For a detailed and exhaustive analysis of how to improve schools' performance, see Hoxby (2004).
38. See IERAL (1999).
39. The main purpose of their analysis is identifying which policies help a society achieve its long-term objectives. They focus on six desirable properties of successful and high-quality public policies: stability, adaptability to new circumstances, coordination and coherence, enforcement, public regard, and efficiency. For details, see Spiller and Tommasi (2007) and Tommasi (2006).
40. The Spiller and Tommasi framework is based on the analyses of a number of political theorists, including Cox and McCubbins (2001).
41. See, for example, http://www.venezuelanalysis.com/news/2204 and Millman and Crowe (2008).
42. See, for example, Lyons (2008).
43. See Viciano Pastor and Martínez Dalmau (2008). See also Salamanca and Viciano Pastor (2004).
44. Viciano Pastor and Martínez Dalmau (2008).
45. See Salamanca and Viciano Pastor (2004).
46. See, for example, Martínez Dalmau (2008).
47. The texts of all constitutions in the region may be found in Georgetown University's Political Database of the America's, at http://pdba.georgetown.edu/Constitutions/constudies.html.
48. See West (1993).
49. See García-Villegas (2001).
50. See Sunstein (1993) and Voigt (1998).
51. See article 303 of the 2008 constitution.
52. Viciano Pastor and Martínez Dalmau (2008), 4. My translation.
53. Ibid., 4–5. Emphasis added.
54. See Viciano Pastor and Martínez Dalmau (2008).
55. Córdoba (2008a).

CHAPTER NINE

1. A video of Chávez's statement after surrendering may be seen at http://www.youtube
   .com/watch?v=VBU0-pYeVfQ.
2. LR21 (2007). My translation.
3. See http://www.venezuelanalysis.com/news/2310.
4. See Rodríguez (2008a).
5. See O'Grady (2008) and CNN.com, "Chavez: Take FARC Off Terror List," January 11,
   2008, http://www.cnn.com/2008/WORLD/americas/01/11/chavez.farc/.
6. See *Wall Street Journal* (2008).
7. Naím (2001), 25. Naím was Venezuela's minister of trade and industry from 1989 to
   1990.
8. See Betancourt (1956). Martz (1995) provides a succinct and very useful overview of
   Venezuelan politics between 1958 and 1994.
9. These data refer to gross domestic product per capita measured in constant what
   economists call purchasing power parity (PPP) dollars. These were the years of the
   lost decade, and in many countries growth was close to zero or even negative. See
   Thorp (1998), 353.
10. Naím (2001a), 26.
11. For a long time Venezuelan politicians and analysts talked of the country's "excep-
    tionality." See Martz (1995) for details. On the poll results, see Templeton (1995), 81.
12. On the evolution of the foreign debt in the 1980s see, for example, Cline (1989) and
    Palma (1989). On the polls results, see Templeton (1995), 87.
13. For a detailed analysis of the acceleration of inflation in Venezuela, see Lovera
    (1986).
14. Hausmann (1995), 261. Hausmann was minister of planning during the Pérez
    administration.
15. Since 1983 Venezuela had had three different exchange rates: official, commercial, and
    a "free" rate that applied mostly to financial transactions. The 1989 adjustment pack-
    age called for a reunification of these rates. The "official" rate went from 14.1 bolivares
    per U.S. dollar to 43 bolivares per U.S. dollar.
16. On the uprising see, for example, López Maya (2003) and the news media articles
    cited therein. See also the 1989 issue of *Politeia*, the journal of the Universidad de
    Venezuela's Facultad de Ciencias Jurídicas y Políticas.
17. A video with images of the riots and looting, as well as the police repression may be
    seen at http://www.youtube.com/watch?v=d9-IY1lw6n8.
18. See Naím (2001b).
19. See Corrales (2006).
20. Neither the Venezuelan congress nor other traditional institutions had control or
    oversight over these funds.
21. See, for example, Ortega and Rodríguez (2008b).
22. See Penfold-Becerra (2007). See also Walker (2008) and Corrales and Penfold-
    Becerra (2007).
23. See Vulliamy (2002).
24. See *Businessweek* (2006).

25. These data were published on the Internet by Chávez supporters.

26. Hsieh et al. (2008), 2.

27. See, for example, Alesina et al. (1996).

28. See Rodríguez (2008a) and the comments on his analysis there. Rodríguez says, "Official figures show no significant change in the priority given to social spending during [Chávez's] administration. The average share of the budget devoted to health, education, and housing under Chávez in his first eight years in office was 25.12 percent, essentially identical to the average share (25.08 percent) in the previous eight years." In Rodríguez (2008b) further support is provided for this contention.

29. See, for example, Edwards (2007a).

30. Rodríguez coauthored with Harvard's Dani Rodrik a well-known paper criticizing a number of academic papers—including one of my own—that had found that greater openness resulted in greater growth. See Rodrik and Rodríguez (2001).

31. Rodríguez (2008b).

32. See Ortega and Rodríguez (2008a). For criticism of Rodríguez's article see, for example, Petras (2008).

33. See, for example, the reply to Rodríguez by Venezuela's ambassador to the U.S., Bernardo Alvarez Herrera, published in the July/August 2008 issue of *Foreign Affairs*. That issue also includes a reply by Rodríguez.

34. Rosnick and Weisbrot (2008). For Rodríguez's reply see Ortega and Rodríguez (2008b).

35. The discussion that follows relies on data provided in CEPAL (2008).

36. Brazil, Chile, Ecuador, and Mexico have done better than Venezuela in terms of the Millennium Goals, which have been set by the UN and are used as an indicator of social progress. The goals on poverty reduction are as follows: (1) Halve between 1990 and 2015 the people living in extreme poverty. (2) Achieve decent employment for all those who want to work, including women. And (3) halve the number of those suffering from hunger.

37. See CEPAL (2008), 17.

38. Rodríguez (2008b).

39. See Hirschman (1963), chapter 3. See also Edwards (2007b).

40. The UN Economic Commission for Latin America (or CEPAL) has provided data on the evolution of basic poverty indicators in Venezuela and other Latin American countries. It has not, however, provided an in-depth and systematic analysis of the specific misiones and other transfer programs. Traditionally, governments and the staff of the World Bank decide jointly on the studies to be undertaken. It is extremely rare for the World Bank to embark on an in-depth evaluation of a country's social policies without the consent of government authorities.

41. For a discussion of the evolution of the PT's policy proposals see, for example, Baiocchi and Checa (2008).

42. See Rabello de Castro and Ronci (1991).

43. Edwin Williamson (1992), 421.

44. Ibid., 423.

45. As pointed out in chapter 4, once they were forced to face international competition

in the 1990s, a handful of Brazilian companies became very efficient and highly productive in the global marketplace. The best known are Embraer, Petrobras, CVRD, and the banks Bradesco and Itaú.

46. *New York Times* (1989).

47. For an analysis of the years leading to the Collor plan see Boughton (2001), chapter 10, and Little et al. (1993), chapter 10.

48. In June 1996 Farias and his girlfriend were found dead in their beach house. Some have called the deaths a crime of passion, while others have argued that it was a way of concealing, forever, additional evidence of corruption. For the *New York Times* story on the deaths, see Schemo (1996).

49. The theory supported by Cardoso was known as "dependência" and was popular among progressive intellectuals during the 1970s and 1980s. It combined Marxist-based theories of imperialism, theories of unequal exchange, and structuralist views on economics. See Cardoso and Faletto (1979).

50. See President Cardoso's fascinating memoirs (2007).

51. Dornbusch (2000), 260.

52. The primary balance is the government balance, excluding interest payments on public debt. Many IMF programs are negotiated on the condition that the country receiving assistance attain a certain fiscal balance. Throughout Lula's presidency Brazil either met or exceeded the primary balance goal set or recommended by the IMF.

53. See Acosta and de Mello (2008).

54. For example, the International Food Research Institute has undertaken an evaluation of the Bolsa Alimentação. See, for instance, Maluccio (2004).

55. World Bank, "Bolsa Família: Changing the Lives of Millions in Brazil," http://web .worldbank.org/WBSITE/EXTERNAL/COUNTRIES/LACEXT/BRAZILEXTN/0,, contentMDK:21447054~pagePK:141137~piPK:141127~theSitePK:322341,00.html.

56. See Tommasi (2006).

57. Fraser Institute (2009).

58. Ibid.

59. See Wilson and Purushothaman (2003).

60. See the Global Competitiveness Report 2008–2009 at http://gcr.weforum.org/gcr/.

61. See World Bank (2009b).

CHAPTER TEN

1. See Edwards (2008b).

2. Krugman (2009), A21.

3. In both countries, however, growth had been negative in the preceding years. To an important extent, the rapid growth of 2004–8 represented a recovery from previous lows.

4. See *La Tercera* (2009), 52.

5. See the directive at http://ftp.fas.org/irp/offdocs/pdd14_house.htm.

6. See Lacey (2009), A1. See also the *Los Angeles Times* coverage on the war on drugs in Mexico, *Los Angeles Times* (2009).

7. See *Los Angeles Times* (2009).

8. See O'Grady (2009), A13.

9. See Meyer (2009).

10. Ibid.

11. See Comisión Latinoamericana sobre Drogas y Democracia (2009), 3.

12. In a 2007 article in *Letras Libres* I suggested that, for most practical purposes, Chile was on the way to not being a true Latin American country. See Edwards (2007a).

13. Comisión Latinoamericana sobre Drogas y Democracia (2009), 3. My translation.

14. See Harwood (2009).

Bibliography

Acemoglu, Daron, Simon Johnson, and James A. Robinson. 2005. "Institutions as the Fundamental Cause of Long-Run Economic Growth." In *Handbook of Economic Growth*, ed. Philippe Aghion and Stephen Durlauf. Amsterdam: Elsevier.

Acosta, Ana Carla A., and João M. P. de Mello. 2008. "Judicial Risk and Credit Market Performance: Micro Evidence from Brazilian Payroll Loans." In *Financial Markets, Volatility, and Performance in Emerging Markets*, ed. Sebastian Edwards and Marcio G. P. Garcia, 155–84. Chicago: University of Chicago Press.

Agosin, Manuel R., and Claudio Bravo-Ortega. 2007. *The Emergence of New Successful Export Activities in Latin America: The Case of Chile*. Washington, D.C.: Latin America Research Network, Inter-American Development Bank.

Ahamed, Liaquat. 2009. *Lords of Finance: The Bankers That Broke the World*. New York: Penguin, 2009.

Alesina, Alberto, et al. 1996. "Political Instability and Economic Growth." *Journal of Economic Growth* 1 (2): 189–211.

———, et al. 2003. "Fractionalization." *Journal of Economic Growth* 8:155–94.

Alonso, Iván. 2009. "José Carlos Mariátegui." In *Veinte Peruanos del siglo XX*, ed. Pedro Cateriano Bellido. Lima: Universidad Peruana de Ciencias Aplicadas.

Alvarez Herrera, Bernardo. 2008. "Revolutionary Road: How Chávez Has Helped the Poor." *Foreign Affairs* 87 (4): 158–60.

Arancibia, Patricia, and Francisco Balart. 2007. *Sergio de Castro: El arquitecto del modelo económico chileno*. Santiago de Chile: Biblioteca Americana.

Aspe, Pedro. 1993. *Economic Transformation the Mexican Way*. Cambridge, Mass.: MIT Press.

Astorga, Pablo, Ame R. Berges, and Valpy Fitzgerald. 2005. "The Standard of Living in Latin America during the Twentieth Century." *Economic History Review* 58 (4): 765–96.

A. T. Kearney. 2005. *Foreign Direct Investment (FDI) Confidence Index (2005)*. Washington, D.C.: A. T. Kearney.

———. 2008. *New Concerns in an Uncertain World: The 2007 A. T. Kearney Foreign Direct Investment Confidence Index*. Washington, D.C.: A. T. Kearney.

———. 2009. A. T. Kearney / *Foreign Policy* Globalization Index. http://www.atkearney.com/main.taf?p=5,4,1,127 (accessed February 2009).

Atkinson, Anthony B. 1970. "On the Measurement of Inequality." *Journal of Economic Theory* 2:244–63.

Baiocchi, Gianpaolo, and Sofía Checa. 2008. "The New and Old in Brazil's PT." In *Leftovers: Tales of the Latin American Left*, ed. Jorge Castañeda and Marco A. Morales. New York: Routledge.

Balassa, Bela. 1971. *The Structure of Protection in Developing Countries*. Baltimore: Johns Hopkins University Press.

Banco de México. 1993. *The Mexican Economy*. Mexico City: Banco de México.

————. 1994. *The Mexican Economy*. Mexico City: Banco de México.

Barrionuevo, Alexei. 2008. "In Argentina's Grain Belt, Farmers Revolt over Taxes." *New York Times*, April 27.

Barro, Robert J., and Xavier Sala-i-Martin. 1995. *Economic Growth*. New York: McGraw Hill.

Bates, Henry W. 1878. *Central America, the West Indies and South America*. London: Edward Stanford.

Baumol, William J., Robert E. Litan, and Carl J. Schramm. 2007. *Good Capitalism, Bad Capitalism, and the Economics of Growth and Prosperity*. New Haven, Conn.: Yale University Press.

Berlin, Isaiah. 1953. *The Hedgehog and the Fox: An Essay on Tolstoy's View of History*. New York: Simon and Schuster.

Betancourt, Rómulo. 1956. *Venezuela, política y petróleo*. Mexico City: Fondo de Cultura Económica.

Birdsall, Nancy, Augusto de la Torre, and Rachel Menezes. 2003. *Washington Contentious: Economic Policies for Social Equity in Latin America*. Washington, D.C.: Carnegie Endowment for International Peace and Inter-American Dialogue.

Blustein, Paul. 2005. *And the Money Kept Rolling In (and Out)*. New York: Public Affairs.

Bonilla, Adrián, and César Montúfar. 2008. "Two Perspectives on Ecuador: Rafael Correa's Political Project." Inter-American Dialogue Working Paper, Washington, D.C.

Borraz, Fernando, and José Ernesto López-Cordova. 2007. "Has Globalization Deepened Income Inequality in Mexico?" *Global Economy Journal* 7 (1): 1–55.

Botero, Juan, et al. 2004. "The Regulation of Labor." *Quarterly Journal of Economics* 119 (4): 1339–82.

Boughton, James M. 2001. *Silent Revolution: The International Monetary Fund, 1979–1989*. Washington, D.C.: International Monetary Fund.

Bourne, Richard. 2008. *Lula of Brazil: The Story So Far*. Berkeley: University of California Press.

Brooke, James. 1989. "Brazilians Vote Today for President in a Free and Unpredictable Election." *New York Times*, November 15.

Bruno, Michael. 1995. "Currency Crises and Collapses: Comment." *Brookings Papers on Economic Activity*, 2:278–85.

Bulmer-Thomas, Victor. 1994. *The Economic History of Latin America since Independence*. Cambridge: Cambridge University Press.

Businessweek. 2006. "Why You Should Worry about Big Oil." May 15.

Bustos, R. Javier, Julio Peña, and Manuel Willington. 2008. "Joint ventures y especialización productiva en la industria del vino en Chile." *Estudios Públicos* 109:225–66.

Calvo, Guillermo A. 1986. "Fractured Liberalism: Argentina under Martinez de Hoz." *Economic Development and Cultural Change* 34 (3): 511–33.

Cámara de Diputados. 2005. *Evolución de las normas que rularon el proceso de privatizacion en Chile, desde 1970 a 1990*. Valparaíso, Chile, January 5.

Carbonetto, Daniel. 1987. "Marco teórico de un modelo de consistencia macroeconómica de corto plazo." In *Un modelo económico heterodoxo: El caso peruano*, ed. Daniel Carbonetto. Lima: Instituto Nacional de Planificación.

Cardoso, Eliana, and Ann Helwege. 1991. "Populism, Profligacy and Redistribution." In *The Macroeconomics of Populism in Latin America*, ed. Rudiger Dornbusch and Sebastian Edwards. Chicago: University of Chicago Press.

———. 1992. *Latin America's Economy: Diversity, Trends and Conflicts*. Cambridge, Mass.: MIT Press.

Cardoso, Fernando H. 2007. *The Accidental President of Brazil: A Memoir*. New York: Public Affairs.

Cardoso, Fernando H., and Enzo Faletto. 1979. *Dependency and Development in Latin America*. Berkeley: University of California Press.

Castañeda, Jorge C. 2006. "Latin America's Left Turn." *Foreign Affairs* 85 (3): 28–43.

Castañeda, Jorge C., and Marco A. Morales, eds. 2008. *Leftovers: Tales of the Latin American Left*. New York: Routledge.

Catan, Thomas. 2002. "Divided They Fall." *Financial Times*, January 2, 12.

Cavallo, Domingo. 1984. *Volver a crecer*. Buenos Aires: Sudamericana Planeta.

Centro de Estudios Públicos. 1992. *El ladrillo: Bases de la política económica del gobierno militar chileno*. Santiago de Chile: Centro de Estudios Públicos.

CEPAL (Comisión Económica para América Latina). 1950. *The Economic Development of Latin America and Its Principal Problems*. New York: UN Department of Economic Affairs.

———. 1951. *Economic Survey of Latin America 1950: Recent Trends and Events in the Economy of Cuba*. New York: UN Department of Economic Affairs.

———. 2008. *Panorama económico y social de América Latina y el Caribe 2008*. New York: UN Department of Economic Affairs.

———. 2009. Latin America and the Caribbean Statistics. http://websie.eclac.cl/sisgen/ConsultaIntegrada.asp?idAplicacion=6&idTema=151&idioma=e (accessed February 2009).

Chen, Shaohua, and Martin Ravallion. 2004. "How Have the World's Poorest Fared since the Early 1980s?" *World Bank Research Observer* 19 (2): 141–70.

Cline, William C. 1989. *United States External Adjustment and the World Economy*. Washington, D.C.: Institute for International Economics.

Coatsworth, John H. 2005. "Structures, Endowments and Institutions in the Economic History of Latin America." *Latin America Research Review* 40 (3): 126–44.

Coatsworth, John H., and Alan M. Taylor. 1998. *Latin America and the World Economy since 1800*. Cambridge, Mass.: Harvard University / David Rockefeller Center for Latin American Studies.

Comisión Latinoamericana sobre Drogas y Democracia. 2009. "Drogas y democracia: Hacia un cambio de paradigma." Statement presented at the Third Meeting of the Comisión Latinoamericana sobre Drogas y Democracia, February 2009. Rio de Janeiro.

Conger, Lucy. 1994. "Transition to Transparency." *Institutional Investor*, January, 111–14.

Conniff, Michael L., ed. 1982. *Latin American Populism in Comparative Perspective*. Albuquerque: University of New Mexico Press.

Cooper, Richard N. 1971. *Currency Devaluation in Developing Countries*. Princeton, N.J.: International Finance Section, Princeton University.

Corden, W. Max. 1994. *Economic Policy, Exchange Rates, and the International System*. Chicago: University of Chicago Press.

———. 2002. *Too Sensational: On the Choice of Exchange Rate Regimes*. Cambridge, Mass.: MIT Press.

Córdoba, José de. 2008a. "U.S. Renews Hard Line on Venezuela." *Wall Street Journal*, February 23.

———. 2008b. "Venezuela's Chávez Urges End to Colombian Insurgency." *Wall Street Journal*, June 9.

Corrales, Javier. 2006. "Hugo Boss." *Foreign Policy*, January–February, 32–40.

Corrales, Javier, and Michael Penfold-Becerra. 2007. "Venezuela: Crowding Out the Opposition." *Journal of Democracy* 18 (2): 99–113.

Council on Foreign Relations. 1996. *Lessons of the Mexican Peso Crisis*. New York, January.

Cox, Gary W., and Mathew D. McCubbins. 1993. *Legislative Leviathan: Party Government in the House*. Berkeley: University of California Press.

Cuadra, Sergio de la. 1974. "La protección efectiva en Chile." Working Paper 22, Instituto de Economía, Universidad Católica de Chile, Santiago.

D'Amato, Alfonse. 1995. *Report on the Mexican Economic Crisis*. Washington, D.C.: U.S. Senate.

Darío, Rubén. 2005. *Antología poética de Rubén Darío*. Buenos Aires: Errepar.

Della Paollera, Gerardo, and Alan M. Taylor. 2001. *Straining the Anchor: The Argentine Currency Board and the Search for Macroeconomic Stability, 1880–1935*. Chicago: University of Chicago Press.

———, eds. 2003. *A New Economic History of Argentina*. New York: Cambridge University Press.

Diaz-Alejandro, Carlos F. 1984. "Comment." In *Pioneers in Development*, ed. Gerald M. Meier and Dudley Seers. Oxford: Oxford University Press.

Dittborn, Julio. 2005. "Comentarios al informe de la Comisión Privatizaciones Cámara de Diputados 2004." *Libertad y Dessarollo*. http://www.lyd.com/noticias/privatizaciones/privatiz.pdf.

Djankov, Simeon, et al. 2003. "Courts." *Quarterly Journal of Economics* 118 (2): 453–517.

Dollar, David, and Aart Kraay. 2002. "Growth Is Good for the Poor." *Journal of Economic Growth* 7 (3): 195–225.

Domínguez, Jorge I. 1997. *Technopols: Freeing Politics and Markets in Latin America in the 1990s*. University Park: Pennsylvania State University Press.

Dornbusch, Rudiger. 1993. "Mexico: How to Recover Stability and Growth." In *Stabilization, Debt, and Reform: Policy Analysis for Developing Countries*. Englewood Cliffs, N.J.: Prentice Hall.

———. 1997. "The Folly, the Crash, and Beyond: Economic Policies and the Crisis." In *Mexico 1994: Anatomy of an Emerging Market Crash*, ed. Sebastian Edwards and Moisés Naím. Washington, D.C.: Carnegie Endowment for International Peace.

———. 2000. *Keys to Prosperity: Free Markets, Sound Money, and a Bit of Luck*. Cambridge, Mass.: MIT Press.

Dornbusch, Rudiger, and Sebastian Edwards. 1989. "The Macroeconomics of Populism in Latin America." World Bank Policy Research Working Paper 316, Washington, D.C.

———. 1991. *The Macroeconomics of Populism in Latin America*. Chicago: University of Chicago Press.

Dornbusch, Rudiger, and Juan Carlos de Pablo. 1989. "Debt and Macroeconomic Instability in Argentina." In *Developing Countries, Debt, and Economic Performance*, ed. Jeffrey D. Sachs, vol. 2. Chicago: University of Chicago Press.

Dornbusch, Rudiger, and Alejandro Werner. 1994. "Mexico: Stabilization, Reform, and No Growth." *Brookings Papers on Economic Activity* 25 (1994-1): 253–316.

Drake, Paul W. 1982. "Conclusion: Requiem for Populism?" In *Latin American Populism in Comparative Perspective*, ed. Michael Conniff. Albuquerque: University of New Mexico Press.

Duhalde, Eduardo. 2002. "Argentina Regrets." *Financial Times*, July 2, USA edition.

Easterly, William. 2001. *The Elusive Quest for Growth: Economists' Adventures and Misadventures in the Tropics*. Cambridge, Mass.: MIT Press.

———. 2006. *The White Man's Burden: Why the West's Efforts to Aid the Rest Have Done So Much Ill and So Little Good*. New York: Penguin.

———. 2007. "Inequality Does Cause Underdevelopment: New Evidence." Center for Global Development Working Paper 1, Washington, D.C.

Easterly, William, and Ross E. Levine. 2001. "What Have We Learned from a Decade of Empirical Research on Growth? It's Not Factor Accumulation: Stylized Facts and Growth Models." *World Bank Economic Review* 15 (2): 177–219.

ECLAC (Economic Commission for Latin American and the Caribbean). 2006. *Shaping the Future of Social Protection: Access, Financing and Solidarity*. Santiago de Chile: ECLAC.

Economist. 1994. "The Clash in Mexico." January 22, 13–14.

———. 2002. "Devaluation's Downbeat Starts." January 12, 34–35.

———. 2004. "Making Poverty History." December 16, 13–14.

———. 2006. "Monopoly Money." November 16, 11–12.

———. 2008. "Order in the Jungle—Economics and the Rule of Law." March 15, 83–85.

Edwards, Sebastian. 1975. "Tipo de cambio sombra y protección efectiva: Un cálculo basado en la metodología del tipo de cambio de equilibrio bajo libre comercio." *Cuadernos de Economía* 12 (December): 127–44.

———. 1989. *Real Exchange Rates, Devaluation, and Adjustment: Exchange Rate Policy in Developing Countries*. Cambridge, Mass.: MIT Press.

———. 1995. *Crisis and Reform in Latin America: From Despair to Hope*. New York: Oxford University Press.

———. 1998. "The Mexican Peso Crisis: How Much Did We Know? When Did We Know It?" *World Economy* 21 (1): 1–30.

———. 1999. *Crecimiento con participación: Una estrategia de desarrollo para el siglo XXI*. San Salvador: Fundación Salvadoreña para El Desarrollo Económico y Social.

———. 2003. *Desaceleración del crecimiento económico en El Salvador: Un análisis exploratorio*. San Salvador: Fundación Salvadoreña para el Desarrollo Económico y Social.

———. 2004. "Financial Openness, Sudden Stops and Current Account Reversals." *American Economic Review* 94 (2): 59–64.

———. 2006. "Crises and Growth in the World Economy: History and Prospects." Paper presented at the Figuerola Lecture at the Seminario de Historia Económica Otoño 2006, Universidad Carlos III, Madrid.

———. 2007a. "Contra la maldición de la distancia." *Letras Libres* 72 (Septiembre): 22–24.

———. 2007b. "Crisis and Growth: A Latin American Perspective." *Journal of Iberian and Latin American Economic History* 25 (1): 19–51.

———. 2008a. "Al sur de la crisis." *Letras Libres* 87 (Diciembre): 30–34.

———. 2008b. "Sequencing of Reform, Financial Globalization and Macroeconomic Vulnerability." National Bureau of Economic Research Working Paper 14034, Cambridge, Mass.

———. 2008c. "Globalization, Growth and Crises: The View from Latin America." *Australian Economic Review* 41:123–40.

Edwards, Sebastian, and Alejandra C. Edwards. 1991. *Monetarism and Liberalization: the Chilean Experiment*. Chicago: University of Chicago Press.

Edwards, Sebastian, Gerardo Esquivel, and Graciela Márquez, eds. 2007. *The Decline of Latin America Economies: Growth, Institutions and Crises*. Chicago: University of Chicago Press.

Edwards, Sebastian, and Daniel Lederman. 2002. "The Political Economy of Unilateral Trade Liberalization: The Case of Chile." In *Going Alone: The Case for Relaxed Reciprocity in Freeing Trade*, ed. Jagdish Bhagwati, 337–93. Cambridge, Mass.: MIT Press.

Edwards, Sebastian, and Roberto Rigobón. 2008. *Capital Controls, Managed Exchange Rates, and External Vulnerability*. Working paper, UCLA Anderson Graduate School of Management.

Edwards, Sebastian, and Miguel Savastano. 2000. "Exchange Rate Economics: What Do We Know? What Do We Need to Know?" In *Economic Policy Reform: The Second Stage*, ed. Anne O. Krueger. Chicago: University of Chicago Press.

Edwards, Sebastian, and Roberto Steiner. 2008. *La revolución incompleta: Las reformas de Gaviria*. Bogotá: Grupo Editorial Norma.

Eichengreen, Barry, et al. 1998. *Exit Strategies: Policy Changes for Countries Seeking Greater Exchange Rate Flexibility*. Washington, D.C.: International Monetary Fund.

Elliott, John H. 1994. "Going Baroque." *New York Review of Books* 41 (17): 31–37.

———. 2006. *Empires of the Atlantic World: Britain and Spain in America, 1492–1830*. New Haven, Conn.: Yale University Press.

El Mundo. 2004. "José López Portillo, el presidente de México que restableció relaciones con España." February 18.

El País. 1990. "Vargas Llosa: 'México es la dictadura perfecta.'" September 1, international edition.

Engerman, Stanley L., and Kenneth L. Sokoloff. 2002. "Factor Endowments, Inequality, and Paths of Development among New World Economies." *Economia* 3 (1): 41–109.

Erzan, Refik, K., et al. 1989. "The Profile of Protection in Developing Countries." *UNCTAD Review* 1 (1): 29–49.

Feldstein, Martin, ed. 1998. *Privatizing Social Security*. Chicago: University of Chicago Press.

Fernández-Armesto, Felipe. 2003. *The Americas: A Hemispheric History*. New York: Modern Library.

Ferranti, David de, et al. 2003. *Inequality in Latin America and the Caribbean: Breaking with History?* Washington, D.C.: World Bank.

Fetter, Frank W. 1931. *Monetary Inflation in Chile*. Princeton, N.J.: Princeton University Press.

Financial Times. 2001. "Investors Wary of Cavallo's Magic Wand.". June 20, London edition.

Fontaine Aldunate, Arturo. 1988. *Los economistas y el presidente Pinochet*. Santiago de Chile: Zig Zag.

Forbes, Kristin. 2005. "Argentina's Latest Tango." Remarks at the World Economic Forum Annual Meeting, January 27, 2005, Davos, Switz.

———. 2007a. "One Cost of the Chilean Capital Controls: Increased Financial Constraints for Smaller Traded Firms." *Journal of International Economics* 71 (2): 294–323.

———. 2007b. "The Microeconomic Evidence on Capital Controls: No Free Lunch." In *Capital Controls and Capital Flows in Emerging Economies: Policies, Practices, and Consequences*, ed. Sebastian Edwards, 171–91. Chicago: University of Chicago Press.

Forteza, Alvaro, and Martín Rama. 2001. "Labor Market 'Rigidity' and the Success of Economic Reforms across More Than One Hundred Countries." World Bank Policy Research Working Paper 2521, Washington, D.C.

Frankel, Jeffrey A., and David Romer. 1999. "Does Trade Cause Growth?" *American Economic Review* 89 (3): 379–99.

Fraser Institute. 2009. *Economic Freedom of the World 2008 Annual Report* data set. Economic Freedom Network. http://www.freetheworld.com/release.html (accessed February 2009).

Freedom House. 2009. Freedom in the World Comparative and Historical Data. http://www.freedomhouse.org/template.cfm?page=439 (accessed February 2009).

Friedman, Milton, and Rose D. Friedman. 1998. *Two Lucky People: Memoirs*. Chicago: University of Chicago Press.

Fukuyama, Francis, ed. 2008. *Falling Behind: Explaining the Development Gap between Latin America and the United States*. New York: Oxford University Press.

García, Pascual. "La evolución de las telecomunicaciones en México." Escuela de Graduados en Administración Pública y Políticas Públicas (EGAP) Working Paper 2007-02, Instituto Tecnológico y de Estudios Superiores de Monterrey.

García Hamilton, José I. 1998. *Cuyano alborotador*. Buenos Aires: Editorial Sudamericana.

———. 2002. *El autoritarismo y la autoridad*. Buenos Aires: Editorial Sudamericana.

García-Villegas, Mauricio. 2001. "Law as Hope: Constitutions, Courts and Social Change in Latin America." Paper presented at 2001 seminar at the Universidad Nacional de Colombia. http://www.eurozine.com/articles/2004-02-25-villegas-en.html.

Geddes, Barbara. 1994. *Politician's Dilemma: Building State Capacity in Latin America*. Berkeley: University of California Press.

Gil-Díaz, Francisco. 1997. "La política monetaria y sus canales de transmisión en México." *Gaceta de Economía* 3 (5): 79–102.

Goldberg, Pinelopi, K., and Nina Pavcnik. 2007. "Distributional Effects of Globalization in Developing Countries." *Journal of Economic Literature* 45 (1): 39–82.

Gonzales, Patrick, et al. 2000. *Highlights from TIMSS-R*. Chestnut Hill, Mass.: TIMSS International Study Center.

———. 2004. *Highlights from the Trends in International Mathematics and Science: TIMSS 2003*. Chestnut Hill, Mass.: TIMSS International Study Center.

———. 2008. *Highlights from TIMSS 2007: Mathematics and Science Achievements of US Fourth- and Eighth-Grade Students in an International Context*. Chestnut Hill, Mass.: TIMSS International Study Center.

Goodwin, Jeff. 2001. *No Other Way Out: States and Revolutionary Movements, 1945–1991*. Cambridge: Cambridge University Press.

Group of Thirty. 1995. *Mexico: Why Didn't Wall Street Sound the Alarm?* New York: Group of Thirty, New York.

Guevara, Ernesto. 1997. *Guerrilla Warfare*. 3rd ed. Wilmington, Del.: SR Books.

Gwartney, James, Robert Lawson, and Seth Norton. 2008. *Economic Freedom of the World: 2008 Annual Report*. N.p. [Canada]: Economic Freedom Network.

Haber, Stephen H. 2001. "Political Institutions and Banking Systems: Lessons from the Economic Histories of Mexico and the United States, 1790–1914." Center for Research on Economic Development and Policy Reform Working Paper 163, Stanford University, Stanford, Calif. http://www.stanford.edu/group/siepr/cgi-bin/siepr/?q=system/files/shared/pubs/papers/pdf/credpr163.pdf.

Hamermesh, Daniel S. 2004. "Labor Demand in Latin America and the Caribbean: What Does It Tell Us?" In *Law and Employment: Lessons from Latin America and the Caribbean*, ed. James J. Heckman and Carmen Pages. Chicago: University of Chicago Press.

Hanhimaki, Jussi. M. 2004. *The Flawed Architect: Henry Kissinger and American Foreign Policy*. New York: Oxford University Press.

Harmon, Maryellen, et al. 1997. *Performance Assessment in IEA's Third International Mathematics and Science Study*. Chestnut Hill, Mass.: TIMSS International Study Center.

Harrison, Ann. 2007. *Globalization and Poverty*. Chicago: University of Chicago Press.

Harwood, Matthew. 2009. "Drugs Are Bad. Fighting Them Is Worse." *Guardian*, February 20.

Hausmann, Ricardo. 1995. "Repercusiones de las finanzas públicas en materia de distribución." In *Políticas de ajuste y pobreza: Falsos dilemas, verdaderos problemas*, ed. José Núñez del Arco. Washington, D.C.: Inter-American Development Bank.

Hausmann, Ricardo, Lant Pritchett, and Dani Rodrik. 2005. "Growth Accelerations." *Journal of Economic Growth* 10:303–29.

Hausmann, Ricardo, and Dani Rodrik. 2003. "Economic Development as Self-Discovery." *Journal of Development Economics* 72 (2): 603–33.

Heckman, James J., and Carmen Pages. 2004. *Law and Employment: Lessons from Latin America and the Caribbean*. Chicago: University of Chicago Press.

Heritage Foundation. 2009. 2009 Index of Economic Freedom. http://www.heritage.org/ Index/Ranking.aspx (accessed February 2009).

Hinds, Manuel. 2006. *Playing Monopoly with the Devil: Dollarization and Domestic Currencies in Developing Countries*. New Haven, Conn.: Yale University Press.

Hirschman, Albert O. 1963. *Journeys toward Progress: Studies of Economic Policy-Making in Latin America*. New York: Twentieth Century Fund.

———. 1979. "The Turn to Authoritarianism in Latin America and the Search for Its Economic Determinants." In *The New Authoritarianism in Latin America*, ed. David Collier. Princeton, N.J.: Princeton University Press.

———. 1984. "A Dissenter's Confession: The Strategy of Development." In *Pioneers in Development*, ed. Gerald M. Meier and Dudley Seers. Oxford: Oxford University Press.

Holden, Robert, and Eric Zolov. 2000. *Latin America and the United States: A Documentary History*. New York: Oxford University Press.

Hommes, Rudolf. 1990. "Una propuesta económica para los noventa." *Estrategia Económica y Financiera* 141:1–17.

Hornbeck, Jeff F. 2002. "The Argentine Financial Crisis: A Chronology of Events." Washington, D.C.: Congressional Research Service.

Hoxby, Caroline. 2004. "Achievement in Charter Schools and Regular Public Schools in the United States: Understanding the Differences." PEPG Working Paper.

Hsieh, Chang-Tai, et al. 2008. "The Price of Political Opposition: Evidence from Venezuela's Maisanta." http://siteresources.worldbank.org/INTMACRO/Resources/ December13-14BrazilMGConferencePAPERSRodriguez.pdf.

Hume, David. 1875. "Of National Characters." In *Essays Moral, Political, and Literary*, ed. Thomas H. Green and Thomas H. Grose. Reprint, London: Scientia Verlag Aalen, 1882.

IERAL (Instituto de Estudios sobre la Realidad Argentina y Latinoamericana) de Fundación Mediterránea. 1999. "Educación para todos." Buenos Aires.

Inter-American Economic and Social Council. 1961. "The Charter of Punta del Este, Establishing an Alliance for Progress within the Framework of Operation Pan America." Charter signed at the special meeting of the Inter-American Economic and Social Council in August 1961, Punta del Este.

Inter-American Development Bank. 2007. *The State of State Reform in Latin America*. Ed. Eduardo Lora. Stanford, Calif.: Stanford University Press, World Bank, and Inter-American Development Bank.

International Country Risk Guide. 2009. International Country Risk Guide Ratings. The Political Risk Services Group. http://www.prsgroup.com/ICRG.aspx (accessed February 2009).

International Herald Tribune. 2008. "Peruvian President Defends Germany's Merkel in Verbal Spat with Venezuela's Chavez." May 16.

International Monetary Fund. 2004. *Evaluation Report: The IMF and Argentina, 1991–2001*. Independent Evaluation Office.

———. 2009. International Financial Statistics. http://www.imfstatistics.org/imf/ (accessed February 2009).

Jean, Diana. 1996. "Politics, Passion and Graft at Issue in Rio Slayings." *New York Times*, June 28.

Junguito, Roberto. 1995. *La deuda externa en el siglo XIX: Cien años de incumplimiento.* Bogotá: Tercer Mundo Editores.

Kaufmann, Daniel, Aart Kraay, and Massimo Mastruzzi. 2008. "Governance Matters VII: Aggregate and Individual Governance Indicators 1996–2007." World Bank Policy Research Working Paper 4654, Washington, D.C.

Kennedy, John F. 1961. "Preliminary Formulations of the Alliance for Progress." Speech presented at a White House Reception for Latin American Diplomats and Members of Congress, March 13, 1961, Washington, D.C.

Kissinger, Henry A. 1979. *White House Years.* Boston: Little, Brown.

Klein, Naomi. 2007. *The Shock Doctrine: The Rise of Disaster Capitalism.* New York: Metropolitan Books.

KOF Swiss Economic Institute. 2009. KOF Globalization Index. http://globalization.kof.ethz.ch/ (accessed February 2009).

Köhler, Horst, and James Wolfensohn. 2003. "We Can Trade Up to a Better World." *Financial Times*, December 12.

Kraft, Joseph. 1984. *The Mexican Rescue.* New York: Group of Thirty.

Krauze, Enrique. 2008. "Looking at Them: A Mexican Perspective of the Gap with the United States." In *Falling Behind: Explaining the Development Gap between Latin America and the United States*, ed. Francis Fukuyama, 48–71. New York: Oxford University Press.

Krueger, Anne O. 1978. *Liberalization Attempts and Consequences.* Cambridge, Mass.: Ballinger.

Krugman, Paul. 1995. "Dutch Tulips and the Emerging Markets: Another Bubble Bursts." *Foreign Affairs* 75 (4): 28–44.

———. 2009. "The Revenge of the Glut." *New York Times*, March 1.

Kuczynski, Pedro-Pablo, and John Williamson. 2003. *After the Washington Consensus: Restarting Growth and Reform in Latin America.* Washington, D.C.: Peterson Institute for International Economics.

Lacey, Marc. 2009. "With Deadly Persistence, Mexican Drug Cartels Get Their Way." *New York Times*, February 28.

La Nación. 2003. "Necesitamos más de cuatro años para volver al mercado de capitales." October 7.

———. 2004. "Por la crisis energética, en la Bolsa reinó un mal clima para los negocios." March 28.

———. 2005. "Chile será la variable de ajuste si falta el gas." April 3.

———. 2007. "Miceli dice que cometió un error, pero no un delito." July 7.

———. 2008. "La corte abre otra puerta al Corralito." April 29.

Landes, David. 2001. "Culture Makes Almost All the Difference." In *Culture Matters: How Values Shape Human Progress*, ed. Lawrence H. Harrison and Samuel P. Huntington. New York: Basic Books.

Landivar, Jorge. 2007. "Bolivia y el socialismo del siglo XXI." *La Historia Paralela.* June 4.

Lang, James. 1975. *Conquest and Commerce: Spain and England in the Americas.* New York: Academic Press.

La Porta Rafael, et al. 1998. "Law and Finance." *Journal of Political Economy* 106: 1113–55.

Lapper, Richard, and Mark Mulligan. 2002. "Government Selects 'Orthodox' Fiscal and Monetary Policy." *Financial Times*, January 15.

Larraín, Felipe, and Patricio Meller. 1991. "The Socialist-Populist Chilean Experience: 1970–1973." In *The Macroeconomics of Populism in Latin America*, ed. Rudiger Dornbusch and Sebastian Edwards. Chicago: University of Chicago Press.

La Tercera. 2008. "Morales nacionaliza por decreto tres petroleras y una filial de Telecom." May 1.

———. 2009. "Pese a la crisis." March 8.

Lavagna, Roberto. 2004. "The IMF and Argentina, 1991–2001." Evaluation Report. IMF Independent Evaluation Office, Washington, D.C.

Lederman, Daniel, and Pablo Sanguinetti. 2003. "Trade Policy Options for Argentina in the Short and Long Run." *Revista Integración y Comercio* 19 (July–December): 205–42.

Le Monde Diplomatique. 2007. "Champ libre pour transformer l'Equator." November, 20–21.

Levine, Ross E., and David Renelt. 1992. "A Sensitivity Analysis of Cross-Country Growth Regressions." *American Economic Review* 82 (4): 942–63.

Levy, Santiago. 2008. *Good Intentions, Bad Outcomes: Social Policy, Informality, and Economic Growth in Mexico.* Washington, D.C.: Brookings Institution Press.

Lewis, Oscar. 1961. *The Children of Sánchez: Autobiography of a Mexican Family.* New York: Random House.

Little, I. M. D., et al. 1993. *Boom, Crisis and Adjustment: The Macroeconomic Experience of Developing Countries.* Oxford: Oxford University Press for the World Bank.

Loayza, Norman, Pablo Fajnzylber, and César Calderón. 2005. *Economic Growth in Latin America and the Caribbean: Stylized Facts, Explanations and Forecasts.* Washington, D.C.: World Bank.

López, Humberto, and Guillermo Perry. 2008. "Inequality in America: Determinants and Consequences." World Bank Policy Research Working Paper 4504, Washington, D.C.

López Maya, Margarita. 2003. "The Venezuelan Caracazo of 1989: Popular Protest and Institutional Weakness." *Journal of Latin American Studies* 35:117–37.

Lora, Eduardo, ed. 2007. *The State of State Reform in Latin America.* Stanford, Calif.: Stanford University Press.

Los Angeles Times. 2009. Mexico under Siege: The Drug War at Our Doorstep. Online series indexing *Los Angeles Times* coverage of "Mexico under Siege." http://projects.latimes.com/mexico-drug-war/#/its-a-war.

Loser, Claudio, and Eliot Kalter. 1992. "Mexico: The Strategy to Achieve Sustained Economic Growth." IMF Occasional Paper 99, International Monetary Fund, Washington, D.C.

Lovera, Aníbal. 1986. "La aceleración inflacionaria en Venezuela." *Pensamiento Iberoamericano* 9: 225–38.

LR21. 2007. "José Vicente Rangel: Chávez es el antipoder." February 19. http://www.larepublica.com.uy/mundo/246849-jose-vicente-rangel-chavez-es-el-antipoder.

Lustig, Nora. 1992. *Mexico: The Remaking of an Economy*. Washington, D.C.: Brookings Institution.

———, ed. 1995. *Coping with Austerity: Poverty and Inequality in Latin America*. Washington, D.C.: Brookings Institution.

———. 1998. *Mexico: The Remaking of an Economy*. 2nd ed. Washington, D.C.: Brookings Institution Press.

Lyons, John. 2008. "Bolivia Nationalizes Pipeline." *Wall Street Journal*, June 2.

Maddison, Angus. 2003. *The World Economy: Historical Statistics*. Paris: Organisation for Economic Co-operation and Development.

———. 2007. *Contours of the World Economy, 1–2030 AD: Essays in Macro-Economic History*. Oxford: Oxford University Press.

Malpass, David, and David Chon. 1994. "Mexican Pesos and Cetes Are Attractive." Bear Stearns newsletter, November 7.

Maluccio, John A. "Effects of Conditional Cash Transfer Programs on Current Poverty, Consumption, and Nutrition. International Food Policy Research Institute." Second International Workshop on Conditional Cash Transfer Programs, São Paulo, Brazil. http://siteresources.worldbank.org/SAFETYNETSANDTRANSFERS/Resources/281945 1131468287118/1876750 1140119752568/Maluccio_En.pdf.

Marichal, Carlos. 1989. *A Century of Debt Crises in Latin America: From Independence to the Great Depression, 1820–1930*. Princeton, N.J.: Princeton University Press.

Martínez, Eloy T. 2004. *Las vidas del general: Memorias del exilio y otros textos sobre Juan Domingo Perón*. Buenos Aires: Aguilar.

Martínez Dalmau, Rubén. 2008. *El proceso constituyente boliviano (2006–2008) en el marco del nuevo constitucionalismo latinoamericano*. La Paz: Editorial Enlace.

Martz, John D. 1995. "Political Parties and the Democratic Crisis." In *Lessons of the Venezuelan Experience*, ed. Louis Goodman, 31–53. Washington, D.C.: Woodrow Wilson Center Press.

Matthews, Herbert L. 1961. *The Cuban Story*. New York: George Braziller.

Maurer, Noel, and Stephen H. Haber. 2007. "Related Lending: Manifest Looting or Good Governance? Lessons from the Economic History of Mexico." In *The Decline of Latin American Economies: Growth, Institutions, and Crises*, ed. Sebastian Edwards, Gerardo Esquivel, and Graciela Márquez. Chicago: University of Chicago Press.

Mauro, Paolo. 1995. "Corruption and Growth." *Quarterly Journal of Economics* 110 (3): 681–712.

Meade, James E. 1951. *The Balance of Payments: Mathematical Supplement*. London: Oxford University Press.

Meyer, Josh. 2009. "Hundreds Arrested in U.S. Probe of Mexican Drug Cartel." *Los Angeles Times*, February 26.

Milanovic, Branko, and Lyn Squire. 2007. "Does Tariff Liberalization Increase Inequality? Some Empirical Evidence." In *Globalization and Poverty*, ed. Ann Harrison, 143–82. Chicago: University of Chicago Press.

Milesi-Ferretti, Gian M., and Assaf Razin. 1996. *Current-Account Sustainability*. Princeton Studies in International Finance 81. Princeton, N.J.: International Finance Section.

Mill, John Stuart. 1848. *The Principles of Political Economy: With Some of Their Applications to Social Philosophy*. Boston: Charles C. Little and James Brown.

Millman, Joel, and Darcy Crowe. 2008. "Chávez to Nationalize Ternium Unit." *Wall Street Journal*, April 10.

Mills, C. Wright. 1960. *Listen, Yankee: The Revolution in Cuba*. New York: Ballantine.

Molina, Evaristo. 1898. *Bosquejo de la hacienda pública de Chile desde la independencia hasta la fecha (1898)*. Santiago: Imprenta Nacional.

Morales, Marco A. 2008. "Have Latin Americans Turned Left?" In *Leftovers: Tales of the Latin American Left*, ed. Jorge C. Castañeda and Marco A. Morales. New York: Routledge.

Mundell, Robert A. 1995. "The International Monetary System: The Missing Factor." *Journal of Policy Modeling* 17 (5): 479–92.

Mussa, Michael. 2002. *Argentina and the Fund: From Triumph to Tragedy*. Washington, D.C.: Institute for International Economics.

Naím, Moisés. 1993. *Paper Tigers and Minotaurs: The Politics of Venezuela's Economic Reforms*. Washington, D.C.: Carnegie Endowment for International Peace.

———. 2001a. "High Anxiety in the Andes: The Real Story behind Venezuela's Woes." *Journal of Democracy* 12 (2): 17–31.

———. 2001b. *The Venezuelan Story: Revising the Conventional Wisdom*. Washington, D.C.: Carnegie Endowment for International Peace.

———. 2006. *Illicit: How Smugglers, Traffickers and Copycats Are Hijacking the Global Economy*. New York: Anchor Books.

Neruda, Pablo. 1950. *Canto general*. Mexico City: Talleres Gráficos de la Nación.

———. 1973. *Incitación al nixonicidio y alabanza de la revolución chilena*. Mexico City: Editorial Grijalbo.

New York Times. 2009. "Brazilians Vote Today in a Free and Unpredictable Election." November 15.

North, Douglass C. 1990. *Institutions, Institutional Change, and Economic Performance*. Cambridge: Cambridge University Press.

———. 1993. "The Ultimate Sources of Economic Growth." In *Explaining Economic Growth: Essays in Honour of Angus Maddison*, ed. Adam Szirmai, Bart van Ark, and Dirk Pilat. Amsterdam: North-Holland.

OECD (Organisation for Economic Co-operation and Development). 2007. *PISA 2006: Science Competencies for Tomorrow's World*. Vol. 1, *Analysis*. Paris: OECD Publishing.

O'Grady, Mary A. 2008. "The FARC's Foreign Friends." *Wall Street Journal*, June 2.

———. 2009. "A Stimulus Plan for Mexican Gangsters." *Wall Street Journal*, March 2.

Oppenheimer, Andrés. 2007. *Saving the Americas: The Dangerous Decline of Latin America and What the U.S. Must Do*. Mexico, D.F.: Random House Mondadori.

Ortega, Daniel, and Francisco R. Rodríguez. 2008a. "Freed from Illiteracy? A Closer Look at Venezuela's *Robinson* Campaign." *Economic Development and Cultural Change* 57 (1): 1–30.

———. 2008b. "A Response to Rosnick and Weisbrot." Available at http://frrodriguez .web.wesleyan.edu/docs/working_papers/Response_to_RW.pdf.

Palma, Pedro A. 1989. "La económica venezolana en el período (1974–1988)." In *Venezuela contemporánea, 1974–1989*, ed. Pedro Cunill Grau et al. Caracas: Fundación Eugenio Mendoza.

Parente, Stephen L., and Edward C. Prescott. 2000. *Barriers to Riches*. Cambridge, Mass.: MIT Press.

Pastor, Manuel, and Carol Wise. 2005. "The Lost Sexenio: Vicente Fox and the New Politics of Economic Reform in Mexico." *Latin American Politics and Society* 47 (4): 135–60.

Penfold-Becerra, Michael. 2007. "Clientelism and Social Funds: Evidence from Chávez's Misiones." *Latin American Politics and Society* 49 (4): 63–84.

Perry, Guillermo, J. Humberto López, William F. Maloney, Omar Arias, and Luis Serven. 2006. *Poverty Reduction and Growth: Virtuous and Vicious Circles*. Washington, D.C.: World Bank.

Perry, Guillermo, et al. 2007. *Informality: Exit and Exclusion*. Washington, D.C.: World Bank.

Petras, James. 2008. "Democracy, Socialism, and Imperialism." James Petras Web site. http://petras.lahaine.org/articulo.php?p=1729&more=1&c=1.

Polity Index Task Force. 2009. Polity IV Project: Regime Authority Characteristics and Transition Database. Center for Systemic Peace. http://www.systemicpeace.org/polity/polity4.htm (accessed February 2009).

Prados de la Escosura, Leandro. 2007. "When Did Latin America Fall Behind?" In *The Decline of Latin American Economies: Growth, Institutions, and Crises*, ed. Sebastian Edwards, Gerardo Esquivel, and Graciela Márquez. Chicago: University of Chicago Press.

Prebisch, Raúl. 1984. "Five Stages in My Thinking on Development." In *Pioneers in Development*, ed. Gerald M. Meier and Dudley Seers. Oxford: Oxford University Press.

Przeworski, Adam. 2008. "Does Politics Explain the Economic Gap between the United States and Latin America?" In *Falling Behind: Explaining the Development Gap between Latin America and the United States*, ed. Francis Fukuyama. New York: Oxford University Press.

Rabello de Castro, Paulo, and Marcio Ronci. 1991. "Sixty Years of Populismo in Brazil." In *The Macroeconomics of Populism in Latin America*, ed. Rudiger Dornbusch and Sebastian Edwards. Chicago: University of Chicago Press.

Reid, Michael. 2007. *Forgotten Continent: The Battle for Latin America's Soul*. New Haven, Conn.: Yale University Press.

Roberts, Kenneth M. 1995. "Neoliberalism and the Transformation of Populism in Latin America: The Peruvian Case." *World Politics* 48 (1): 82–116.

Robinson, James A. 2008. "Latin American Equilibrium." In *Falling Behind: Explaining the Development Gap between Latin America and the United States*, ed. Francis Fukuyama, 161–93. New York: Oxford University Press.

Rodó, José, E. 1900. "Ariel." In *Ariel*, trans. F. J. Stimson. Boston: Riverside, 1922.

Rodríguez, Francisco R. 2008a. "An Empty Revolution: The Unfulfilled Promises of Hugo Chávez." *Foreign Affairs* 87 (2): 49–62.

———. 2008b. "Revolutionary Road? Debating Venezuela's Progress." *Foreign Affairs* 87 (4): 160–62.

Rodrik, Dani. 2006. "Goodbye Washington Consensus, Hello Washington Confusion? A Review of the World Bank's Economic Growth in the 1990s: Learning from a Decade of Reform." *Journal of Economic Literature* 44 (4): 973–87.

Rodrik, Dani, and Francisco Rodríguez. 2001. "Trade Policy and Economic Growth: A Skeptic's Guide to the Cross-National Evidence." In *Macroeconomics Annual 2000*, ed. Ben Bernanke and Kenneth S. Rogoff. Cambridge, Mass.: MIT Press for National Bureau of Economic Research.

Rodrik, Dani, Arbind Subramanina, and Francesco Trebbi. 2002. *Institutions Rule: The Primacy of Institutions over Geography and Integration in Economic Development.* Cambridge, Mass.: Kennedy School of Government, Harvard University.

Rosenstein-Rodan, Paul. 1974. "Why Allende Failed." *Challenge* 17 (May–June): 1–14.

———. 1984. "Natura Facit Saltum: Analysis of the Disequilibrium Growth Process." In *Pioneers in Development*, ed. Gerald M. Meier and Dudley Seers. Oxford: Oxford University Press.

Rosnick, David, and Mark Weisbrot. 2008. "'Illiteracy' Revisited: What Ortega and Rodríguez Read in the Household Survey." CEPR Reports and Issue Briefs 2008-16, Center for Economic and Policy Research, Washington, D.C.

SAC (Sociedad de Agricultores de Colombia). 1991. "La apertura, el entorno macro-económico y su incidencia en el sector agropecuario." *Revista Nacional de Agricultura* 896:35–42.

Sachs, Jeffrey. 2002. "Duhalde's Wrong Turn: Dollarisation Would Have Been a Better Bet in a Chronically Indisciplined Country like Argentina." *Financial Times*, January 11, 13.

Salamanca, Luis, and Roberto Viciano Pastor. 2004. *El sistema político en la Constitución Bolivariana de Venezuela.* Caracas: Vandell Hermanos.

Sarmiento, Domingo F. 1845. "Facundo: Civilization and Barabarism." In *Facundo: Civilization and Barbarism*, trans. Roberto González. Berkeley: University of California Press, 2003.

———. 1849. "Viajes en Europa, Africa i América, 1845–1847." In *A Sarmiento Anthology*, ed. Allison Williams. Princeton: Princeton University Press, 1948.

Schemo, Diana Jean. 1996. "Politics, Passion and Graft at Issue in Rio Slayings." *New York Times*, June 28.

Schetinno, Macario. 2007. *Cien años de confusión: México en el siglo XX.* Mexico, D.F.: Taurus.

Schumpeter, Joseph A. 1939. *Business cycles: A Theoretical, Historical, and Statistical Analysis of the Capitalist Process.* New York: McGraw-Hill.

Sheahan, John. 1987. *Patterns of Development in Latin America: Poverty, Repression, and Economic Strategy.* Princeton: Princeton University Press.

Smith, Adam. 1776. *An Inquiry into the Nature and Causes of the Wealth of Nations.* Ed. Edwin Cannan. London: Methuen and Co., 1904.

Soto, Hernando de. 2000. *The Mystery of Capital: Why Capitalism Triumphs in the West and Fails Everywhere Else.* New York: Basic Books.

Spiller, Pablo T., and Mariano Tommasi. 2007. *The Institutional Foundations of Public Policy in Argentina: A Transaction Cost Approach.* Cambridge: Cambridge University Press.

Stein, Barbara H., and Stanley Stein. 1970. *The Colonial Heritage of Latin America: Essays on Economic Dependence in Perspective*. New York: Oxford University Press.

Stiglitz, Joseph E. 2002. *Globalization and Its Discontents*. New York: Norton.

———. 2006. *Making Globalization Work*. New York: Norton.

Stokes, Susan C. 2001. *Mandates and Democracy: Neoliberalism by Surprise in Latin America*. Cambridge: Cambridge University Press.

Sunstein, Cass R. 1993. "The Negative Constitution: Transition in Latin America." In *Transition to democracy in Latin America: The Role of the Judiciary*, ed. Irwin P. Stotzky. Boulder, Colo.: Westview Press.

Syme, Ronald. 1958. *Colonial Elites: Rome, Spain and the Americas*. London: Oxford University Press.

Taylor, John. 2002. "Argentina Economic Update." Testimony before the Subcommittee on International Monetary Policy and Trade of the House Financial Services Committee, February 6.

Teijeiro, Mario. 2001. "Una vez más la política fiscal." Centro de Estudios Públicos, Buenos Aires. http://www.cep.org.ar/articulo.php?ids=156.

Templeton, Andrew. 1995. "The Evolution of Popular Opinion." In *Lessons of the Venezuelan Experience*, ed. Louis Goodman, 79–114. Washington, D.C.: Woodrow Wilson Center Press.

Tenembaum, Ernesto. 2004. *Enemigos: Argentina y el FMI, la apasionante discusión entre un periodista y uno de los hombres clave del Fondo en los noventa*. Buenos Aires: Grupo Editorial Norma.

Thorp, Rosemary. 1998. *Progress, Poverty and Exclusion: An Economic History of Latin America in the 20th Century*. Washington, D.C.: Inter-American Development Bank.

Tocqueville, Alexis de. 1835. *Democracy in America*. New York: Signet Classics, 2001.

Tommasi, Mariano. 2006. "The Economic Foundations of Public Policy." *Economia* 6:2.

Transparency International. 2009. Corruption Perceptions Indexes. http://www.transparency.org/policy_research/surveys_indices/cpi (accessed February 2009).

Uchitelle, Louis. 1998. "Ounces of Prevention for the Next Crisis." *New York Times*. February 1.

U.S. Department of State. 1975. *Covert Action in Chile 1963–1973*. Washington, D.C.: U.S. Government Printing Office.

———, Bureau of Democracy, Human Rights and Labor. 2007. *El Salvador: Country Reports on Human Rights Practices*. http://www.state.gov/g/drl/rls/hrrpt/2006/78891.htm. March 6.

Valdés, Juan Gabriel. 1995. *Pinochet's Economists: The Chicago School of Economics in Chile*. Cambridge: Cambridge University Press.

Vanhanen, Tatu. 1997. *Prospects of Democracy: A Study of 172 Countries*. New York: Routledge.

Vargas, Mauricio. 1993. *Memorias secretas del revolcón: La historia íntima del polémico gobierno de César Gaviria, revelado por uno de sus protagonistas*. Bogotá: Tercer Mundo Editores.

Vargas Llosa, Alvaro. 2005. *Liberty for Latin America: How to Undo Five Hundred Years of State Oppression*. New York: Farrar, Straus and Giroux.

Vela, Abraham. 1993. "Three Essays on Inflation and Stabilization: Lesson from the Mexican Solidarity Pact." PhD diss., University of California, Los Angeles.

Véliz, Claudio. 1980. *The Centralist Tradition of Latin America*. Princeton: Princeton University Press.

———. 1994. *The New World of the Gothic Fox: Culture and Economy in English and Spanish America*. Berkeley: University of California Press.

Viciano Pastor, Roberto, and Rubén Martínez Dalmau. 2008. "¿Ganar o perder? La propuesta de reforma constitucional en Venezuela y el referendo de diciembre de 2007." Centro de Estudios Políticos y Sociales Working Paper, Valencia, Spain.

Vinogradoff, Ludmila. 2009. "El Gobierno de Chávez califica de 'falso' el informe de EE.UU. sobre los derechos humanos." February 27. http://www.abc.es/20090226/internacional-iberoamerica/gobierno-chavez-califica-falso-200902262107.html.

Voigt, Stefan. 1998. "Making Constitutions Work: Conditions for Maintaining the Rule of Law." *Cato Journal* 18 (2): 191–208.

Vulliamy, Ed. 2002. "Venezuela Coup Linked to Bush Team." *Observer*, April 21.

Wacziarg, Romain, and Karen H. Welch. 2008. "Trade Liberalization and Growth: New Evidence." *World Bank Economic Review* 22 (2): 187–231.

Walker, Ignacio. 2008. "Democracy and Populism in Latin America." Kellogg Institute for International Studies Working Paper 347.

Wall Street Journal. 2008. "Venezuela's Chávez Urges End to Colombia's Insurgency." June 9.

Weber, Max. 1958. *The Protestant Ethic and the Spirit of Capitalism*. Translated by Talcott Parsons. New York: Scribner.

Weil, David N. 2005. *Economic Growth*. Boston: Addison-Wesley.

Wessel, D., P. B. Carroll, and T. T. Vogel Jr. 1995. "Peso Surprise: How Mexico's Crisis Ambushed Top Minds in Officialdom, Finance." *Wall Street Journal*, July 6, eastern edition.

West, Robin. 1993 "The Aspirational Constitution." *Northwestern University Law Review* 88 (2): 265–71.

Weyland, Kurt. 2003. "Neopopulism and Neoliberalism in Latin America: How Much Affinity." *Third World Quarterly* 24 (6): 1095–1115.

———. 2007. *Bounded Rationality and Policy Diffusion: Social Sector Reform in Latin America*. Princeton: Princeton University Press.

Wilde, Oscar. 1899. *An Ideal Husband*. London: L. Smithers and Co.

Williamson, Edwin. 1992. *The Penguin History of Latin America*. London: Penguin.

Williamson, John. 1990. *Latin American Adjustment: How Much Has Happened?* Washington, D.C.: Peterson Institute for International Economics.

Wilpert, Gregory. 2007. "Venezuela to Introduce Local Currencies." Venezuelanalysis.com, March 30. http://www.venezuelanalysis.com/news/2310.

Wilson, Dominic, and Roopa Purushothaman. 2003. "Dreaming with BRICs: The Path to 2050." Goldman Sachs Global Economics Paper 99. http://www2.goldmansachs.com/ideas/brics/book/99-dreaming.pdf.

World Bank. 1992. *Trends in Developing Economies*. Washington, D.C.: World Bank.

———. 2003. *Inequality in Latin America and the Caribbean: Breaking with History?* Washington, D.C.: World Bank.

———. 2006. *Poverty Reduction and Growth: Virtuous and Vicious Cycles* Washington, D.C.: World Bank.

———. 2008. *Raising Student Learning in Latin America: The Challenge for the 21st Century*, Washington, D.C.: World Bank.

———. 2009a. Doing Business data set, 2008–9. The World Bank Group. http://www.doingbusiness.org/ (accessed February 2009).

———. 2009b. World Development Indicators. http://ddp-ext.worldbank.org/ext/DDPQQ/member.do?method=getMembers&userid=1&queryId=135.

World Bank. 2009c. Worldwide Governance Indicators, 1996–2008. http://info.worldbank.org/governance/wgi/index.asp.

World Economic Forum. 2008. The Global Competitiveness Index Rankings and 2007–2008 Comparisons. World Economic Forum. http://www.weforum.org/pdf/gcr/2008/rankings.pdf (accessed February 2009).

———. 2009. *The Global Competitiveness Report 2008–2009*. Geneva: World Economic Forum.

Yen, Goh C. 2006. "EU, Japan Propose New WTO Treaties to Prevent Export Taxes." Third World Network, April 24. http://www.twnside.org.sg/title2/twninfo396.htm.

Index

Acemoglu, Daron, 29, 31, 239n12

Aerolíneas Argentinas, 81–82

AES Corporation, 184

Africa, 83

Agosin, Manuel R., 244n22

Ahamed, Liaquat, 138

Alesina, Alberto, 199

Alianza Popular Revolucionaria Americana (APRA), 237n12

Allende, Isabel, 45

Allende, Salvador: Chile under, 102–4; overthrow of, 32, 102, 104–5; populism of, 7, 165, 171; socialist leaders in Latin America and, 237n1

Alliance for Progress: Cuban Revolution and, 48–50; income inequality and, 36–37, 174–75; as pause from U.S. neglect, 45; versus Washington Consensus, 64

Alvarado, Juan Velasco, 165

Amadeo, Eduardo, 156

Anaconda Copper Mining Company, 44

Annan, Kofi, 211

Antofagasta PLC, 96

APRA (Alianza Popular Revolucionaria Americana). *See* Alianza Popular Revolucionaria Americana (APRA)

Arbenz, Jacobo, 48

Archilochus, 239n23

Arcor (Argentina), 96

Argentina: aid from Venezuela to, 193; Austral versus peso in, 145, 246n6; banking sector in, 151–55; Baring Crisis in, 33–34; Chile and, 108, 161; constitution of, 187; Convertibility Law in, 145–49, 151–53, 158–60; Coparticipation Law in, 148, 154; currency crises in, 33–34, 94, 178; data manipulation and, 202; debt default of, 81, 143, 155–59; democratic rule in, 84; despotism in, 41; dollarization and, 157; ease of doing business in, 89; economic crisis in, 143–62; economic growth in, 51; economic progress in, 224–25, 252n3; economic recovery in, 159–60; education in, 180, 182–83; Emergency Law in, 155; exchange rates in, 137, 140, 145–53, 155–58; expropriation in, 81–82; external economic shocks and, 148–50; failure to learn from Mexico's mistakes and, 137; federal-provincial relationship in, 148, 153, 155; fixed currency values in, 138, 143–44; foreign investment and, 145–46, 152–53, 160; future prospects of, 225, 234; government deficits in, 147–49, 154; growth transition in, 16; health care system in, 150; in *An Ideal Husband* (Wilde), 32; income distribution in, 36–37, 175; inflation in, 51, 59, 63, 99–100, 144–45, 202; informal sector in, 89; judiciary in, 79; labor market in, 98, 149–50; labor movements in, 77; landownership in, 36, 173; literacy in, 174; lost decade of 1980s and, 63; Mercosur and, 94, 146–47; monetary policy in, 67; per capita income in, 145, 159; pesification in, 155–59; policy weaknesses in, 147, 184; populism and neopopulism in, 165, 171–72; poverty in, 9, 175, 178; presidential succession in, 143; profit-